THE OWNLEY INN

By JOSEPH C. LINCOLN

CHRISTMAS DAYS
ALL ALONGSHORE
BACK NUMBERS

By FREEMAN LINCOLN

NOD

REBOUND

SAM

By JOSEPH C. LINCOLN
AND FREEMAN LINCOLN

BLAIR'S ATTIC
THE OWNLEY INN

THE OWNLEY INN

By

JOSEPH C. LINCOLN

and

FREEMAN LINCOLN

COWARD-McCANN, INC. NEW YORK

Manufactured in the United States of America

Van Rees Press, New York

CONTENTS

CONTENTS

PROLOGUE

What the Hurricane Brought to Sepatonk

Told by Seth Hammond Ownley

I

THAT DAY, as I recollect it, began pretty much like any other day of that season of the year, which was along in the last week of August. The sun was shining pretty middling clear, although there was a kind of watery haze—a "smur" the fishermen call it—hanging low on the skyline. When I come down to breakfast, I always go out to take a look at the ship's barometer hanging by the front door of the Inn—'twas my father hung it there more than twenty years ago—and this morning I noticed that it read lower than it had when I went to bed. A falling glass and the "smur" are pretty sure signs of a change of weather, but I did not pay much attention to them this time. I went into what I call my private office, the little room back of the regular office, and sat down to look through the Boston newspaper, which had come, with the Island mail, on the steamer from Brandt, which is the nighest good-sized town opposite Sepatonk on the main land.

The door of the private office was open, and I could see out over the clerk's desk and the cigar counter and across the lobby. Most of the boarders were in the dining room, having breakfast, but a few of the men folks were lounging around, smoking and talking. A small crowd compared to

3

the week before, but it would be smaller still in another week. The season was edging on to its end. A fortnight more and the Ownley Inn would close its doors until May. I hated to think of the long months ahead of me. Of course I am postmaster and town constable and do a little insurance business once in a while and those odd jobs keep going the year around, but the Inn is always my main interest. I have lived on Sepatonk Island all my life, same as my father did afore me, and I've owned and managed the Ownley Inn since I was twenty-four. Every spring I open it up and every fall I shut it down, but I declare I don't ever seem to get reconciled to the shutting down part. A bear holes up every winter, so they tell me, and sleeps contented until warm weather comes again. There are times, along about the middle of February, when I would not much mind being a bear.

This was August, though, and I still had plenty to do besides sleep. After I had given the newspaper the once over, it would be up to me to go out and treat the boarders to their "Good mornings" and smiles. That's one thing a hotel man can't ever forget—smiling. He must smile sympathetic when old Mrs. Foster comes groaning to him with her mile-long complaints about her digestion, and he must smile apologetic when old Commodore House tells him that the Inn coffee is made out of peanut shells. He might— the hotel man, I mean—hint to Mrs. Foster that an appetite like hers would encourage dyspepsy in a horsefoot crab, and he might remind the Commodore that the coffee is exactly the same brand he had been drinking all summer and had praised so high only the week before. I say he *might*—but he don't. If he is a sensible hotel man, he just smiles and gets what comfort he can later on, when he looks over the House and Foster bills.

There was nothing much in the paper. A half column or so about a tropical hurricane which was supposed to be moving north from the West Indies; but hurricanes in those latitudes are always breaking out, like measles in a schoolhouse, and their northerly moves end somewheres below Hatteras. A real, honest-to-the-Lord hurricane hitting sleepy old Sepatonk seemed about as likely a notion as the Methodist chapel running a poker party in the vestry. Nothing much out of the common ever happened on Sepatonk Island, or ever would happen. That is how I felt that morning, and it just goes to show how little we know what is in store for us.

I had just folded up the newspaper and was getting up to start on my smiling cruise, when Hettie came in. She is my first cousin, daughter of my Aunt Lucinda, who was Father's sister. Hettie—that's short for Henrietta—is a widow. Her husband, Ezra Bassett from over to Denboro, died in '28, and Hettie has been housekeeper here at the Ownley Inn ever since. She is a capable woman and a good manager, but, Lord, how she can talk! I don't know what I should do without Hettie, although I own up that there are times when I don't know what to do *with* her.

She came bustling in like a schooner with all sail set, same as she always does, and the first breath out of her was a groan that sounded as if it had started from underneath her keel somewheres. I could see, of course, that she wanted me to ask what the matter was, so I obliged.

"Matter!" says she. "Matter? I— But there, *you* won't be interested. You'll just say it's nothing when I tell you, so what's the use?"

"Don't know," I said; "but if you do tell me perhaps we can find out. If nothing makes you suffer like this, I am thankful it isn't something."

She sniffed, disgusted. "Can't you *ever* stop trying to be funny?" she snapped. "I vow I believe you'll make jokes at your own funeral.... Oh, dear!" with a catch of her breath. *"What* made me say that? It's another sign! That's what it is, another sign! Oh, Ham, I dreamed about you last night."

"That must have been pretty tough, I own up. What did you eat for supper?"

"Oh, stop! Do stop and listen! I woke up screaming right out loud. Oh, Hammond, *please!*"

Perhaps I might as well say right here that my father's name was Seth, I have always been called Hammond. About everybody shortens it to Ham. Hettie does too, except when she wants to be extra solemn, which was the case just that minute.

"It means something, of course," she went on. "It was a warning sent. If I only knew what or when or where or who it was to, I should—"

"Here, here!" I cut in. "Who is what to and to what? What kind of language is that anyhow? Hettie, your talking machine is running off-center."

There was more of this, but she straightened out after a while, and the upshot of it all was that she had dreamed she saw me out at sea somewheres on a little rock all surrounded by great waves. And I looked *so* distressed, as if I didn't know what would happen next.

"Should think I might have risked a guess. If the rock—"

"It wasn't all rock. There was some sand—or seems to me there was."

"Liable to be, around here. Anyhow, if the rock and sand place was as small as you say and the waves as high, I should figure that about only one thing could happen."

"But I haven't told you all of it. You were setting on that rock, with a pencil in your hand, working at one of those ridiculous newspaper puzzles you are always wasting time on. . . . Now what does it mean? that is what I want to know. It was sent to you and me—that dream was—as a warning, one of them per—pre—predicaments, the Spiritu'list folk'd tell about."

I laughed out loud. "I'd say predicament was a good word for it, Hettie, but I judge what you were fishing for was 'premonition.' What do you calculate this premonition was sent to warn us against? For me to quit doing crosswords, or for you to lay off clam fritters?"

She said I was what the minister called a "scoffer." Anyhow she knew as well as she did that she was sitting there—she was standing up at the time—that that dream *was* a—a—one of them what-you-may-call-its, and that it meant something was going to happen, something connected with the sea and rocks and sand and her and me and puzzles and—

"And fried clams. All right. Now let's talk about boarders and hired help and keeping hotel, for a change."

That is what we did talk about, and I forgot all about her premonition dream. It was ridiculous enough, of course, and I should not write about it now, only, as I look back at it in the light of what came afterward, it *was* kind of queer. Something—a whole lot of somethings—did begin to happen right away; and as for puzzles—well, no newspaper or book puzzle that I ever tackled, and I am a great hand at them, was a patch on the puzzles that old Sepatonk Island handed me and Dick Clarke and the rest of us, beginning that very night and lasting through the coming fortnight.

II

The forenoon was quiet and everyday enough. I spent it
at the Inn and at the post office, talking with the boarders
and seeing that George Silver, my clerk at the Inn, and
Mamie Bearse, my helper at the post office, took care of
their chores. It was clouding over by eleven, and I recollect telling Pete Holley and Commodore House—"Souse,"
the chambermaids and waitresses call him behind his back,
for reasons—that I did not believe they had better go off
in Cahoon's boat after mackerel that day. The Fosters—
Edgar T. and his wife—were playing what they called
"double-dummy bridge" in the sitting room; Grace Hunter
and Maizie Fay, the two schoolteachers, were out taking
what they called their "constitutional" around the Island;
and Charles Drake, a new boarder with us this summer and
an odd stick if ever I saw one, was out too, nobody seemed
to know where or why. For the matter of that, nobody ever
knew much about Drake; he was a great hand for keeping
his own company. Oscar Grover—he had been with us a
month or so and all hands called him "Doc" although he
insisted he wasn't a doctor at all—was away on the mainland, Boston or New York or somewheres. He was coming
back though, to stay till the Inn closed.

That accounts for all our boarders. A pretty small list,
but, as I have said already, the season was almost over.

The only other person I recollect seeing that morning,
outside of Hettie Bassett and the help and maybe half a
dozen of the village folks, was Perry Hale, the rich fellow
who owns the big property on the north shore a mile or so
from the Inn. He dropped in to tell me he was entertaining
what he called a small house party at his place the next

few weeks and would I have their mail put in his box at the post office. Hale is a bachelor, forty years old maybe, and his main job—while he is on Sepatonk, anyhow—is seeing that he and his friends have a good time. No reason, far as I could see, why they shouldn't have one. With a big house, servants to wait on you, and a motor boat and an automobile, and, judging by the looks, money to chuck around loose for anything you might want, 'most anybody could enjoy life. Course I never tried it, but I should think they might.

I will say this for Perry Hale though. He had always been open-handed and pleasant and got along first-rate with the Sepatonkers. He built his place some six or seven year ago, and, though there was a few who didn't like him, that was more their fault than it was his, from what I ever heard.

It was after dinner, about one o'clock, when the wind began to blow—really blow, I mean. It had been breezing on steady all forenoon, but now it rolled up its sleeves and squared off. It was more than a high wind, it was a gale even then, and word came from the life-saving station at High Point that orders had been sent from the Weather Bureau to set hurricane signals.

By supper time it was as bad a storm as I could remember and getting worse every minute. The sky was as nigh black as a daytime sky can be, and it was raining like Noah's flood. Down in the Cove, where the steamer lands and most of the fish boats are moored, the owners of those boats were hustling, making things fast on deck and putting out extra anchors. The village folks were lashing shutters tight and fetching loose odds and ends into homes. George Silver and I went around the Inn porches, moving chairs and settees to places in the lee; and Hettie had Maggie Dolan and Minnie Ryder, our two combination chambermaids and waitresses, flying around upstairs shutting blinds and stuffing towels under loose window sashes. It really began to look as if that tropical hurricane the paper told about was going to call at Sepatonk, after all.

Long afore that night was over, any doubts I might have had were wiped out. *What* a night! The wind didn't just howl, it screeched. The Ownley Inn is a pretty well-put-together building, but those gusts shook it till, more than once, I began to think it would rattle to pieces. I spent the heft of my time padding barefoot up and down stairs lugging a lamp and looking for leaks. I found some, too, mainly by stepping into the puddles on the floor underneath them.

The very worst of it was over by five o'clock, and I was settling down for a half-hour catnap before getting up for good, when Hettie knocked on my bedroom door. Phin Burgess was down in the kitchen, she said; and, according to him, some kind of craft had been drove ashore over at Snow's Ledge on the south side, and one body had been landed already. Phin was going right over, and didn't I want to go with him.

Well, one way I didn't—the bed felt mighty good—but in another I did, at least I thought maybe I ought to, so I put on thick clothes and oilskins and rubber boots, and Phin and I started.

I could use up considerable time and paper telling about that tramp of ours across the Island, but I won't. Between rain and wind and puddles and trees down across the path and limbs and chunks of bushes flying by our heads, it was some cruise. We got there finally, though, and found that we was a little too late. Most of the excitement was over.

There was quite a little crowd on the shore, which is high and—for Sepatonk, which is mainly sand—pretty rocky just there. The life-saving crew was on hand, and the others were village folks like myself. I asked one of them—it happened to be Half Pound—what was going on. According to his tell, the wrecked boat was a motor cruiser from Bridgeton, Connecticut, and her name was the *Nellie B*.

"Her sternpost and a piece of the hull washed in a spell ago," Half said. His right name is Augustus Pound but us Sepatonkers call him "Half," because, so far as worthwhileness is concerned, he isn't more than half a pound and scant weight at that.

"The name was on the stern board, that's how we know," says Half. "She was a little craft, about thirty foot or so, and, judging by the wreckage, not much good. Solon Briggs"—Solon is captain at the life station—"cal'lates she lost her bearings, or the engine quit or something, and she drove on the ledge broadside to. The beach patrol sighted her just daylight. She was in the trough then and heaving in shore fast."

"How about them aboard her?" I asked. "What's this about a body being washed in?"

Well, it wasn't a body exactly, Pound said; not a dead body. It was a man and they all figured he was dead when they hauled him up on the beach, but it turned out he wasn't—quite. Unconscious, though, and they were not certain that he would pull through.

"Where is he now?" I asked.

"They've carried him over to Doctor Farmer's place. The doctor cal'lates he can 'tend to him there better than anywheres else. Been gone quite a spell, they have. Should have thought you and Phin would have met 'em lugging the stretcher when you come across."

"We came across lots and all we met was what was blown into our faces and eyes. Was this fellow alone on that boat?"

"Don't know. Looks like it. Anyhow no other human thing has come ashore yet. Ain't got any spare tobacco with you, have you, Judge?"

I am justice of the peace here on Sepatonk, so a few of the year-'rounders call me "Judge." Half Pound always does when he wants something, same as he wanted the tobacco. I told him I hadn't any, so he said, "So long, Ham," and went off to find a more promising prospect. I hung around a few minutes longer and then headed back home.

I followed the road this time and it was a little improvement on the path, but not much. On the way I stopped at the doctor's house to ask if there was anything I could do there to help. Doctor Farmer lives just across the way from the entrance to the driveway to Perry Hale's big place.

Martha Pound is the doctor's housekeeper and cousin or some kind of relation to Gus. Nobody ever called *her* a half pound though; half a ton would be a nigher estimate. She was all a twitter of excitement. Yes, they had brought the castaway there, and he was in the best downstairs front room, with the doctor working over him. She had had just one look at the poor soul when they fetched him in, and he looked like death itself. No, she was certain there was nothing I could do just then. Some of the neighbors had been in to ask if they couldn't help, but Doctor Farmer had said no, he would call them if there was. "But, oh, Mr. Ownley, ain't it awful? Did you ever know such a terrible storm in your life? Why, there was times last night when I thought—"

I didn't want to hear about her thoughts, having plenty of my own. I left word to tell the doctor I'd stop in again later in the day and tramped and waded back to see how much of the Ownley Inn was still on an even keel.

Of course, if I had had the least notion of what was ahead of us all, if I had had a hint that that fellow in Doctor Farmer's spare room was to be responsible for— but there! no use to talk that way. I didn't have any such notions or hints. Why should I have had them—then?

And here, for a while, is where I step out of this story. What I have told so far is the part I was in on first, the beginning of it on Sepatonk Island. There was another beginning somewhere else and that I was not in on. Dick Clarke was, though, and it is his turn to come on watch. After he has spun that part of his yarn, I will pick up the next part of mine.

PART I

What Happened in the Library

Told by Dickson Clarke

I

To me this story has the shape of an elongated letter Y. Ham Ownley starts at the top of one of the arms, and I at the top of the other. We move separately but simultaneously until we meet. Then we go on together. It seems simple enough, and still I am a bit puzzled. I don't quite know where my part begins.

I might choose the so-called "strong room" of the Knowlton Library of American Literature at Bainbridge University, Bainbridge, Connecticut, for a start. The time would be the early afternoon of a day in this past August. The day doesn't need a number to identify it, for to the residents of New England it will be known for years to come as the day of the Big Blow. To me, personally, it will always have another significance, totally unrelated to hurricanes. To me it will always be the day when I walked into the Knowlton Library strong room and saw what I saw.

The wind was not blowing at the time. The air was heavy and lifeless, and the dusty leaves of the ancient elms outside the library windows hung wearily still. Inside, the customary library hush seemed intensified. My heels clicked sharply with tiny little echoes as I walked rapidly across the marble floor of the reading room to the strong room door.

That tall door was of plate glass fronted by heavy iron grillwork, and was invariably kept locked even when someone was working inside. I say "invariably" only to contradict myself immediately, for at this time the door was not locked. It was ajar. That fact I noticed as I raised my hand to touch the little electric signal button set in the jamb. It was enough. It caused my scalp to prickle unpleasantly as I stepped inside.

Dr. Samuel Payson, curator of the library, lay quietly on the strong room floor. He was a little man in a neat gray tweed suit, and the hair of his head was only slightly less white than the squares of marble upon which he had crumpled. His eyes were half open but they saw nothing.

As I ran to his side, bits of glass crunched under my feet and I kicked something else out of the way. Later I was to learn that what I had kicked was a leather case made to hold the tiny old book that was the library's most prized possession. At the time I did not know, and would not have cared. All that I cared about was Dr. Payson. He lay strangely still. A little trickle of blood had come from the corner of his mouth. The blood made a design like a drunken question mark, bright red on the white of the strong room floor.

That picture—I shall never forget it—might make the best beginning for my part of this story. It is sensational enough to be tempting; but as I look back I wonder if there aren't other, even if more prosaic, milestones in my unimportant life that might better serve the purpose.

I might turn the clock back to an afternoon in the previous May. For two hours that afternoon I had been sitting in a shadowy corner of the Knowlton Library reading room, but I hadn't been reading. I had merely been parking in one of the big leather chairs and staring intently at nothing in particular. Finally Dr. Payson, from whom I had taken a couple of courses in American Literature, came up and spoke to me. I don't know whether he had a purpose or whether he was just being civil. Anyhow, he spoke, and I spoke back.

"Maybe you ought to have me thrown out of here, Doctor," I told him. "I'm just a gate crasher. I'm not improving my mind or anything else. To tell you the truth, I don't know exactly what I *am* doing." Then on impulse I added, "Maybe I'm hiding."

Payson didn't do what a lot of other people would have done. He didn't jump to the conclusion that I was wanted by the police, or that some girl's husband was after me with a knife. He just smiled and said, "People choose different ways of hiding. Some go to sea. Some get drunk. Some bury themselves in libraries." He nodded. "As a matter of fact, a library isn't a bad place to hide. How would you like to try it this summer?"

I looked at him. "Do you mean a job? Here?"

He nodded again. "Yes. That's what I mean."

Well, it sounded funny enough at first, even to me. The thought of Puss Clarke, recent tackle on a more than average tough Bainbridge football team, working for Doc Payson in the Knowlton Library of American Literature, would have made almost anybody laugh. As a matter of fact it *did* make people laugh, because eventually I took the job.

I took the job; and I got to know Samuel Payson; and I got to know something about rare American books; and I got to know a lot about perhaps the rarest of them all, the very early edition of the New England Primer; and in the end I got mixed up in the weird tangle of events that form the reason for this story. That is why I say that my little talk with Doc Payson in the reading room might be as good a place to start my tale as the scene in the strong room that I've already told. They're both good, so to save myself the trouble of making a choice I won't use either. I'll start instead—I mean business this time— by accepting a bit of simple advice. I'll follow my nose.

A man doesn't usually pay much attention to his nose. He uses it for the purpose of sniffing, blowing, and perhaps for poking into the business of other people. Otherwise it is merely an integral part of his face and of no great importance. My nose was different, for the simple reason, God help us, that it happened to have a Grecian cast.

My earliest memory in life has to do with my nose, and with a lady who commented on it. I could not have been more than three or four years old at the time, so the picture is not very clear. All I can recall is a vague, mountainous female in swirling draperies who remarked upon me to my mother, "What a perfectly beautiful child, Mrs. Clarke!" I am sure that her tone must have been sugary and that she richly deserved a sharp kick on the shin. "His nose," she continued, "is genuinely classic! And how beautifully he is proportioned. Why, he's only a tot and yet already he looks like a little Greek god!"

Sickening, of course, but it must be told because it is significant. I had been born with a good build and a nasal column that caught the feminine eye. I had been born with them and I grew up with them, and I only wish I could truthfully say that I paid no attention to them at all. I like to think that I was as virile and unselfconscious as the next growing boy, but the fact remains that I was told about my manly beauty so repeatedly and in so many different ways that I'm afraid I finally began to take some stock in it myself.

Anyhow, the Hope of Hollywood grew up and went to Bainbridge University where his father and his uncles had gone before him. There he was not particularly popular with his fellows, who seemed to regard him with a certain amount of suspicion. Perhaps he was a little bit too "pretty." He played tackle on the Freshman football team, adequately but without inspiration. Perhaps he was unconsciously protecting the famous beak. Anyhow he was quietly unhappy, and in a fair way to become more so, until the afternoon he met a gentleman from Scranton, Pennsylvania. The Pennsylvanian, who played end for an opposing Freshman team, used his orange clad elbow with telling effect. With it he spread the historic Clarke nose all over the astonished Clarke face and left it there for dead.

I'll never forget the scene when the adhesive tape finally came off and for the first time I faced the boys in the locker room. They took one look at me and burst with one accord into wild laughter. When the mirth finally subsided, a voice from the rear spoke the thoughts of all. "What a puss!" said the voice in a tone of genuine awe. "What a magnificent puss!"

Right then I became "Puss" Clarke, and Puss Clarke I remained. As Puss I continued to play football and played better than anyone had believed possible. As Puss my acquaintances dropped their reserve and became friends. As Puss Clarke I was no longer a possible ornament to the silver screen, but for the first time in my life I was completely happy. Thoughts of plastic surgery quickly vanished when I found that I took a quiet pleasure in standing before the mirror to observe my unique and slightly ludicrous countenance.

Event number one, then, of my Bainbridge career was the busting of the beak. Event number two was the appearance of Anne Francis.

II

A lot of rot has been written and said and thought about Fifth Avenue. To some it is the exemplification of excess wealth, greed, glitter, show, arrogance, and snobbery. To me it means something very different. I like to think of Fifth Avenue as it is on any clear, cold winter evening. All traces of dirt and tawdriness have gone with the daylight. The lights are sharp and bright. The buildings seem white and clean and severely classical—like my *soi disant* nose. The shop windows are uncluttered, dignified, well bred. In the lines of traffic the cars give the impression of all being black, shining, quiet, and quietly powerful. The women in them are all lovely, beautifully groomed, beautifully bred. Like their men they have background, dignity, intelligence, stability, and purpose. It is all an illusion, of course, but to me Fifth Avenue on a winter's night represents all that life could be if a man had the will and the ability to make it that way.

Anne Francis gave, and gives me, the same impression. No surface glitter. No cheapness. Everything on display is genuine. The poise that goes with background. Expensive, of course. Everything that is worth having is expensive in one way or another. Lovely, of course. Intensely human, and warm. Sometimes *too* warm. There is a light in her eye that should warn any man, and seems to warn none. To state the case baldly she may be the essence of my cockeyed impression of Fifth Avenue, but she is a hell-cat when she wants to be—which is about three-fifths of the time.

Yes, I liked the girl. We met at a prom in the fall of my first year at Bainbridge, and I went down before her with the magnificent finality of a great tree falling. She didn't dislike me, either. She overlooked the rah-rah glory that went with my being captain of the football team, and she even forgave me my face. "It isn't such a bad face," she told me with a smile that first evening. "It's ugly of course, but it isn't ugly ugly. It's sort of *nice* ugly."

A couple of months later I asked her something else about my face. I asked her if she could take the idea, and the fact, of kissing it—not just once but for good. She said that she could, so we were engaged.

There is a hazy period after that in which I moved in a sort of glow of the species known as rosy. I could not believe my good fortune, and neither could other people. They envied me and did not hesitate to say so. "You, Puss Clarke," said my roommate not altogether facetiously, "are a lucky stiff. If you fell down a drain, you'd emerge covered with diamonds. Look what happens. You follow that horror, loosely known as your nose, to a dance, and what happens?" He sighed lugubriously and totted off the items on his fingers. "One, you find a nice girl, about whom the worst thing that can be said is that she can look at you and still relish her victuals. Two, by some foul means you lure her into saying that she'll marry you. Three, her father and mother are what are known as charming people. Four, her father is senior partner in one of the oldest and best law firms in New York. Five, and don't forget it, he has oodles of the stuff that counts. Six, our class graduates from this institution a year from next spring. After that, the rest of us will be rushing around trying to find jobs at nothing a week, but not Puss. Oh, no! Puss will be politely ushered into a large office with his name in gilt letters on the door. Puss will get along. He will win his 'B' in life. In no time at all Palm Beach and Nassau and the run of giant tuna off Nova Scotia will know him well. Puss will be considerable potatoes, and why? Why, because he is a lucky stiff!"

"I know." I felt quite humble. "I'm very lucky. She's a swell girl."

My roommate sort of snorted. "Love, sweet love. Yes, Puss, she's a swell girl. But don't forget the other items I've mentioned. They count. They count like hell."

Well, he was right. I soon found out that the other items counted, even if they didn't count in quite the expected way.

Anne lived in Greenwich, and I spent a lot of time in that village before I was through. I got to know her family and friends, and to like them. Who could help it? I'll have to admit that the Francis way of life rather made me catch my breath, even though I knew that I had no reason for standing in awe. The Clarkes, generations of them, had lived in the Genesee valley for years, and were respected there. They were still known as gentlefolk, even if a steadily waning income had rubbed off some of the gloss. Perhaps the Clarkes were what is known as "decayed gentility." If so there was nothing decadent about the Francises.

I spent my spring vacation that year at a small island near Bimini, fishing for blue marlin. I caught one, and had my "pitcher" in the papers—not the sporting pages, if you please, but the society section. That summer I spent some time at the Francis place in Canada. It was Atlantic salmon this time, and I loved every minute of it.

The crack-up was gradual, hard to explain, and long in arriving. I won't go into it except to say that everything was much too smoothly oiled. I was accepted and added to the Francis family with no more fuss than it takes to add cream to coffee. The only difference was that cream changes the color of coffee. I didn't change the color of anything. I just lost my own.

Anne and I were to be married three weeks after my graduation from Bainbridge, but we weren't. We chose, instead, one bright May morning in which to quarrel and to call the whole thing off.

I won't try to argue the point as to who was right in the quarrel. Maybe we both were right—or both wrong. The night before Mr. Francis had told me about the position I was to take after Anne and I had come back from our European honeymoon, the latter to be financed, of course, by a Francis check. The position was with a canning company, and one that my roommate, or almost any right-minded young man, would have grabbed with a loud cry of joy. I was not right-minded. I expressed due thanks but said that I wasn't sure the canning business was what I wanted—thereby knocking the lid off of things in a big way.

Mr. Francis was very gentle with me, and so was Anne when she talked with me the next morning. At least she was gentle at first. It did not last long, that gentleness. I'll skip the scene, all except the highlights. In essence Anne wanted to know if I was mad as well as ungrateful and lacking in a sense of duty. I inquired if she would like to spend her honeymoon on my place in the Valley instead of in Devon. I also inquired how she would like to have a crack at gentleman farming instead of the canning business. She laughed bitterly, and I laughed bitterly. When the smoke blew away, I was minus a fiancée, and Anne was minus an engagement ring.

Anne, on her way out of the morning room where we had been talking, disdainfully dropped the engagement ring into the deep water of a large goldfish bowl standing on the window sill. It was her way of adding the human touch to a grande dame exit.

III

Not so many days later I found myself working under Doctor Samuel Payson in the Knowlton Library of American Literature at Bainbridge University. My title was that of Assistant Curator and my salary was something not visible to the naked eye.

How I got there is fairly easy to tell, even if it doesn't make much sense. My life, for the moment, had more or less come to a standstill. I had cut myself entirely free from the Francis family, which was the thing, as I told myself over and over, that I most wanted to do. On the other hand I had lost Anne, and toward her, personally, I still felt exactly as I had felt ever since I first laid eyes on her. I suppose I was suffering. I know I was miserable. I know I didn't want to explain things to people, or to talk to people.

That was why I went to the library reading room and just sat there. That was why I told Doc Payson that perhaps I was hiding. That was why I finally took the job there. The Doc had said that a library was a good place to hide for a time, and I needed one badly.

Samuel Payson did a lot for me. He must have sensed what was the matter with me, even though I never told him, and even though he never mentioned it. He took the line of trying to interest me in something entirely new, that subject being the study of American literature in general and of rare old American editions in particular.

Being an authority and an enthusiast, the Doctor liked to talk to somebody, and I wasn't such a bad somebody. Being nine-tenths numb, I never argued with him, and, having nothing else to do, I listened a little in the beginning and more as time went on. After a couple of weeks I even discovered that during a day there were intervals of as long as fifteen minutes when my attention was fixed on Cooper, Emerson, and the rest, and not on myself at all. Thoughts of self gradually grew more brief and finally disappeared altogether under the spell of a musty little volume known as the New England Primer.

Ever heard of the New England Primer? Well, I hadn't either until a few weeks after I had taken up the scholarly life. Then I heard about it with a vengeance, you can believe me, for I happened to find one.

I make that statement simply, for with it I have small hope of causing my audience to gasp with awe. Its reading of necessity being largely confined to market reports and the daily papers, my audience will merely raise its collective eyebrow in polite and bored interrogation. I hasten to raise an offensively superior eyebrow in return, my implication being tut-tut and fie for shame.

The New England Primer, oh ye of expensive education and little savvy, is an early American children's book. It was produced for the education, edification, and perhaps even for the entertainment of the young in early Colonial days. The young must have liked it, for authorities say that between the years 1680 and 1830 more than six million copies of it were printed.

That figure is impressive and must put the Primer on any list of Best Sellers. It also might lead to the belief that there are any number of the little books still kicking around. Well, there aren't, because the Primer was rather flimsy, and because children are notoriously tough on books. The earliest issue extant was printed in Boston in 1727. If you can go up in grandma's attic and come down with a similar or earlier copy, I advise no delay. I might even urge extreme haste.

Let's be crass and material about the whole thing. A good copy of a very early New England Primer is worth important money. How much? That's hard to say. Fifty thousand dollars—a hundred—a hundred and fifty? I don't know. I only know that it is worth what you can get for it, and you can get plenty.

I repeat, and this time with more assurance of respectful attention, that I, Dickson Clarke, found an early copy of the New England Primer.

It was bull luck, of course. Under the watchful eye of Doc Payson, I was working one afternoon at the dreary task of sorting a big collection of books and pamphlets that had come to the library on the settlement of some Vermont estate. It was dusty and seemingly trivial work, and I experienced no premonitory thrill at all when I picked up the book that was to create such a stir in the world of letters, and more personally to bring about such an upheaval in my own life.

It was a little bit of a thing, measuring only about four by three and a half inches, and bound in dingy calfskin over boards. The printing inside was irregular and the woodcut illustrations crude. I blew off a layer of dust, glanced through the pages, and spoke to Dr. Payson. "What shall I do with this thing?" I inquired casually, handing him a good-sized fortune as though it were so much peanut brittle. "Shall I put it with the kid stuff or give it the chuck?"

What happened after that can easily be imagined. Doc Payson took one good look and went white as a sheet. I thought he was going to faint, but he didn't. He rushed off to his office and slammed the door behind him. He stayed there so long that he should have been calmer when he came out, but instead he was so excited that he was only about half a jump ahead of a Grade A fit.

His incoherence was such that it took me quite a time to find out what all the shooting was about, but finally I did. It seems that the item that for two cents I would have heaved into a wastebasket was a copy of the New England Primer. It had been printed in Boston by Rogers and Fowle, for the Booksellers. The date was 1749.

"This must be our lucky day," I told him, sort of marveling to myself how steamed up a collector could get over a thing that wouldn't cause anybody else to turn a hair. "It's kind of rare, I gather."

Well, he gave every indication that he was about to choke to death, but finally refrained. It appeared that hitherto there had been only one known copy of that issue in existence. Dr. Rosenbach, the Philadelphia collector, owned that, and it was minus two pages. Ours was complete.

"Only one other copy in the world?" I was gradually beginning to get the hang of things. "Why, in that case, this little book must be worth some money."

Dr. Payson looked at me with pity. "Money? Why, a

good-sized fortune wouldn't buy it. I couldn't put a cash value on it. It's beyond that. It's priceless!"

A good-sized fortune! I didn't believe him, of course, but I soon learned that he knew something about what he was saying. If our New England Primer could have been priced in proportion to the disturbance it created it would have fetched a million on any man's newsstand. As soon as the news got around, which was soon, the Knowlton Library took a new lease on life. Letters arrived in bunches, the telephones kept ringing, telegraph boys came in and out. I even got my picture in the papers once more. This time I wasn't holding a football and looking grim. I was hanging onto a dingy little book and looking silly. Underneath I was labeled as "The discoverer of the Knowlton Library's New England Primer." Such is the nature of fame.

Doc Payson, naturally, was in the seventh heaven of delight. He was so happy that he almost made me happy myself. He went about with a perpetual grin, and he kept telling anybody who would listen that at last the Knowlton Library had a Relic. It had a Relic, he maintained, that would cause scholars to flock to its door like pilgrims to Mecca. "Just wait!" he crowed, grabbing my elbow hard with his wiry fingers. "Just wait till Phil Semphill sees our Primer. He'll be so jealous that the eyes will pop right out of the old buzzard's head!"

Professor Phillip Semphill of Columbia University was another authority on American Literature. He was also Payson's arch rival and closest friend. His had been the first congratulatory telegram received after the discovery of the Primer. He had followed that with almost daily letters to Dr. Payson. The pair discussed intricate points about the Primer in long, expensive telephone calls. The

Professor was coming to Bainbridge the first moment he could get away from some pressing work that he was doing in New York. That was why I was not surprised one morning in late August when a calling card came in which read "Richard Sanger." The name meant nothing to Dr. Payson, but the words underneath in pencil did. They said "Secretary to Professor Phillip Semphill," and that was enough.

IV

Dr. Payson happened to be in my office at the time, so I had a good look at the Sanger man. He was of medium height, stockily built; and even though his hair was nearly white, he gave the impression of being on the right side of forty by several years. His bright black eyes were fronted by silver rimmed dark glasses. His jaw was square and his mouth rather thin. He was dressed in a plain gray suit of conservative cut. His tie was black. His voice was low and not unpleasant, and he did not overwork it. As a matter of fact he was almost taciturn, merely saying that Professor Semphill had asked him to come up, have a look at our New England Primer, and bring back a report. Would Dr. Payson mind?

Dr. Payson, of course, did anything but mind. He announced himself as more than delighted to show the Primer to his friend's secretary; and in a little while the pair went off in the direction of the strong room, leaving me behind to sit scowling at the blotter on my desk.

I wasn't scowling because I had a headache, either. It was because of Mr. Sanger's shoes.

Mr. Sanger's shoes were made of much cracked patent leather, and had long pointed toes. They did not lace but were fastened up the side with round shiny black buttons. They were foreign-looking affairs, and perhaps it was only natural for me not to like them; but why should they make me uneasy—as they most definitely did?

I scowled over that question and could not answer it except to tell myself that such shoes were not items to be found on any secretary to Professor Phillip Semphill. They did not fit the picture. Perhaps, I followed my complete lack of logic further, this Sanger man was not what he pretended to be at all. Perhaps he was a ringer. Perhaps he had come to the library to steal our Primer and was even now throttling my boss and friend in the latter's own strong room. Perhaps I ought to go down there to make sure.

It was nothing but a hunch, of course, but it was such a strong one that I would have followed it at once if fate had not taken a hand. And if fate hadn't horned in— Oh, well. What actually happened was that I was halfway out of the chair on my way to the strong room when I looked up. Standing in the doorway and smiling at me was Anne Francis.

The hunch vanished then. Everything vanished except a rush of feeling that I can't even attempt to describe. Anne was smiling at me, and she was lovelier than a person has any right to be. All the not-so-old longings and heartaches I had tried to forget came back with a bang, and I supposed I gulped at her like a freshly boated fish.

She walked over to the desk and looked down at me. "Perhaps I shouldn't have done this," she said simply. "Perhaps it is a mistake. Do you mind?"

"No." I shook my head stupidly. "I don't mind."

She took the only other chair and sat down in it. "My

alleged reason for coming here," she told me, "is to apologize for what I did with your ring—dropping it in the goldfish bowl, I mean. It was a childish trick and I'm genuinely sorry. I don't know why I was such a fool. It just seemed the indicated thing to do at the moment. Will you forgive me, Dick?"

"Of course." I was gradually getting my bearings. "For that matter I should apologize for smashing the bowl on the hearth to get the ring back. Was it an expensive bowl?"

"Very."

"I thought so. Was your mother furious?"

"Very."

"Did the goldfish die?"

"No." She laughed, and I liked the sound of it. "Marie picked them up—or was it Charlotte? Anyhow, the fish are getting on swimmingly, if you'll pardon the pun. Or is it a pun?"

We just looked at each other.

"Are you happy?" she asked at last.

"No." I shook my head. "I thought I was, but I'm not. Not now."

I didn't have to explain. "Perhaps we made a mistake," she said softly. "Do you think we made a mistake, Dick?"

That was kind of a dirty trick, for she must have known the power she had over me. Anyhow, I tried to rally. "No. I'm quite sure we didn't. The situation was impossible."

"Impossible? You mean my family?"

I closed my eyes. "Let's not argue, Anne. I honestly don't feel up to it. Let's not fight."

She shook her head quickly in the old, familiar way. "I don't want to fight—or argue. I just want to be sure we didn't make a bad mistake. That's why I came here."

I felt weak and tired, and I wished she had not come. "I thought it was all decided. I thought it was over and done with."

"I know." She nodded soberly. "I felt sure that it was —at first. Now I'm not so positive. You and I meant something to each other—something very important. Don't you think so, Dick?"

"Yes."

"And we didn't quarrel for personal reasons, you'll admit that. We quarreled on account of circumstances which were more or less beyond our control."

"That's true," I told her miserably, "but sometimes circumstances can change a lot of things. Sometimes they can change plans and even lives. It seems to me they have changed ours."

"I know. I'm wondering if perhaps we were wrong in letting them change anything. If this thing between us was so very important, perhaps we should have told circumstances to go to the devil."

I looked at her. "Perhaps. But let me ask you one thing. If I ask you, will you come to the Valley with me and have a go at farming?"

"I don't see why I should." There was a trace of new color in her cheeks. "I don't see why I should, any more than you—"

I finished the thing for her. "Than I should go into the canning business and live in Greenwich." I shrugged. "Don't you see, Anne? We're right back at the place we left off. In a minute we'll be quarreling—if we let ourselves. Let's not."

"That's right. Let's not." She picked up the pair of

gloves that lay in her lap and twisted them. "I don't know why I came here, Puss. I was afraid it might be a mistake. Still, I wanted to be absolutely sure—before I went away."

There was a sort of finality about her words that gave me a queer sinking feeling. "Where are you going, Anne?"

She laughed a little—uncertainly. "I make it sound as though I were taking a world cruise. I'm not. I'm just going to an island off the Massachusetts coast for a visit."

Something in her tone made me ask another question. "Do I know the people?"

"No." She shook her head. "It isn't people, really. It's a man named Perry Hale—a bachelor—older than we are. He's asked a married couple you don't know, either, and me, to come to his summer place for a few weeks."

"He's in love with you." There wasn't the faintest doubt in my mind about the thing. "He wants to marry you, of course."

Anne said, "He's very nice, Puss. You'd like him."

I tried to laugh. "I'm sure I'd just love him! Do you? Are you going to marry him?"

She paid no attention to the bitterness that must have been in my voice. "I'm not sure. That's why I came here —before I went away."

The situation was not an easy one. I had a feeling that if I took my chance, then, I could steal her from this man, Hale, and from everybody else. But what if I did? If we were engaged again, what would happen? It would be the same thing all over again, and I felt that that would be wrong for both of us.

"I'm sorry, Anne," I told her, trying to keep my voice steady. "I wish I had something new to offer you, but I haven't. Not now. With time I might be able to face the canning business. You might be able to swallow the idea of farming. Who knows? With time anything might happen, but not now. I'm afraid things will have to stay the way they are, and that you'll have to go—wherever you are going."

"I'm going," she said faintly, "to Sepatonk Island."

"Sepatonk." I grabbed the word as an escape from intolerable emotional strain. "Why, I own a little cottage on Sepatonk Island. It was left to me."

She smiled with wooden politeness and got to her feet. "That's nice, Puss. We might meet down there."

I came around the desk and stood beside her. "We might."

She looked up at me. "Would you mind very much," she asked in a small voice, "kissing me—just once? Sort of good-by?"

"No. I wouldn't mind at all."

I had every intention of making that kiss the most brotherly of salutes. But Anne was very lovely, and very near, and I felt the way I felt. So the kiss was not brotherly. It was everything that a kiss should be, and so far as I was concerned it might have gone on indefinitely. Anne, however, finally pulled away.

"Thank you," she said breathlessly. "I'm sorry. I hope you don't lose your job?"

"Lose my job?" I didn't know what she was talking about. "Why should I lose my job?"

"Someone saw us just now." She seemed suddenly quite happy. Almost radiant. "Someone went by the door. He was running."

"Nonsense!" I said roughly. "Nobody ever runs in this place. And what of it? Come here!"

But she didn't obey. She said something bright and cheerful about seeing me on Sepatonk perhaps, and was gone.

V

How long I stood still in my tracks I don't know. It probably was not more than half a minute, but it seemed a long time. When I came to, it was with the memory of something Anne had just said. She said that someone had gone by the office door while we were kissing—that he had been running. She must have been wrong. Nobody ever ran in the Knowlton Library.

It was then that I remembered the patent leather shoes with the pointed toes and the shiny black buttons. They and their owner had gone to the strong room with Doc Payson to have a look at our Primer.

I've already told what happened after that. I didn't exactly run to the strong room, and I didn't exactly walk. My premonition and I, however, made the distance in pretty fast time, and I can still hear the hollow little clicking noises that my heels made on the floor.

When I first saw Dr. Payson, I was quite sure that he was dead. He lay so absolutely still and looked so horribly crumpled, and his face was such a blank white, that the assumption was reasonable. The jagged question mark of bright red blood on the white marble did not help things, either.

I must have yelled for help, although I don't remember it. In any event, I was still on my knees beside Payson and had just determined that he was not dead, but unconscious from a vicious blow on the forehead, when the room suddenly filled with people. They all milled about, and exclaimed, and babbled as people do in moments of excitement, and I'm afraid I wasn't much better.

I scrambled to my feet and grabbed hold of the arm of the nearest person I knew—he happened to be a history instructor and, luckily, a man with a level head. "Take charge of this, will you?" I begged him rapidly, and I knew my hand was shaking. "Get a doctor. Call the police. Call an ambulance. Get these people out of here. Do what has to be done, for God's sake! I can't stay."

"Of course, Clarke. I'll do what I can." The fellow was remarkably calm. "But where on earth are you going?"

I told him. "I'm going to find the guy who did this— a bird with patent leather shoes. And when I find him I'm going to jam his front teeth right through the back of his skull!"

Big talk, of course, for how I thought I was going to find Sanger I don't yet know. If he was the man who had run past my office door, he had at least a five minute start, and Bainbridge is a fairly big city. All the odds were in favor of his being completely and finally lost by this time, and I didn't even think of that. In a short space I had run through a list of emotions that included shock, horror, pity, and remorse, and I had ended in a white hot rage. All I asked of life, and I demanded that, was to get my hands on the man who called himself Sanger.

Without having the slightest idea where I was going, I boiled out of that building before anybody had a chance to try to stop me, and by dumb luck I ran into a gold mine right at the front door.

The gold mine was in the shape of a taxi driver named Paddy who had a regular stand there. Paddy listening to my panting description of the man I wanted and stifled a yawn as he nodded. "Sure. That guy come out a couple of minutes back and took the cab in front of me—Frank's cab."

"Did you hear where he wanted to go?"

"Sure." Everything hung on his answer but he did not seem to care. "The New York boat."

I was in the back of that cab almost before the last word had been spoken. "The New York boat!" I ordered. "And go like hell! When does she sail?"

Paddy stepped on the starter and got the car on its way. "In about seven minutes," he observed briefly.

"Can you make it?"

"Don't know," was the answer. "I can try."

Well, we didn't make it. A couple of wrong lights saw to that; and when I got out on the wharf, the New York boat was out in the river, and she was just swinging to start the trip down stream. I shook my fist at her and shouted remarks that were not benedictions, and for two cents I would have cried.

I must have made something of a spectacle of myself, for after a few seconds a little man in a blue uniform spoke to me. "Tough luck, Mister," he said soothingly, "but there's no call to take on so. If you're in an awful hurry, you can get a train that will get you to New York just as soon."

"That's an idea!" I turned on him. "I can meet the boat in New York! Tell me something. Did a white-haired man drive up here in a taxi just before the boat sailed? Did he make it all right?"

"Now that's a funny thing." The little man seemed pleased that I had asked him such a question. "A white-haired man, just like you said, druv up here in a cab just about two minutes before the *Marie* sailed."

That was all I wanted to know. "Then he's on it!"

"That's the funny thing." The official scratched his chin with an air of satisfaction. "That's the funny thing, mister, because he *ain't* on it."

"You're crazy!" I stared at him. "What are you talking about?"

The little man did not seem to resent the insult. He chuckled. "I ain't crazy," he said mildly, "though I don't blame you for thinking so. Let me tell you about it. The white-haired man druv up, just like I said. He paid off the cab and walked up the *Marie*'s gangplank."

"Then—"

"And then!" A triumphant finger was pointed at me. "About two shakes before we hauled the gangplank back to the dock, Mr. Whitehair walked down it again!"

"But—but—" I was floundering. "Why—?"

"I know, Mister." He was all sympathy. "I know just how you feel. I felt the same way—but that was how it happened. Mr. Whitehair walked up the *Marie*'s gangplank. Then he walks *down* again and lets her sail without him. Last I saw him, he was walking fast that way"— he pointed—"up the street along the river."

Well, it was not very long before I, too, was walking up that street along the river, but there was very little hope in my heart. On my left were rows of buildings separated by streets leading off at right angles up to the heart of the town. On my right were the piers, some covered and some open, thrusting out into the river. There were hundreds of places all about where the man, Sanger, would be safe from my eyes, even if he did not know I was following him. Further search seemed absolutely silly on the face of it, and yet for some reason I kept on.

Once more, bull luck came to my aid. I had not been

walking and looking for more than five minutes when I spotted Sanger.

He was standing about halfway out on one of the piers talking to a big man in blue jeans and a dirty undershirt. His back was toward me, but I knew him at once; and just by way of helping the identification along, he exposed his white hair, as I watched, by taking off his hat and tossing it into the cockpit of a small cabin cruiser that lay moored alongside.

I don't suppose that many seconds passed before I began to run in his direction, but in that time the entire scene was photographed vividly in my mind. A long, low building ran along one side of the pier, and the other side was open water. The cruiser into which Sanger had thrown his hat was a neat white craft with fast lines, and I even noticed her name. She had the words *Nellie B.* in big gold letters on her stern.

Sanger, as I say, had his back toward me, but he heard my footsteps as I came pounding out onto the pier. He turned sharply, then, and uttered an exclamation. He had very little time in which to make up his mind what to do, but he made it up quickly. Shouting something to the man in the blue jeans, he darted across the dock and vanished into the building on the other side.

Blue jeans tried to stop me, but he had no chance. I shot past him and crashed against the door Sanger had just slammed. It flew open, and I was in a long corridor without doors. There being no one else there, I did the indicated thing. I ran down its length, bounced off the end wall, and started off again at right angles. My trip came to an abrupt end when something was thrust between my feet and I fell to the floor with sickening violence.

I am slightly tough, and the fall did not knock me out.

It shook me up very badly, however, and I groaned as I scrambled to my hands and knees. My vision cleared and the first thing I saw, about twelve inches from my nose, was a pointed patent leather shoe with round black buttons. Above me, with a kind of mean grin on his face, was brother Sanger.

There was something short and black in the hand he was swinging down toward my head. I tried to dodge but was not quick enough. The lights went out then, for me, in a resounding clap of thunder.

They tell me that that was the afternoon of the great hurricane. I, personally, wouldn't know.

PART II

Doctor Farmer's Patient

The Story Continued by
Seth Hammond Ownley

I

DICK CLARKE, thanks to the thump on the head which he got up there at the Bainbridge pier and which he has already told you about, wasn't much interested in the weather for the rest of that night and the following day. The hurricane up along that part of the shore wasn't nigh as bad as it was down our way, and, if it had been, he wouldn't have cared. With us, though, on Sepatonk Island, it was different. For a spell it looked like the end of the world and, when it was over, as if we were in a world of our own.

When we came to, as you might say, on the morning after the typhoon, we found that Sepatonk was practically cut off from the rest of creation. Not that we had time to sit down and feel lonesome. There was enough for us to do. Every Islander was busy taking account of damage to boats and roofs and henhouses and trees, so playing at Robinson Crusoe didn't trouble us much. The steamer from Brandt didn't cross, so there was no mail; and, although the Brandt telegraph and telephone wires, being underwater cables, were clear, the wires on the mainland were down, and the only news we got was from the radio.

The second day, though, telephone service beyond Brandt began to get going, although not on full schedule, and word came that the steamer would make its regular trip the following morning. Perry Hale's phone was out of kilter, so he used ours at the Inn and, after waiting an hour or so and heaving overboard a deckload of swear words, finally got in connection with Rye, New York, and fixed it up about his house party folks coming soon as they could get here comfortable. His place wasn't much hurt by the gale, he told me.

That evening, about eight or so, Clarke called up from Bainbridge, in Connecticut. I call him Dick now, but he was Mr. Dickson Clarke to me then; for we had never met, although we had written each other a few times during the past winter and this summer. Clarke, as he has told you, owned a small cottage on the northeast beach at Sepatonk—it had been willed to him by an uncle who died in October—and he had put it in my charge to collect the rent and help out the tenants, when there were any. Clarke himself had never laid eyes on the property.

The telephone wire he was talking over was in pretty poor shape, but, in spite of the mosquito buzzings and the thumps, we could make out to hear each other. He was calling, he said, to ask whether that cottage of his was still on Sepatonk, or, if it had been blown out to sea, where he had better start dredging for it. I told him it was still here and, except for a blind or so missing and the roof of the front porch being up in a neighbor's tree, it was doing as well as could be expected. He was lucky, I told him.

"Um-hm," he said. "Then my luck is all at your end, Mr. Ownley. Unless a fellow with a broken leg is lucky that it isn't his neck. I am in the hospital just now."

"What that?" I sung out. "Your leg broke? That's pretty tough. How did it happen?"

"It didn't. My legs are all right, as a matter of fact. It

is my head that is tough. It must be, considering the crack it got."

"Well, well! Something fall on you, did it?"

"It didn't fall, it was pushed. But don't worry about me, I am all right now. How did that island of yours get through the tornado?"

I gave him what Sepatonk news there was. It was when I told about the motor boat wreck and the poor fellow fetched ashore from her that he woke up and got real interested.

"Wait a minute! Hold on!" he cut in. *"Where* did you say that motor boat came from?"

"According to the lettering on her stern board she hailed from Bainbridge, Connecticut. That's right up your way, ain't it? Her name was the *Nellie B.*"

That seemed to stir him up more still. The mosquitoes had stopped buzzing for a second, and I heard him muttering—to himself, I judged, for I couldn't catch the words.

"What?" I asked.

"Say that name again, will you?"

I said it.

"And she was a motor boat from Bainbridge?"

"According to her labeling she was—yes."

He didn't speak for right off. When he did, he asked another question.

"This man they brought ashore; what does he look like?"

I couldn't tell him that. Nobody but Doctor Farmer and Martha Pound, the doctor's housekeeper, had seen him since he was carried into their house.

"I asked Martha about him this morning, and she said he was lots better but had to be kept in bed. She said the doctor had ordered her not to let anybody from outside so much as peek at the patient.... Eh? Hello! Mr. Clarke, you still there?"

"Yes.... Yes, I am here. Humph! Was he alone on that boat? Anybody else with him?"

"Not so far as we know. If there was anybody, he, or they, have gone to the bottom. That stern board and a cabin door and half the rudder are the only sizable pieces of the craft that have been picked up so far. The rest of her is splinters."

Clarke seemed to be thinking "This fellow at the doctor's house?" he asked. "Did he bring anything ashore with him? Have they been through his pockets?"

"Pockets! Good Lord! I don't know as he had any pockets! He did have a cork life jacket buckled around him and that is how he kept afloat."

"And you say he will be there at your doctor's for a day or two at least?"

"Liable to be there for a fortnight, I judged from Martha Pound's story."

"I see.... Well, this is certainly a miracle—if it is what it looks to be.... Say, Ownley, is the Sepatonk steamer running regularly?"

"Starts running tomorrow, I understand."

"Good!... Well, so long."

"Eh? Wait a jiffy, Mr. Clarke. I want to know what you want done about fixing up your cottage."

But the line was dead; he had been cut off or had hung up or something. Considering how long it must have taken him to get me, he was in a terrible hurry to finish, seemed to me.

The next morning I went outdoors after breakfast and stood on the front grass plot by the old cannon looking out across the sound, trying to sight the steamer. That old cannon is one that was buried in the sand on the beach of Abel Ellis's property for nobody knows how long until a no'theaster washed it into sight again. It was so old-fashioned that folks figured it must have come from the wreck or some man-of-war craft—British, most likely—of the time afore the Revolution. Father bought it from Abe for little or nothing and set it up in front of the Inn.

I have got considerable free advertising out of that old cannon, just as I have from the name of the little hotel itself. The Ownley Inn is the only inn on Sepatonk Island, and city folks get a great laugh out of that feeble joke. When they ask me what the cannon is there for, I tell them "To repel boarders" and that *always* makes a hit. They repeat it all over creation and tell people that I am a "character"—which is a fine reputation for a hotel man to have in a place like Sepatonk. The average summer boarder is forever hunting "characters" and forgetting to look in the looking glass for a specimen.

Commodore House drifted out of the Inn while I was standing by the cannon and stopped to hail. This was his third summer with us, and we didn't know now what he had ever been commodore of, any more than we did when he first came. He is medium height and broad in the beam —although he would not have liked it if you called him fat —and his hair and little needle-pointed mustache were white. Against his red face that mustache shows up like a whitewashed stick in a bonfire.

Where he lived in the winter time none of us know. He engaged his room with us for the next season afore he left in the fall, and he always showed up the second day after the Inn opened. What he did for a living—if anything, he never told anybody, but he always seemed to have money in his pocket. His nickname "Souse," or "Old

Souse," was pinned on him by the Dolan girl chambermaid—who has considerable Irish fun in her—and if you walked past him any time after eleven in the morning you could smell the reason why. Not that he ever took aboard enough to give him a list; he was always on an even keel, and dignified and important.

"Good morning, Ownley," he hailed, clearing his throat, as he always did. He could make "Ahem" sound as important as a shot across the bows.

"Good morning, Commodore," said I. "And it *is* a good one, too."

"Very fine—very fine. Yes—ahem—yes. You were looking for the—er—steamer, I judge."

"Yes. I think that's her now, just heaving in sight."

He looked where I pointed. The steamer wasn't much more than a speck with a smudge over it.

"Hum—yes. Good eyes you have, Ownley—very good indeed, considering your age."

I am reaching the point where my age is one of the things I don't like to consider, but I didn't tell him so. As we stood there, Maizie Fay and Grace Hunter came swishing down the path, all rigged up in white skirts and sweaters.

"We are going down to the landing to meet the steamer," says the Fay girl. I call her and the Hunter one "girls" because I have a habit of looking on the bright side of things.

"Yes," chirped in Miss Hunter. "Watching something coming from somewhere else will be quite exciting after our isolation."

They swished away, all snap and sparkle. Charlie Drake came down the steps. He walked by us, just waving his hand but saying not so much as "Hello." He wasn't bound for the landing, I judged, for he turned to starboard after he went out of the front gate, and moved toward the upper end of the village.

"Now where is he going, in that direction and at this time in the morning?" says House. "Alone, too, as he always is. Odd fellow, isn't he? Yes—ahem—er—very odd. What do you know about him, Ownley?"

"Just about as much as you do, Commodore. To get anything about him *out* of him a man would need a cold chisel."

The Commodore let that sink in for a half a minute or so and then he began to chuckle.

"Yes, yes, very good," he said. "Very good indeed. Might call him the Sepatonk Island mystery, eh? Ha, ha!"

I hahaed too and thought no more about it—then. If he had said it afterward, I might have said: "Yes, one of them."

The steamer was in plain sight now, and Old Souse strutted off down the hill toward the landing. I had a notion to go along, but then I decided not to and went back into the Inn. I heard the steamer whistle for her landing; and, a few minutes afterward, I heard Pete Holley, who was out in the lobby, sing out. "Why, hello, Doc! Back again, eh? Glad to see you."

So Oscar Grover had been one of the boat passengers. I knew he was liable to come back from New York, or wherever he had been, most any time now, but I hadn't hardly looked for him that day. I walked out from the office to meet him.

"Welcome home," says I, as we shook hands. "Have a good trip?"

"Fairly good," he told me. "Business, and not very

exciting. I understand you have had more excitement down here."

"Why, yes, the weather folks gave us a surprise party and it was considerable of a blow-out. Where's your baggage? Or aren't you planning to stay with us over night?"

That was intended as a joke, for of course I knew his intention was to stay till the Inn closed, but he seemed to take it serious. He looked at me kind of funny, I thought.

"Stay with you?" he said. "Why shouldn't I stay with you? Have you heard anything to make you think I had changed my mind?"

"Eh? Why, no. You haven't changed it, have you? I hope you haven't."

He smiled. He had a way of smiling that made you wonder whether he was amused or just being polite. He was always polite—yes, and quiet. With his thin face and gray-black hair and manners he would have made you notice him anywhere. "A born aristocrat," that is how the Hunter girl ticketed him the first time she and he met. He seldom talked about himself, but, somehow or other, some boarder had learned that he had been professor in a college out West—that is why we called him "Doctor"— and that his health had broke down and he had come to Sepatonk to rest and put it together again. In spite of his quiet ways, he was one of the most popular summer folks on the Island. Perry Hale invited him to dinner up to the big house every once in a while.

He told me he shared my hope—that about staying to the end of the season.

"Although," he said, "there is a chance that a business matter may change my plans. My baggage? Oh, I took only a suitcase with me, and that is at the pier. I arranged with a boy to bring it up. By the way, Hammond, have any letters, or telegrams, come for me since I left?"

"Not a thing. But, so far as that goes, we haven't had any mail on Sepatonk since the gale. Probably some came on the steamer with you, though."

He went up to his room right after that, and I was turning to go back to the private office when another somebody came in at the Inn front door. I turned back to see who it was.

A big young fellow, a stranger, with a traveling bag in his hand.

"Good morning," says he. "This is the Ownley Inn, isn't it?"

"So the sign says," I told him. "And it is old enough to know what it is talking about."

Pretty fresh way to put it, I own up; but, you see, I had a notion that he was a drummer come to sell me something, and I was getting kind of tired of drummers. He laughed.

"I am all right so far, then. And now if I might speak to Mr. Ownley."

"You might. Far as that goes you are doing it now. I am Ownley."

He put down the bag and held out his hand. "Glad to look at you, Mr. Ownley," says he. "You and I have spoken before and recently, but this is our first look. My name is Dickson Clarke."

II

I was surprised to see him and said as much. Before I could say any more, he asked if I had a room to spare.

"Got more to spare than I have taken just now, Mr. Clarke. Calculating to stay with us a spell, was you? That's fine; only I suppose I ought to tell you that the season will be over, and we shut up shop in another ten days."

He said that would be plenty long enough for him, and we went to the desk together. I picked out his room myself, a nice corner room on the second floor corridor. As we were on the way upstairs, he asked if there were many folks still in the hotel.

"Not many. I'm afraid you'll find it kind of dull, Mr. Clarke."

He grinned. "Oh, maybe not," he said. I liked that grin of his; he grinned with his eyes as well as his mouth. While he was signing the register, I looked him over. He would have been more than common good-looking if it hadn't been for his nose; that looked as if it had been broken sometime or other. When he took his hat off, I noticed a place on the top of his head where the hair had been cut away and strips of plaster stuck on. I recollected he said over the phone that his head had been hurt.

He liked his room first-rate and said so. He ought to have liked it, for it was one of the best rooms in that part of the house. And quiet now, too, for there was nobody left along that hallway now but Charlie Drake and Doc Grover. I said he must have had to hustle to get from Bainbridge to Brandt and catch the boat so early in the morning. He said hustle was the word.

I was just going to leave him alone so as he could unpack his suitcase when he asked me if I was very busy just now.

"This morning, I mean," he said. "I'd like to have a talk with you when it's convenient, Mr. Ownley."

"My front name is Hammond," I told him. "Ham for

short. I'm absent-minded sometimes, and I might answer quicker if you hailed me that way."

He laughed. "Fair enough!" says he. "And I am Dick. Don't forget it. Now, about that talk?"

"How about ten minutes from now? I'll be up then if you say so."

I was there in just ten minutes by the clock. First thing he did was make me sit down in the rocker by the window, next was to offer me a cigarette. I told him I was much obliged but I had smoked tobacco for forty-odd year and it was a little mite too late in life to change. That tickled him, and he lit up a cigarette while I loaded my pipe. Then he stepped across the room and turned the key in the door.

"Looks mysterious, doesn't it?" he said, with one of those grins of his. "Well, darn it, that is exactly what it is. I've got a lot of things to tell you, Mr. Ownley—Hammond, I mean—"

" 'Ham' saves space," I reminded him.

"Right you are. Well, Ham, I've got to talk to somebody, and, from what I used to hear my uncle say about you, you are exactly the one to talk it to. There is just one thing"—he reddened up a little—"and that is—well, I must ask you to keep all this I am going to tell you under your hat. You haven't told anyone about my phoning you, have you?"

"No."

"Fine! Did you notice that I registered from Springfield; not from Bainbridge?"

I hadn't noticed and I said so. I spoke pretty short, I guess, for, to tell the truth, all this "don't tell" business riled me a little. When a man had kept hotel long as I have he listens to a whole lot of private history; and, if he was in the habit of spilling what was poured into his ears, he wouldn't last long at his trade.

"I know it sounds queer," he went on, "but—well, if anybody asks you, you don't know anything about me except that I am here to see about that cottage of mine. I'll explain—"

"There, there! You needn't explain anything, or say anything, unless you want to. If you do say it, you can count on my mouth staying shut without having buttons sewed on it."

He laughed. "I would have bet on that after our first five minutes together," he said. "Well, here is my yarn."

It was a long yarn, and a lot of it he has written down already. He spun it till he got to the part where he got that crack over the head. The next thing he knew he was in bed in the Bainbridge hospital. By the time he got this far I was sitting on the edge of my chair. I read a good many detective books in the winter time—the circulating library at Brandt sends them over to me—and this was beginning to sound like a chapter out of one of them. I told Clarke so.

"It sounds more that way as it goes on," he said. "It is like one of those 'Tune in Mondays for our next installment' things on the radio."

Lucky for him, and no thanks to the fellow that hit him, there wasn't any of what the doctors call "concussion." He was knocked out of time, and it was a day or so before the hospital folks let him sit up or see anybody. The first thing he wanted to learn was news from the Knowlton Library, what had happened there, and how his friend, the Payson man, was getting along. They let him see the newspaper after a spell, but there wasn't a word in it about Payson. The hurricane news was filling the paper, and he couldn't find even a paragraph about any happening at the Library. They had learned from some letters in his pocket who he was and had, so they told him, notified Doctor Payson already. Payson had phoned two or three times to ask about him and was coming to see him as soon as he was well enough.

And, the following morning, he did come. He was all right too, Payson was, not hurt serious at all. But he was dreadful worried and upset. He had a story of his own to tell, and when Clarke heard it, he could understand what the worry was about.

Seems that Payson and this collector's secretary fellow, the one who had come especial to look at the rare Primer book the Knowlton Library had, were in the little room they called the "strong room" together. Payson had locked the door behind them when they came in, same as he always did when he took anybody to that room, and they were alone. Payson had laid the door key on the table instead of putting it back in his pocket, and doing that was something he blamed himself especially for.

"Careless, careless!" he kept on saying during his talk with Clarke. "I am not offering any excuse and I told the Trustees so."

He had taken the Primer out of the safe where it was kept, and the secretary man had taken the book out of the leather case it was kept in and had it open before him on the table. He was saying how wonderful it was and in what remarkable condition. He called Payson's attention to the date or something, and Payson stooped over him to see what he was pointing at; and just as he did, this secretary rascal stood up sudden and knocked the Doctor's nose glasses off and on to the marble floor where they smashed all to pieces. Payson, according to Clarke, is blind as an owl in daylight without his specs, and, naturally, he got down to grope round and make out what damage was done. The secretary kept saying how sorry he was, but— as the Doctor remembered later, although he didn't think anything of it then—he stayed at the table instead of getting down to help.

Then Doctor Payson recollected that, for a wonder, he had his spare pair of glasses in his jacket pocket. He rummaged them out, put them on and stood up. And then, he saw that the secretary fellow was putting the Primer back in its leather case. Got through looking it over mighty quick, seemed to the Doctor.

"Oh," says Payson, "don't bother to do that, Mr. Sanger; I'll attend to that."

He reached for the Primer, and, the minute he got hold of it, he sensed something queer. The book didn't—well, feel just right, or look just right, or something.

"Why—why—" says he. "What—"

And that was the last word he had a chance to say. The next thing he knew, he didn't know anything, as the saying is. When he came to, people were mopping his head with cold water, the secretary had gone, and, when they looked for it, the real Primer—the rare one—had gone too. There was an imitation one there, but it was the shoddiest kind of a make-believe, just something the same shape and size that might have fooled a nigh-sighted person without glasses until he came to look it over.

It was all a put-up job, of course. The secretary wasn't the real collector's secretary at all, and the letter introducing him wasn't real either. They were both part of a plan to steal that Primer book. Smashing Payson's glasses was done on purpose; and if the Doctor hadn't happened to have the spare pair with him, the fake Primer would have been back in the case and back in the safe, and the swap might not have been noticed for weeks. As it was, that secretary scamp had to think and act quick. He probably had a blackjack or a sandbag handy, and he used it. Then he picked up the strong room key from the table, unlocked the door, and cleared out. If Clarke had come only a minute sooner—but he didn't.

Poor Doctor Payson was too badly shook up and dazed to realize all this that day. He asked for Clarke and Clarke had gone, nobody seemed to know why or where.

Payson told the Library trustees the whole story, keeping nothing back. They were very nice to him, he said. They didn't say what they must have thought, but he realized, all too well, the mess he was in. That Primer was one of the Knowlton Library's finest and rarest ownings, and he—he kept repeating this to Clarke there at the hospital—was responsible for its safety. His carelessness, and taking too much for granted, were responsible for its loss. Unless it could be found and brought back, he would lose his position. "And I have been curator and librarian there for thirty years. It was my life work."

Clarke said it was pitiful to hear him.

Dick tried to cheer him up, make him promise not to resign or anything like that for a few weeks at least. Made believe there was a chance to locate the book and the rascal that stole it and talked all the encouragement he could think of; but it was mostly bluff, and both of them knew it. Clarke told the old man about his following the fellow and about being knocked out, but he said little or nothing about seeing the rascal talking to somebody on a motor boat. He didn't consider that part important; not then he didn't.

But when I told him, over the phone, about a motor

craft named the *Nellie B.*, registered from Bainbridge in Connecticut, being wrecked on Sepatonk Island and about a man having been brought ashore from her, the possible importance hit him and hit him hard. The first place he headed for, after he left the hospital, was the wharf in Bainbridge. The night watchman there told him that the *Nellie B.* belonged to an old fellow named Blake or Burke —some such name—who had lived in the town only a few months, and nobody knew much of anything about him. He made a little money fishing or taking out parties. The watchman said the *Nellie B.* left the pier the afternoon of the day Clarke was hurt and nobody knew where she was bound or had seen hide nor hair of her since. It was the watchman's guess that the hurricane had got her, same as it got so many small craft.

Clarke asked if there was anybody aboard her late that afternoon except this Blake man. The watchman didn't know for sure, but he had a sort of notion that there was— one other. That was enough for Dick Clarke. He hurried back to the hospital, threw some clothes and duds into a bag, caught a night train for Brandt, and took the steamer to Sepatonk Island.

By this time I was in about as excited a state of mind as he was himself. Here was a mystery yarn that hadn't come from a circulating library and hadn't been worked out for me by any book author. The sort of thing that was right up my back alley, as you might say. I had a couple of hundred questions to ask, and I asked some of them.

"Then it is your notion, Mr. Clarke," says I, "that this castaway in Doctor Farmer's spare room may be the bird that knocked out the poor old Payson man, stole that Primer thing you say is so important, and then whacked you out of tune?"

"He might be, mightn't he? If he went away on the *Nellie B.* and the *Nellie B.* was wrecked on this island."

"But you are not dead certain he did go on the *Nellie B.?*"

"No, but I am guessing he did. He was talking with this Blake fellow aboard her there in Bainbridge, for I saw him."

"Um-hm. And the *Nellie B.* is here—what there is left of her—and somebody from her is in the doctor's house. Of course he might be the Blake one. Have you thought of that?"

"Yes, I have thought of it. It is about fifty-fifty, I suppose. If I could only see him. Darn it all, Ownley, I have *got* to see him!"

"That can be arranged somehow, I should think. He ought to be well enough for folks to look at pretty soon. But as for his still having your Primer book, providing he ever had it, that's no chance at all. A big book like that—"

"Who told you it was big? The New England Primer is a tiny little thing. Three inches square, or thereabouts. He could carry it in his vest pocket, almost."

I stared at him. "As little as that!" I sang out. "And—and valuable! Don't seem possible! What sense is there in robbing and murdering to get hold of a midget book like that? Could it be sold for anything worth while?"

"Depends on what you call worth while. Our edition of the New England Primer is, so far as anyone knows, among the very earliest in existence. And in fine condition. Almost any big library would pay thirty thousand for it. A rich collector of Americana might pay twice that."

I caught my breath. "Good Lord above! Sixty thousand dollars! Sixty *thousand!*"

"Some collectors—the unscrupulous kind—would pay that and ask no questions.... Well, Mr. Ownley, *now* don't you think I ought to see this castaway chap as soon as I can? Will you help me to see him?"

I drew another long breath. "I'll help you," says I. "You shall get a good sight of that man if we have to break and enter. Yes, and go to jail afterward. I am with you, Mr. Clarke, right through past the stake boat."

III

Dick was for going right up to Farmer's that very minute. As I look back at it now, it might have been better if we had, but then it didn't seem wise to me. Nine chances to one, the doctor, who is a stubborn old boy, wouldn't let us do it unless we told him our reasons. Dick didn't like that idea at all. The stealing of the Primer, he felt, ought to be kept a secret for a while anyhow. Nothing had been given out to the newspapers about it yet, and, provided the man at Farmer's was our thief, he mustn't suspect that anybody on Sepatonk was on to him. "For poor Payson's sake," says Dick, "the less this business is advertised the better. If we can't get the Primer back, it will have to be, of course, but not now."

I saw the point and agreed with him.

"Then we'll take it slow for a few hours anyhow," I said. "That fellow at the doctor's is bound to stay there because he is too weak to get away. As for you—"

"As for me," cut in Dick, "I am down here to see about having my cottage fixed up. If they notice my plastered head, you can tell them I am subject to fits and fell down stairs."

I had intended to drop in at Doctor Farmer's that afternoon, just to ask a few innocent questions about how the castaway was getting on, but the doctor himself saved me the trouble. He happened into the Inn that afternoon, and we had quite a talk. He said his patient was doing well, was conscious, but too badly shook up to talk much or be allowed to do anything.

"First thing he wanted to know," the doctor told me, "was where he was. When I told him he was on Sepatonk Island, he was the most surprised person you can imagine. Said the name over again and swore out loud. I told him swearing was a good healthy sign but that he mustn't get excited. I was just going to tell him how he happened to be there when he broke in to ask what day it was. I gave him the name and date and he swore again. Vowed he was going to get up and dress. I settled that notion in just one minute. The next thing he asked about was what had become of the things in his pockets."

"Oh! He did have things in his pockets, did he?"

"Yes, a few. In the inside pocket of his vest, they were. And I could understand why he was anxious about them. He had a hundred and ten dollars in his pocketbook, a fifty dollar bill, and three twenties. They were in a state, too. Sopping wet, of course."

"They must have been. Anything else?"

"Let me tell you about the money first. When my housekeeper saw those big bills, so wet they would scarcely hold together, she was in a flurry. I don't suppose Martha Pound had ever seen a fifty dollar bill before, and three twenties all together was like an exhibition of fireworks to her. She was sure the money was ruined, and I declare I thought she was going to break down and cry. I cheered her up by telling her they could be dried careful and then pressed with a flatiron and they would be as good as ever. She figures that this fellow must be a millionaire."

He laughed again. I laughed, too, but my laugh ended sooner than his did. I had some more questions to ask.

"Anything else in his pockets?" I asked, trying to make it sound casual.

"Eh? O yes, a watch—that *is* ruined, I'm afraid—and a little flat thing done up in oilskin, with oiled silk under that. I only undid the outside wrapping, for the silk underneath was dry. It felt like a memorandum book, I thought. That's why I didn't unwrap it."

You can imagine how this item of news hit me. I had to turn my head so the doc wouldn't see my face.

"Must have been a pretty important memorandum book," I said, "for him to wrap it up careful as all that."

"Oh, it was. He is a traveling salesman for a wholesale liquor house, so he says, and this little book has the names and addresses of all his New England customers in it, the state of their credit and all that. I took it and the watch to him and told him the money would be brought in soon as it was dry and ironed. He was grateful enough, poor chap."

Hindsight is always so much better than foresight. *Then* was the time I ought to have come right out with Dick's yarn about the Primer. I didn't because I thought I had better speak to Dick first.

Doctor Farmer went on to say that his patient's name was Kelly—John Kelly. "That's Irish," says the doctor, "but he looks more like a Frenchman or Italian. Maybe his mother was Italian. I'll ask him sometime."

The fellow might have been part Chinese for all I cared. That didn't interest me, but I remembered some other things Dick had told me.

"He must have a pretty tough constitution to pull through the way he has," I said.

The doctor and I were in my private office while we were talking so far, but now he looked at his watch and declared he must be going along.

"I have things to attend to," says he. "Can't sit around and loaf the whole afternoon. I'm no hotel man, I'm a hard-working practicer of medicine, Lord help me."

He went out into the lobby, and I followed him. Pete Holley and Grover and Drake were playing dominoes by the window. How they ever got Drake to join in I don't know. Usually he wasn't as sociable as that. Doctor Farmer said hello to them, and they helloed back.

"The doctor has been giving me the news about the fellow up at his house, the one from the wreck," I said, by way of general information to all hands. "I was just saying that he must have a healthy constitution for his age."

Farmer turned to look at me. "Age?" says he. "What do you mean? He can't be more than thirty."

"Oh, is that so? Somehow or other I got the notion he was along in years. Maybe 'twas the shock that turned his hair white. I've read about such cases, in books."

The doctor was disgusted. "You read too much trash, Ham, that's what ails you. You know what this boarding-house keeper here does all winter long?" he added, turning toward the domino players. "He reads every wild-eyed detective yarn he can get hold of. Looks hard-boiled and antique enough, too, but he isn't; he's just an oversized kid."

Everybody laughed; that is everybody except Charlie Drake and even he looked up long enough to smile. Farmer, having got their attention—he does dearly love a congregation to preach to—went right on.

"Shock!" he snorted. "If shocks whiten hair, mine, what little I've got left, would have whitened long ago. A man on this island owed me a bill for seven years. The other day he came in and paid it. If *that* wasn't shock enough to bleach anybody's hair, nothing could. Who told you this wreck wash-up of mine had white hair, Ham?"

I sputtered some excuse; that I guessed I must have dreamed it, or something like that. Everybody laughed again. The doctor shook his head.

"White hair!" he sniffed. "His hair is jet black, and so are his eyebrows and eyes. He's a husky-built specimen, too. Got a crooked left arm. Tells me he broke it out hunting one time and 'twas badly set. First thing I noticed when I got his clothes off."

Just then Holley or Grover or Drake—each one accused the other of it afterward—jolted the table and half the dominoes fell on the floor. That ended the talk. Farmer went out, and I hurried upstairs to find Dick. Dick was all upset over the news about the "memorandum book."

"It's the Primer!" he vowed, thumping his fist down on his knee. "It's our Primer; I'll bet on it! Shall we go up there and take it from him?"

"Wait a minute. Suppose he says it *is* a memorandum book, his own private list of customers and all that? Suppose we ask him to let us look at it and he tells us where to go? What then?"

"Why—but, hang it all, Ham, we—"

"Now, now, take it easy! Would you recognize that bogus secretary if you saw him again? In different clothes —or in pajamas or a nightgown, or whatever the doctor has fitted him out with?"

Dick pulled at his port ear, a habit of his.

"Well," says he, kind of troubled, "I think I would—yes. Of course I didn't look him over item by item—why should I? An oldish man. Glasses—kind of dark glasses, they were, and whitish eyebrows and a mop of white hair."

"There's no glasses now and no white hair, either. This liquor drummer's hair and eyebrows are black, and, according to Farmer, he can't be more than thirty. That don't fit in, even if the memorandum book does."

"But—but he might have worn a wig."

"Certain sure he might, but who's going to prove it? No, no, we mustn't ruin our chances by rushing. And yet we've got to see the inside of that flat package. When we've settled what is inside it, we've settled everything—friend Kelly included."

"But if it is the Primer, he won't *let* us see it. You just said so, yourself."

"And if it is his own private memo book, why should he? ... But we mustn't stay up here together any longer just now. Hettie and half the boarders are probably wondering where I am by this time. I'm going downstairs."

He said he would follow right along, so I left him. I went down to my little private office, the place where I can generally figure on being alone as much as a hotel man can ever be anywhere, and sat down to do some heavy thinking. Silver, the bookkeeper, had gone to the post office, the domino party had broke up and gone outdoor; so I had the whole front lower floor to myself. I was sitting in the little office, with my feet up on the desk, when I heard Dick come downstairs.

I was just going to sing out to him when I heard the front door open. Then somebody said:

"Dick Clarke! Dick!"

The voice didn't sound familiar to me. It was a woman's, but I couldn't place the owner of it. I got up from my chair and looked out into the lobby. There was a young woman there—a stranger to me she was. She was looking at the Clarke fellow as if she was mighty surprised—yes, and kind of excited and pleased, too. As for him, he looked surprised but more fussed and sheepish than pleased, I thought. He looked the way a young-one does when he's caught with his fist in the cooky jar.

"Dick Clarke!" she said again. "In person and on Sepatonk Island!"

Dick's face was red. "Hello, Anne," he said.

The name gave me my clue. George Silver had told me that the Hale houseparty had arrived; Perry Hale had gone over to Brandt in his motor boat and fetched them across the night before. Silver said there was a married couple named Folger and a young woman named Anne Francis. "She's a peach, too," says George. "I saw her when the launch came in."

So that's who the girl in the lobby was—the Anne Francis one; she couldn't be anyone else.

"I came in to buy a few postcards," she went on; "but I certainly didn't expect *this!*"

Dick's words were snapped out. "I know what you're thinking. You think I followed you down here. Well, you're wrong. I didn't. Nothing of the kind."

"Of course not." She spoke in a gentle, soothing kind of voice. "Why should I flatter myself to that extent?"

"I told you I owned a house down here." He was talking fast. "Well, I wanted to see what the hurricane had left of it, so—so I came down here."

"Of course."

She said the words real soft, and I couldn't see as they

were anything to make anybody mad; but they seemed to make Clarke that way. "Don't look so darn smug," he says, raising his voice a little and getting redder in the face. "You can think what you please, but I'm not chasing you. I tell you I came down here to see about my house!"

"So you said. And how is your house?"

"It's all right. Only a few shutters blown off."

"That's too bad."

"Thanks a lot."

"I mean it's too bad for me. Since your house is all right you'll probably be leaving right away."

I had heard this much afore it crossed my mind that I was listening to what wasn't my business at all, something no outsider was expected to hear, or ought to. I ought to show myself right off; but, if I did, that would be kind of awkward too. Awkward for all hands. While I was trying to settle what to do, they went right on talking. The upshot of it was that I decided to keep quiet and do my explaining to Dick afterward. I tiptoed back to my chair. I couldn't see them now, but I could hear plain enough.

Dick mumbled something about maybe having to stay on for a few days. "But don't worry," he snapped. "I won't bother you. I'll keep out of the way."

She was keeping her patience remarkable well, I thought. "I wish you wouldn't be like this," she said. "Can't we be friends even if we aren't engaged any longer? I would like you to meet the Folgers. You'd like them. You would like Perry Hale, too."

"Oh, sure!" sarcastic. "And I'll bet Mr. Hale would just love to have your ex-fiancé hanging around his premises."

"Why shouldn't he? Perry has no claim on me."

"No, but he'd like to have. . . . Never mind. It doesn't matter. I won't purposely see you again even if I stay here for a month."

"A month? Why, how wonderful! But how about the big job? Don't you have to get back to that?"

"Why—"

"And that reminds me of another reason why you should meet my friends. Fred Folger is tremendously interested in rare books, and the minute I tell him you're with the Knowlton Library—"

That shook him up. I could tell by the way he broke in on her.

"You mustn't do that!" he ordered, sharp. "You mustn't tell him a word about my being with the Library."

"What! Why—why on earth not?"

"Well—well, because I'm not with the Library any more. There—there was trouble there and I had to get out. I don't want to talk about it to you—or anybody else. Do me a big favor, will you, Anne? Promise me that you won't say a word to a soul about my ever having had any connection with the Knowlton Library. Promise!"

"Well, I'll be darned! This is all very sudden and odd. What's the mystery?"

"No mystery. I just don't want to talk about the Library, that's all. I want to forget it. Will you do me that favor— and help me?"

"I'm not sure. . . . I might."

"Then promise."

She took a second or two before answering. Then she said, slow: "If I do you this favor, will you do one for me?"

"Of course. What is it?"

"Nothing very tremendous. I'll promise to keep your

dark secret dark if you'll promise me to be reasonable about me and Perry and the Folgers."

"What do you mean, 'reasonable'?"

"I mean that I want you to let me introduce you to them. Then, if you're asked for tennis or swimming or dinner, I want you to accept. I'm just asking you to be friendly with us. That's all."

Dick didn't like that notion, anybody could tell.

"I can't do that, of course," he growled.

"Why not?"

"Don't be absurd. A man doesn't play around with a girl and her friends just a few weeks after she has given him the bounce. It isn't done."

"If it isn't done, it's time it was. Why can't we be friends? You don't hate me, do you?"

"Of course not."

"And I don't hate you. Q.E.D."

"I'm sorry. I can't do it."

And then she did put her foot down, in a way.

"Well," she said, "I won't argue. You've asked me to do you a favor—a rather peculiar one, I might say. I'll do it, if you'll do me one in return. Not unless."

You could tell she meant it. Dick Clarke took a little time, but finally he gave in. "It's insane," he vowed, "but I haven't any choice. I agree."

"Good. Shake hands on it."

They shook hands, I judged, for there was a little break in the talk. Then I heard the Francis girl ask: "Why, what is the matter with your head?"

"Something hit it. Hurricane accident, nothing important. My wits aren't any duller, I hope."

"That's a relief. And you will be friends with the Folgers and Perry?"

"Yes. Oh, yes, if they will let me. And you'll keep my secret?"

"No one shall learn it from me. I can't help it, of course, if any of them have already heard you worked at the Library."

"Not much chance of that. I'll have to take the risk, anyhow."

Perry Hale called to her from the front yard then. "Anne, where are you!" She called to him that she was coming and hurried out. Dick Clarke stood where he was for a minute and then wandered off down to the other end of the lobby. I grabbed the chance to slip out through the side way into the kitchen.

Thinking over what I had heard, I decided not to mention having heard it—not yet, at any rate. As I said, it wasn't my business. The news about the broken-off engagement was news, of course, and, up to just then, I had no notion that Clarke and Hale had a friend in common. But none of that was my business, either. So, when Dick and I met a little later, I told him not a word. He and Anne Francis wasn't the only ones who could keep secrets.

IV

Nothing in particular happened the rest of that day or during the daylight hours of the one after it. Hettie Bassett came to me that second forenoon with a yarn that Sophronia Ryder—Laban Ryder's wife, she is, and the Ryders live next house to Doctor Farmer—had told her at Eastern Star lodge meeting. Seems that Martha Pound, the Farmer housekeeper, had come running to Sophronia in a peck of trouble and scared to death. Martha had, according to her boss's orders, dried and ironed out the bills in the Kelly man's pocketbook and the flat iron was too hot, or something, and the bills had got scorched in places. Martha was scared they could never be used for money again, but Sophronia went over and looked at them; and she told Hettie that the scorches were just black smudges and wouldn't do a mite of harm. She advised the Pound woman to put them right back in the pocketbook and put the pocketbook with the Kelly man's watch and things in his bureau drawer.

"Nine chances to one he'll think the scorched places are just dirt," Sophronia said, "that is if he ever notices them at all." So Martha did that and felt considerable better.

Hettie made a tremendous yarn of it, mainly on account of the Kelly man being rich enough to have all those big bills with him. He must be a millionaire sure, so she and Sophronia figured. The whole story sounded to me like a hurrah over nothing, and I put it out of my head altogether. Shouldn't mention it now, only, later on, I was reminded of it in an unexpected way.

That evening, more to soothe down some of Dick Clarke's fidgets than anything else, I suggested that he and I take a walk over in the general direction of Doctor Farmer's place.

"We can look the land over, if nothing more," I said. "I know the ground floor room that our Kelly chum is in, and the window is liable to be open a warm, fine night like this. If the shade is up and the lamp lighted, you might get a sight of him. Even without the white hair and specs there might be something about him that looked familiar."

I didn't take much stock in our seeing anything worth while, but the walk would keep Dick from fretting and getting more impatient. He was crazy about the idea; so, after the bunch in the lobby had thinned out—'most everybody turned in early—he and I started out by way of the side door. We followed the main road a ways and then took the path across the fields and through the pine grove which is on the little hill back of the Farmer property.

When we hove in sight of the doctor's house, I left Dick at the edge of the pines and went ahead by myself to take an observation, as you might say. The doctor's office was dark, so I judged he was out; but the kitchen window was lighted, and I could see Martha Pound's shadow moving in there.

I went back and told Dick the coast was clear and to come ahead. "The spare room," I said, "is in the front so I couldn't see whether or not there was a light in it. We will have to be quiet and keep our heads down."

Dick had a question to ask. "Hush!" he said to me. "Listen!"

I listened, but except for the wind in the tops of the pines and the surf growling on the Hale beach I heard nothing.

"*I* don't now," he said, "but I did just before you came back, a minute or two ago. Something or somebody was going along that path we just came up by. It was too dark for me to see, but I heard. It wasn't on the path exactly, but near it. It sounded as if it was in a hurry, too."

"Humph! Can't think who would be traveling that path this time of night. This is late for Sepatonk, I'd have you know. Which way did the noise seem to be moving?"

"Back, the way we came."

Whatever it was, or wasn't, it had gone now; so we started on our cruise, keeping behind the barn and the henhouses until we turned the corner and then in the lee of the front fence until we got to the big lilac bush by the gate. Even afore we got that far, though, I could see that we'd had our tramp for nothing. The window of the spare room was black dark; patient was in bed and asleep, no doubt. We might have expected it, but it was disappointing.

"Too late," I whispered. "Might as well about ship and head for home."

Dick Clarke swore, under his breath. "Darned if I am going back yet," he vowed. "Light or no light I am going to look in that window."

He was over the fence and tiptoeing across the yard afore I could stop him. No sense in it; he wouldn't be able to see his man, and the doctor might show up any time and catch us at it. However, I couldn't very well let him go alone, so I swung over the fence and tiptoed in his wake.

The window was wide open, the lower half of the sash pushed up far as it would go, and the shade run up clear to the roller. A queer way for a sick man's window to be fixed at night, I recollect thinking. We scooched down on the grass and peeked over the sill.

We could see precious little. The shape of the bureau against the end wall, the loom of a rocking chair, and the side of the big double bed. But the person in the bed we couldn't see at all. Everything was awful quiet. Not a rustle, nor a loud breath, to say nothing of a snore. Mr. Kelly was an easy sleeper, I could say that for him.

And then we got a surprise. There was a knock on the bedroom door, on the side nighest the back of the house. Then a voice—Martha Pound's voice, saying: "Mr. Kelly ... Oh, Mr. Kelly."

I put my hand on Dick's shoulder and pushed him down. We scooched as low as we could.

Another knock and then another, a loud one this time.

"Mr. Kelly," says Martha, raising her voice. "Mr. Kelly, I'm so sorry to disturb you, but it is time for your medicine. The doctor said you must be sure and take it. . . . Oh, Mr. *Kelly!*"

But Mr. Kelly didn't so much as move, to say nothing of answering. The door opened just a crack; then it opened wide, and the Pound woman came in holding a lamp in one hand and a teacup with a spoon in it in the other. Perhaps I might as well explain right here that the Hale place and the Ownley Inn are the only buildings on the Island fitted up with electric lights. Hale has his own electric outfit and I hire the Inn current from him.

"Mr. Kelly," said Martha Pound, "I am dreadful sorry to have to—"

She said this much, and then she screamed out loud. I lifted my eyes above the level of the sill, and then I could have screamed, too. Except for the Pound woman herself, there was nobody in that room. The bed had been slept in, but it was vacant now. So were the chairs. Mr. Kelly, the poor sick man who was too shook up and feeble to talk to anybody or even be seen by anybody except the doctor, wasn't among those present, as the newspapers tell about. Unless he was under the bed or in the closet he had gone —cleared out—vanished.

Martha Pound put the lamp and cup down on the bureau and ran—or as nigh running as a craft of her build could make it—over to the bed. She began pulling the sheets and quilts apart; she even lifted up the pillows as if she expected to find her missing patient hid under one of them. All the time she was groaning and exclaiming and talking to herself.

"Mr. Kelly! Oh, Mr. Kelly! Where are you? What *shall* I do?" And the like of that.

It was that minute that Dick Clarke picked out to step on a dry stick and break it. Martha turned toward the window and saw us looking in at her. The screech she gave then was like the Point fog whistle. One or two more like it and the Ryder neighbors would hear her and come galloping. I figured it was time to cut in.

"There, there, Martha!" I said. "Shh! Hush! Put a muffler on it. It's all right. Nobody but me—Ham Ownley. What's the trouble?"

She just gurgled and glared and flapped her hands. I climbed in over the sill and Dick followed after me. I soothed her down best I could, made some sort of explanation about how Mr. Clarke and I were passing by and heard her scream, and so on. Then I asked again what the matter was.

I knew, of course, before I asked. It was the disappearance of the sick man that had set her going. I suggested maybe he was around the house somewheres, gone to the bathroom perhaps. That didn't help much because the bathroom in the Farmer house had been added on within a couple of years and it opened off the kitchen. She had been in that kitchen all the time and if he had gone there she would have seen him.

"He was too sick and—and rickety to go anywhere," she vowed. "He was right in this very bed an hour and a half ago because I seen him there with my own eyes. Oh, it's terrible! He's gone off his poor head and—and got outdoor somehow. He'll die—he'll die of—of dipthery or—or pneumony or something. *What* will Doctor Farmer say to me?"

She was close to hysterics—and there was so darned much of her to get hysterical. All I could do was keep pouring on the soothing syrups, telling her he must be in the house, and if he was, we would find him right off. Dick, though, was more practical.

"Mrs. Pound," he broke in. "Mrs. Pound, was that window open when you left him? Open as far as it is now, I mean?"

She looked at the window and went off into another conniption. No, oh no, it wasn't—it wasn't. It was open only a little crack. That's how he had gone. But he couldn't, because he wasn't strong enough. Oh—

Dick, who was keeping his head like a Major, asked another question. "Where are his clothes?" he wanted to know.

His clothes—the ones he had come ashore in and the only ones he had—were in the closet; Martha herself had put them there after she had dried and pressed them. But what difference did that make? He had on one of the doctor's nightshirts. He had wanted to get up and down but the doctor wouldn't let him.

Dick took the lamp and went over and opened the closet door. "What sort of clothes were they?" he asked.

Martha said there was a coat and vest and pants and—and a shirt and shoes and— Dick didn't want to hear the rest. "There is a shirt here," he said, "but no coat or trousers or shoes that I can see. Humph! well, Ownley, it looks as if the window was the answer. He did dress—part way, anyhow—opened that window and vamoosed. Now why—and where?"

I couldn't imagine, unless Martha was right and he had been struck crazy. No time to argue and guess about it, though; he must be hunted. Sick as he was and rampaging around in that night air—whew!

"Mr. Clarke and I will find him," I told Martha. "Got a lantern on the premises, have you?"

She didn't have any lantern, but there was one of "them electric flashlight things" in the doctor's room. After a little more persuading and more soothing syrup, she fetched it to us. Then, making her promise to hunt the house over on the chance that the Kelly patient might be somewheres inside after all, and not to call the Ryders or anybody till she heard from us, Dick and I got out of the window again and started on our hunt.

"What in the devil do you suppose this means?" Dick wanted to know. "I wonder if he was as sick as he pretended to be. If he could get up and dress and open that window— But why did he do it, anyhow? Do you suppose he was running away?"

"Where could he run to on Sepatonk Island?"

There didn't seem to be any answer to that, so we went down the road a piece and then back a piece the other way. No sign of anybody. The town folks' houses were all shut up and dark and the only lighted windows were those in the big Hale house down by the shore. Wherever he might go it wouldn't be there, half-dressed as he was.

We kept on along the road until we came to where the cross-lots path Dick and I had come over by joined on. Then Dick said he was wondering.

"I have been doing nothing but wonder since we started," I said. "Is your wonder anything particular or just general?"

"Don't know, but—well, I was thinking of that noise I heard when you left me alone over in the woods yonder. Something or somebody went by close to me then. Do you suppose—"

"That it was chum Kelly? By the everlasting, it might have been! Let's go up that way."

We followed the path till we came to where I left Dick when I went ahead to spy out the Farmer premises.

"It was here I heard it," says he. "It sounded over there to the left."

To the left was pines and beachplum bushes and, a little further on, an open space. A big pine stood all by itself on the far edge of the clearing. Dick had the flashlight and he moved over that way. A minute later I heard him call.

"Ham! Come here!"

He sounded excited. I stumbled to where he was. He was kneeling on the pine needles and there was a black lumpy shape on the ground beside him. He turned the flashlight on it. It was a man, dressed in trousers and a jacket over what looked like a nightshirt. The collar of the jacket was turned up around his neck and he was bareheaded. I caught my breath hard.

"Is it—is it him?" I asked.

"Looks as if it might be, doesn't it?"

"Is he—is he—"

"Don't know yet, but— Good God, look at his head!"

In the light from the flash we could see a big bruised cut on the side of the fellow's head, by the temple. It had bled considerable and was bleeding a little yet. I got on my knees and put my ear down to listen for a breath. I couldn't hear any, nor I couldn't feel any pulse either.

Dick made a clicking kind of noise in his throat. "Well?" he asked.

I shook my head. "I'm afraid he's gone," I said. "And it's Kelly, all right. Look here!"

The man was lying across a big branch that the hurricane had blown off the tall pine overhead. One of the twigs had caught the edge of the jacket sleeve and had pulled it and the sleeve of the nightshirt up a foot or so. The arm was bare almost to the elbow.

"There's the crooked wrist," says I. "It's Kelly. Is he the one you followed there at Bainbridge?"

Dick took a long look. "I don't know," he said. "The white wig—if it was a wig—has gone and—no, I don't know.... Say, Ownley!"

"Yes?"

"I was thinking. That noise I heard when I was waiting for you didn't seem to come from right here. It sounded a good deal more to the left—almost behind me—and moving in the direction you and I came from. It must have been this man, though. Of course it was. Who else could it have been?"

PART III

The Twenty Dollar Bill

The Story Continued by
Seth Hammond Ownley

I

WHAT we had done and said since we found the body takes longer to tell about than it did in happening. We hadn't been on the spot more than five minutes, if that, and we both realized that this was no time to guess or speculate. We must get help and get it right off.

"One of us must stay here with him," I said, "and the other go. The doctor must be located first—let's hope he's home by this time—and we'll need others. Shall I go or will you?"

Dick said he would go and started on the gallop, leaving me to stand watch. I picked up the flashlight and stooped over the man on the ground.

He was dead, I couldn't doubt that. The big branch he had fallen across had a sharp point at the place where it had broken from the tree, and his head was close beside that point. If he fell full length and his temple had connected with that sharp edge, why—

The only thing was why did he fall? And what on earth was he doing there, away off the path? Crazy, most likely, or he wouldn't have climbed out of the window, to say nothing of starting off pellmell into the woods. Well, maybe we would know a little more after the doctor come.

Meantime I had something I thought ought to be done and now was my chance to do it.

It wasn't a pleasant job, but if it turned out right it would settle Dick Clarke's trouble and old Doctor Payson's, too. Two people would breathe easier, not to count in the trustees of the Knowlton Library. And there wouldn't have to be a lot of newspaper hurrah, either.

I set my teeth and went to work. Kelly—if this man was Kelly, and I couldn't doubt that—was wearing a coat and trousers over a nightshirt, so there wasn't many pockets to go through. Feeling like a combination sneak-thief and body-snatcher, I went through every one of them, taking care to miss nothing. And nothing was what I did miss—or find, either. Every pocket was empty, not so much as a nickel or a jackknife in any one of them. That was that.

I got to my feet, shaking considerable and wiping my forehead. If the flat package wrapped up in silk and oil-skin was the Primer—or even if it was just a memorandum book—he didn't take it out of his room with him. Or, if he did, he had lost it or hid it afore Dick and I found him. One of the coat pockets did look as though it had been turned inside out, but probably that was the way Martha Pound left it when she finished her drying and pressing.

No, the flat package which might or might not be the Primer was, with his watch and pocketbook, still in or on the bureau in the spare room of the Farmer house. It was up to me and Dick Clarke to get it as soon as we possibly and decently could.

Clarke was back in a surprisingly short time, bringing Doctor Farmer and Labe Ryder and two or three other men folks with him. The doctor drove his old horse and buggy —he was too old-fashioned to buy an automobile—into the yard just as Dick got there. Farmer was business-like, I'll say that for him, and he never spoke a word until he had given the body a thorough examining. Then he stood up and shook his head solemn.

"Dead, poor chap," he said. "Died instantly, I should say, and only a little while ago. No doubt about what killed him, either. When he fell, he struck his head on that sharp limb there. If he had been strong and in normal condition the blow might not have been fatal, but in his weak state, the shock was too much for him. It was really the shock, quite as much as the fall, that finished him. Dear, dear! And he had seemed so much better."

Everybody said "Well, well!" and "Too bad." Ryder told the doctor not to blame himself, it wasn't his fault. I didn't say anything. Dick Clarke, though, asked a question.

"What do you suppose he was doing out here, in this wilderness?" he asked.

"Off his head, that's all. Reaction from the strain of the storm and what he had been through. Wandered off in delirum. Things like this do happen, they are not rare. Dear, dear! Well, we can take him back now."

The doctor had a stretcher at his place, and they had brought it along. Long afore we got to the Farmer house we had an escort of a dozen, at least, and as many women as men. Martha Pound and Sophronia Ryder were amongst the first to meet us, and their tongues were going full steam. The clack sounded like a toy windmill in a stiff breeze. We carried poor John Kelly into the spare room and laid him on the bed he had run away from.

All hands were crowding around, asking Clarke and me how we come to find the body, and all that. I was trying to get clear of them so he and I could talk by ourselves when the doctor came out of the house.

"Ham," he said. "Ham Ownley, are you there? Don't go just yet. I want you to take charge of some things for me, if you will. That pocketbook of this poor fellow who has just died is in the room there, with his watch and another piece of property of his. There is a good-sized sum of money in the pocketbook, and, now that he has gone, I don't want to be responsible for it. You've got a safe down to the Inn. Suppose I give the stuff to you, will you put it in your safe and keep it there until we can locate his heirs, or relatives, whoever they are?"

Anybody but him would have been liable to take me to one side and ask me this in private, but not the bossy old doctor—no sir. The idea had just struck him and he thought it was a good one, so, naturally everybody else must think so, too. Well, there wasn't any real reason for keeping it secret, of course.

Anyhow, he hollered it out, and everybody's ears picked up. I caught Dick's eye as he looked at me over the heads of the folks. I didn't dare look at him more than a second, but the way his face lighted up was enough. Here was luck! I was wondering how we were to get a look at that oilskin package and now it was going to be handed to us on a platter, as you might say.

I tried not to sound too eager, even tried to act as I was a little doubtful of taking so much responsibility, myself. "I'll do it if you say so, of course, Doctor," I said. "Although—"

"Fine! Fine! I'll give it to you right away. Come into the kitchen."

I followed him into the kitchen and motioned for Clarke to trail along, too. The rest of the bunch would have joined us, only Farmer was too quick for them and shut the door. He ordered us to sit down a minute and went off to the spare room to get the Kelly belongings.

Dick and I looked at each other. The same thought was in both our minds, I guess, for we spoke at the same time.

"Well," I said, "it looks as if our biggest question was close to settling, don't it?"

Dick's eyes were shining. "Now we're going to *know*," he vowed. He was so fidgety he couldn't sit still; he got up and walked around the kitchen. It was just as Martha had left it when she ran out to join the neighbors in the yard: kettle on the stove, dish towels hanging on the rack, and an old pair of shoes over in one corner. I saw Clarke pick up one of the shoes and look at it. I remember wondering why he did it, but I wasn't interested enough to ask.

The doctor was gone longer than I expected, and when he did come, he looked, I thought, upset and queer. I asked him what was the matter.

"Matter enough. Ham, they aren't there."

"Not there? Where? What?"

"Those things of Kelly's, the pocketbook and the watch and the little package. They were in his top bureau drawer this morning, for I saw them there, myself. They aren't there now, they are gone. The drawer is empty."

I stared at him. "Good Lord!" I said. "Maybe Martha put them somewhere else."

He shook his head. He was a good deal fussed up, and it takes a lot to fuss him. "Where could she have put them?" he snapped. "I looked in the other drawers, in the table drawer, in the closet, and even under the pillows. His pockets are empty, too; I looked there. Those things of his are not in that room. Now where are they?"

Dick was as fussed as the doctor; I wasn't what you

might call cool myself. Some idea of what this might mean was beginning to get hold of me.

"Martha," I said, and headed for the door. Doctor Farmer sang out for me to stop.

"Martha doesn't know any more about them than I do," he declared. "I'll get after her later, but I don't want her in here now. I don't want anybody here but us, and I don't want anybody to know the stuff is missing. Don't you see, Ownley? If the things aren't in this house then he—Kelly, I mean—must have taken them with him when he got out of that window. He must have."

"But—but what did he do with them?" It was Dick who asked this.

"How do I know? Hid them, or lost them. He might have chucked them into the surf; he was crazy, or he wouldn't have gone out at all. Tut, tut, tut!... Well, there is nothing we can do about it tonight. I have sent for Crusit"—Abel Crusit is our Sepatonk undertaker—"and he will be here any minute. You and I and Mr. Clarke here, if he is willing to help, must have a hunt along that path and the locality where you found him; but we'll have to wait till daylight for that. Tut, tut! The devil! Who could have expected anything like this?"

I couldn't, sure, and I hadn't. Poor Dick looked like the boy that found nothing but a hole in his Christmas stocking. Doctor Farmer had had more time to think than the rest of us, so he went on talking.

"I'll give Martha a cross-questioning when she comes in," he said, "but if the things aren't in that room they aren't in the house, I'll bet on it. Well, we'll have our hunt early in the morning. Meantime, though, I think we three better keep our mouths shut. Let everybody think you have the Kelly pocketbook and the rest in your safe, Ownley.

That is where I wanted them to be, and it is where all Sepatonk might as well think they are. If that poor lunatic," with a jerk of his head in the direction of the spare room, "lost them anywhere, I don't want every Tom, Dick, and Harry setting out to find them—not yet, anyhow. Our people here are as honest as the average run of humans; but there was a hundred and ten dollars in that pocketbook, and that's a lot of money—on Sepatonk Island, anyhow."

Just plain common sense, that was, and I said so. Dick Clarke didn't say anything; he was smashed flat. He had probably seen himself headed back to Bainbridge next day with the forty thousand dollar Primer in his pocket. And *now* look!

We agreed to meet Doctor Farmer by the big pine at six o'clock in the morning. We left his house—by the side door, for the gab fest was still going on in the back yard —and tramped back to the Inn. With our ears down and our tails between our legs, too.

I tried to say something cheerful. "Well, in the morning—" I began. He didn't let me finish.

"Oh, blah!" said he. "We won't find anything in the morning; you know it, Ham. If this Kelly bird took them out of that house at all, he probably stuck them into a woodchuck hole or fired them out to sea, as Farmer said. Of course," a little more hopefully, "we aren't dead sure that he did take them out of the house."

"There are so many things we aren't sure of. We aren't sure that that package of his had the Primer in it. A few minutes ago I thought we were going to be, but now we're not. Far as that goes, we aren't even sure that this Kelly man was the Library thief."

"Oh yes, we are! That's one thing we did settle to-night."

"What do you mean? How? What settled it?"

"Shoes."

"Shoes? Kelly's, do you mean? He had on a pair of old slippers when we found him. Farmer lent them to him, probably."

"I know; but there was a pair of shoes in the doctor's kitchen. I noticed them right away and picked one up to look at it. Those shoes were old patent leathers with button tops. If they weren't the shoes that Sanger crook wore when he came to our Library, I'll eat them."

So one of our questions was answered, after all. John Kelly was Sanger, the man who stole the New England Primer. And, that being so, there wasn't a reasonable doubt that the said Primer was in the oilskin package. But where that package was now was farther from being settled than ever, or so it seemed to me.

Dick had an idea that, providing we found nothing when we hunted in the morning, we might put up a bill in the post office. "Offer a good-sized reward," he said. "That would set others hunting, don't you think?"

"Yes, and tell the whole Island the things are missing. Farmer wouldn't like that notion, nor do I—yet. If anyone who was decent and straight found the stuff, he or she would turn it in, of course. But suppose the finder wasn't straight. In the first place, the reward would have to be more than a hundred and ten dollars, or it would pay him better to say nothing. And, in the second place, suppose he or she had found it in a place or in a way that might be risky to mention."

"What do you mean?"

I told him about the pocket in the jacket Kelly had on. "I can't swear that pocket had been turned inside out, but it did look as if it had."

He whistled. "Are you trying to tell me that someone else found him before we did?"

"And searched him afore I did? Well, they might have, mightn't they? There's a possible chance."

"But who?"

"That is one more question. Nobody probably; Kelly most likely hid the things himself or lost them. But there is that noise you heard in the bushes. That is still kind of interesting—to me, anyhow."

II

Prompt at six Dick and I met the doctor by the big pine where we found the Kelly man—might as well keep calling him Kelly to save trouble—and we went through the half acre of woods and weeds and scrub, went through it foot by foot. When we got through, our backs were lame, and our hopes were lamer. All we found was considerable many late huckleberries and an empty whisky bottle. The bottle had been empty so long that there was no smell to it and the huckleberries were pretty well dried up.

We three held a committee meeting, if you might call it that, and decided on a few points. I was to get in touch with the Bainbridge police folks and find out if anything more had come to light about the *Nellie B.* or her skipper, the Blake man. I asked Doctor Farmer if, in any of his talks with his late patient, Kelly had said anything about how he came to be on the motor boat or where she was bound when the hurricane caught her.

He said Kelly was in no state to talk about it much—any mention of the wreck got him all nerved up; but from the little he did say, the doctor gathered that he—Kelly—was going somewheres along the coast—Providence or Fall River—on business, and that his hiring the *Nellie B.* was just chance, as you might say. It looked like good weather when they started, and Kelly thought the boat trip would be a nice change from the train riding he had to do so much of. Farmer purposely hadn't said anything about the Blake man, but Kelly had asked Martha Pound about him, and Martha—she wouldn't have any notion of holding anything back—told Kelly that the Blake fellow hadn't been saved, nor his body come ashore.

"I asked her," the doctor said, "how he took that bit of news, and she said he wasn't as shocked and affected as she was afraid he would be. The poor chap was in no shape to realize it fully, I suppose," said Farmer.

I didn't go on with the subject, although I had my own ideas. Knowing what Clarke and I now knew about the Kelly-Sanger crook, I could think of a reason why he wasn't more shocked to hear of Blake's drowning. It was barely possible that Blake knew Kelly and perhaps something of what he had been up to; that the hiring of the *Nellie B.* wasn't chance at all, but part of the plan for Kelly's getaway. In that case the death of the man who could "spill the beans," as the boys say, would be a load off Kelly's mind, rather than something to cry about. Unless, of course, the pair had loved each other like brothers, which I doubted.

We decided, too, at that committee meeting in the pines, that we would keep on saying nothing about the Kelly belongings being lost. The doctor didn't know about the Primer, of course; what he was anxious about was the other things, the watch and money. Farmer said he was going to keep his eyes and ears open amongst the village folks with the idea that somebody might have seen Kelly out of door that night.

"Even if they didn't recognize him, which they wouldn't probably, they would have known he was a stranger. If we could only learn where he went before he came up in these woods, we might have a better chance of finding those things of his, providing he hid them. If he lost them or threw them away—why, well, they may turn up. Lord knows I hope so."

Dick and I, in our talk afore we turned in the previous night, had agreed to keep quiet about the Primer. If the other things were found, that would be found, too. And, if the right person found it, we should learn of the finding as quick as anybody.

Kelly's body was took charge of by the undertaker and put in the receiving tomb in the Sepatonk cemetery. The doctor's decision that death was caused by shock following a fall wasn't questioned. Everybody knew how sick and weak poor Mr. Kelly was and was sure he wandered away while out of his head.

Dick Clarke, naturally enough, was down in the mouth. Waiting around and doing nothing was mighty hard, especially when we had come so nigh getting what he was after. He was worried for fear that, providing somebody did find the book, they might realize it was valuable and get across with it to the mainland.

"No all-the-year Sepatonker would think a little child's book, same as you say that one is, was worth a cent," I told him. "And if one of the Inn crowd found it they would fetch it home and ask questions about it. I am keeping track of the steamer passengers every trip and nobody from here has gone on her since the night Kelly died. I am keeping tabs on the fish boats, too, well as I can."

The letter from the Bainbridge police, when it came, wasn't a mite of help. The Blake man had been in Bainbridge only a little while, had no friends to speak of, and nobody knew where he came from. All of Farmer's nosing and listening around Sepatonk had dug up nothing so far. Of course, the whole island was still buzzing about the Kelly accident, and all hands knew his watch and money was in my safe waiting for heirs and relations to turn up. The Inn boarders were as interested as anbody. They talked and guessed and speculated about who the poor man was, whether he had a wife and children somewhere waiting to hear from him, and all that. Old Mrs. Foster was all foamed up over what she called "our Island tragedy." "It is like a romance," she vowed. "Nothing ever happens on nice, quiet, matter-of-fact old Sepatonk, nothing out of the common, I mean; and now, all at once, we have a mysterious stranger coming from nobody knows where—"

"Oh, he came from Bainbridge," I cut in. "We know that."

"Yes, but where did he come from before that? He comes, he is cast up by the sea, he dies in a strange way, and *still* we don't know anything about him. Hammond, some time, when you open your safe, I want you to show me that watch of his, or the pocketbook, anything that actually belongs to him. It would make it seem more real: I think I could almost believe it then."

Well, I should have been just as glad to look at those things as she could be—gladder, I guess—but looking in the Inn safe wouldn't fetch me any nigher to them. I had

had enough experience lately looking for things where they wasn't.

I hadn't said a word to Dick about my overhearing his talk with the Anne Francis girl. I was a little ashamed of having heard it, although it wasn't really my fault that I did. The Hale houseparty was busy, boating and fishing and picnicking. I met the Folgers—they seemed like nice folks—and they and Anne were in and out of the Inn two or three times a day. The Francis girl and Clarke were friendly enough, talking together and, once in a while, walking along the beach or down to the steamer landing. Perry Hale was trotting at her heels most of the time, and, it seemed to me, he wasn't too happy about things in general. He came in one day and asked me if I had seen Anne since lunch time.

"Yes, she was here just now," I told him. "She and Mr. Clarke are out somewheres now. Gone down to watch the fish boats unload, I believe."

He threw his cigarette into the corner, missing the ash bowl by a good foot.

"How long is this Clarke guy going to hang around here?" he asked. "What is he here for?"

I told him Dick had had an accident, hurt his head, and he was under doctor's orders to take it easy. "Then, too," I said, "he is keeping an eye on that cottage property of his. That had to be fixed up after the hurricane, you know."

"Bunkum!" He said it pretty impatient. "That two-for-a-cent shack wasn't damaged much. If that is all that is keeping him, he is making a devil of a fuss over nothing."

"Well, that head of his—"

"Doesn't seem to keep him from having a good time. . . ."

Hello, Anne! I have been looking for you. We were going out in the motor boat. Had you forgotten?"

Anne was all aglow after her climb up from the landing, her hair was blown about a little, her cheeks were red and her eyes shining. If I noticed all those things myself, and I am old enough to be her father, it didn't seem likely that two young fellows like Dick Clarke or Perry Hale would miss them. By the way they looked at her, I sort of gathered they didn't.

"Sorry, Perry," she said. "I know I'm late. Dick and I had a grand walk down around the Cove and back, and I'm afraid I forgot to look at my watch. Swell day, isn't it?"

Hale didn't bother with the weather. He took her by the arm, mumbled something about their having to hustle, and headed for the door.

"See you later, Dick," she called, over her shoulder. "It was a nice walk."

They went out together and Clarke watched them go. Then he turned on his heel and went upstairs to his room. I sat down for a smoke. It did seem to me that there were complications enough on Sepatonk already without a pretty girl dropping in to add another one.

It was the morning after this that I noticed about the insurance policies. The safe in the Inn office is an old-fashioned thing, one Father bought years ago. Holley and Drake and Commodore House are always guying me about it. They call it the "tea caddy," and I recollect one time Holley's offering to bet me that he could open it in twenty minutes if I would lend him a can-opener. I didn't take the bet; told him I was afraid I might never get the can-opener back. "You fellows, most of you, pay with checks," I said, "and I never hold them long. Just endorse them over to the Brandt grocery and market folks and let *them* take the risk."

Well, that morning I opened the safe soon after I came downstairs, same as I always did. The combination was the simplest kind, and I could have worked it in my sleep. As I swung the door back, the first thing I saw was one of my insurance policies lying on the safe floor. I always keep those policies in a certain pigeonhole with a rubber band around them. I have a habit of arranging them in regular order, the one nighest due—the premium, I mean —on the top of the packet. I hadn't looked at them for a long spell; and, when I saw the one on the safe floor, I wondered how it got there. When I picked it up, I saw it wasn't the one from the top of the pack, but one that wouldn't expire for a year.

I took the packet from the pigeonhole and shuffled the policies over. They were not in regular order now, same as I would have sworn I left them, but hit or miss without any regard to dates. And there was no rubber band around them either.

The next thing I did, you can bet, was take out the cash drawer and go through that. The bills and silver totted to a cent with the amount on the slip that Silver, the bookkeeper, had handed me the night afore. There were two checks and both of them were there. I went over every single paper in that safe and, so far as I could see, not one was missing. Everything was just as it should be and as it ought to be except those insurance policies. None of them was missing either, but they certainly had been shifted around and I couldn't find the rubber band anywhere.

Mighty little to stir up suspicion, I own up, but I had

had so much mystery lately that I could catch suspicion the way a summer girl catches ivy poisoning. Common sense told me that no sane person would take the trouble to break into a safe unless it was to steal and that, as nothing had been stolen, the safe hadn't been touched. And it was locked all night. I had to spin the combination to open it myself.

But notwithstanding which, I couldn't get those policies out of my head. If that pesky Primer book had been in the safe, and anybody knew it was there and how valuable it was, I could have seen a reason for trying to steal it and leaving the twenty-odd dollars in the cash drawer. But nobody but Dick Clarke and me knew there was such a Primer—nobody else, not even Doctor Farmer. So *that* didn't explain anything. I decided my suspicions were just foolishness and to put them out of my head. I must be getting into a state where I would be suspecting Hettie Bassett of making love to Old Souse pretty soon. I had to be careful.

And then Doc Grover paid his board bill.

III

In one way there was nothing unusual about that. Oscar Grover's bills were always paid regular and prompt. He always paid cash, too, and that's the way he paid it this time. He paid it to George Silver and got his receipt and went out. All this was ordinary enough, but when Silver and I were figuring up takings and spendings that evening, something that wasn't so ordinary turned up.

George had counted the bills and coins, and then, as he always did, he shoved the pile across the desk for me to count. I was thumbing through the bills and all at once I stopped. I guess likely I must have caught my breath or spoken or something, for Silver looked around at me.

"What?" he asked.

I didn't answer right off. The electric light hung over his end of the desk, and I pushed him to one side and held what I had in my hand up to that light.

"What—" he began again; but I didn't give him a chance to finish. It was a twenty dollar bill I was holding to the light, and that bill had a black smudge on it. In one place it looked as if it had been scorched.

"Where did this twenty come from?" I asked, sharp.

"Eh? Why? Anything wrong with it?"

"Not as I know of. What I want to know is where it came from. How did it get here?"

"H'm. Why now, let's see. . . . H'm. . . . Must have been paid in by somebody."

"Lord above! I didn't think it *flew* in. Who was the somebody?"

"Well, now—let me think. . . . Holley, he paid for some cigars and Souse—I mean the Commodore—he paid his bill; but he gave me a check, I remember that now."

"You don't need to, because here is the check. And Mr. Holley—you notice *I* say 'Mister' Holley—didn't ask you to change a twenty, did he?"

"Eh? Oh, no, no. He gave me a couple of half dollars. . . . I tell you who gave me that bill, Mr. Ownley. It was Oscar—I mean Doctor Grover. His bill came to thirty-seven dollars and eighteen cents this week, extras and all, and he gave me one twenty dollar bill and a ten and a five and two ones and a—a dime—and—"

"Never mind the coppers. So Doctor Grover gave you this, eh? You're sure?"

He was sure. It was the only twenty that came in that day. Why? Was it a counterfeit? Hadn't he ought to have taken it? Plain enough that he hadn't noticed the smudge; maybe I wouldn't if I hadn't been looking for scorched bills ever since the Kelly pocketbook disappeared.

I tried to act careless, told him the bill was all right, put it back with the others and into the safe with them, too. He hadn't been out of the Inn two minutes, however, afore I had that twenty out of there and into my vest pocket. Then I started to find Dick Clarke.

Dick was out—with Hale and Anne Francis and the Folgers, I found out afterwards. Didn't come in to supper, either, and it was close to eleven when he did show up. I was waiting for him, though; that scorched twenty was heating up my pocket lining.

We went into the private office, and there I showed it to him and told him Silver's story of where it came from. He looked at me as if he thought I was crazy.

"Grover!" he said. "Doc *Grover!* That dignified, precise fuddy-duddy! Oh, horse feathers! Ham, you can't believe for a minute that *he* was ever a pal of that Sanger-Kelly tough mug! I'd as soon think of—"

"Sshh! Sshh! I didn't say I was thinking of anybody or anything in that way—yet. Just now let's think no farther than what we know. And, according to George Silver, we *know* that it was Oscar Grover who paid in this twenty dollar bill."

"But— Oh, let's look at that bill again."

We looked at it together. There wasn't any doubt in either of our minds that it was one of the bills Martha Pound had dried and pressed and put back in the Kelly pocketbook. There was a three-cornered mark left by the nose of the hot flatiron.

"Grover!" says Dick again. "Grover, of all people! Well, I'll be damned!"

"So will I, so far as that goes; but how far does it go? Grover had the bill, but where did *he* get it?"

"Where could he have got it except from that pocketbook? If Kelly had the pocketbook with him and, as you have suspected all along, somebody searched Kelly's body before we did—"

"Yes, yes. But that somebody—if there was such a one —must have done his searching only a few minutes afore we showed up. And Doc Grover went up to his room here at the Inn early that evening, and nobody saw him come out of it till next morning. I have just questioned the Dolan girl—the chambermaid on your corridor and his— and she saw him go into that room around nine o'clock. His light was still on at ten, for she saw it over the transom. She thinks she heard him in there, too. It might have been Drake, their rooms are right next to each other, but she is almost sure it was Grover. And Grover is—well, I'd have called him about as respectable a person as anybody on the island. No, no, Dick, we can't go off half cocked; must be mighty careful. I'm keeping hotel, and I can't accuse one of my best boarders of being a thief without a better reason than we've got so far. We've got to have a talk with Grover, of course; but we must handle that talk tender—mighty tender."

We spent some time planning and contriving. We had to have an excuse, other than the real one, for being so interested in that bill. At last we cocked up a yarn that I thought would pass the customs, and it was agreed that I should tackle Grover in the morning.

But he was out and away until noon time and went out again after lunch, so it was close to five afore I got hold of him. Then I took him into the back office, and, trying hard to look innocent while I was lying like a book agent, I began my yarn, the one Clarke and I had agreed on.

I commenced by reminding him that he had paid his bill the day before. He remembered that all right and asked if there had been any mistake in the bill. I said no, there hadn't, but that something was worrying me a little. I happened, for my sins, to be constable on Sepatonk, I told him, and consequently I was supposed to help out the mainland police once in a while. Well, a week or so ago, I had had word from the Fall River police to be on the lookout for bad ten and twenty dollar bills that were being distributed around in our part of the state. That much was true, only it was last year and not last week. Yesterday evening, when the bookkeeper and I counted the cash, I said, we found a twenty in the drawer and we were a little mite suspicious of it. Silver said that the only twenty he had taken in that day was paid by him—Doctor Grover, so—

He was fussed and troubled. "Oh, dear me!" he said. "Is that possible? Mr. Ownley, I hope you don't think—"

I cut in to tell him I never thought *he* knew the bill was bad. It wasn't likely I'd think *that*. No, no. But if he could remember where that particular bill came from we might be able to trace how it got on the Island. Naturally, he asked if he might see the bill. I said "sure" and showed him *a* twenty, only it was not the scorched one, but a twenty that Dick Clarke had happened to have in his own wallet. There had been considerable talk around the village about Martha's burning the Kelly money, and we figured we had better keep the one with the flatiron mark out of sight.

Grover looked the bill over, shook his head, and said it appeared all right to him; no reason why it shouldn't for

that bill *was* all right. But he kept looking at the bill in
an odd sort of way, I thought, and seemed to be thinking.
I was going on with another question when he saved me
the trouble.

"Are you sure this bill came from me, Ownley?" he
asked.

"George Silver is sure."

"H'm," he said. "Well, well!" And then, always speaking in that prim, precise way of his, he went mooning
along, kind of half to himself and half to me. "This is—
er—this is peculiar," he said. "I cashed a check while in
New York, so I have a fair-sized sum on hand; but I make
it a point not to carry too much about with me. I went
fishing yesterday forenoon with—er—Augustus Pound—
I believe Augustus is the name—and I remember counting the—er—contents of my pocketbook before starting.
There was but twenty-five dollars or so there, and your
hotel bill, Hammond, was in the pocketbook, so I added
enough to pay that bill when I returned. There was, as I
recollect, about sixty dollars altogether. Now was there
a twenty dollar bill in the lot? I can't seem to remember
that there was. And yet there must have been, of course,
if your bookkeeper is so sure he took that bill from me."

I said it looked that way. "You didn't give anybody
some small bills in change for a twenty, I suppose?"

"No. When I went out in the boat I paid—er—the
Pound man his five dollars—that was his price for taking
me fishing—before we started. Then I had him put my
pocketbook in the—er—cabin of his boat. I thought it
would be safer there than in the pocket of the old coat
I was wearing. When we got back to the pier, I reminded
him of the pocketbook and he went in and got it for me.

I came back to my room, changed, and went down to lunch. After lunch I paid my bill at your desk here."

"I see." All this sounded straight enough, but it didn't explain where the scorched twenty came from. That he didn't get it when he cashed his check in New York I was dead certain; it wasn't likely that any of the Kelly money had got as far as that. And that the bill with the flatiron mark had been part of the Kelly roll I was ready to swear on the Bible.

He was still thinking hard. "It is very odd," he went on. "When I paid the hotel bill I might not have noticed the twenty, if it was there. But when I counted my money in my pocketbook before I went fishing, I— Well, I am certainly under the impression that there was nothing larger than a ten. Humph! I must be getting absent-minded."

I couldn't think of any answer to that. Best I could say was that I would pump Silver again and was sorry I had bothered him about it. He started to go and then he turned back.

"May I see that bill once more?" he asked. I showed him the twenty; not the burned one, of course, but the one I showed him afore.

He gave it a pretty thorough examining this time. Turned it over, rubbed it through his fingers, and held it to the light.

"I confess I can't see anything the matter with it," he said. "What makes you think it may be counterfeit, Ownley?"

"Don't know as it is, Doc. Maybe I'm just suspicious in the wrong place. That letter from the Fall River folks, you know."

He looked at the bill again and then at me. "Humph!"

he said, and went out of the office. I didn't like the sound of that "Humph!" Thinks I: "Ham Ownley, you haven't done a very smart job. Now *he* will be wondering what's up."

His story had been straight as a string. If he lied, he did it awfully well. The twenty dollar bill had been paid in by him—yes; but I knew that afore. And his alibi—as the detective yarns call it—for the night of the Kelly man's death was, according to the Dolan girl, sound as a fresh egg. I had got nowhere, and I should have to tell Clarke so.

I sat there going over what Grover had said word by word. And then, all at once, something he had said put me on a new track. I started on that track and the further I followed it, the more possible it looked: not promising perhaps, but—yes, just possible. I jumped from my chair and went to locate Dick Clarke.

IV

Augustus Pound—Half Pound to all Sepatonk—lived alone by himself in a little story and a half shanty down nigh the little inlet where he kept that old fish boat of his, the one he and Grover had gone codding in the day before. It was about nine that night when Dick and I hove in sight of the shanty, and there was a light in the back room.

"He's to home," says I. "That's one bit of good luck."

"And just about our first," said Dick; he was pretty blue over my talk with Grover coming to nothing. "I wish I could believe that this wild-goose chase we're on now might bring us more."

"You never can tell. Better let me do the heft of the talking, Dick. I know this eight ounces of nothing better than you do."

Pound opened the door in answer to my knock. He never was any blue ribbon beauty, even when he was dressed up; but now, when he was taking his ease in the shade of his own vine and fig tree, as you might say, in his shirt sleeves and with his collar off, he was something to see once and then try to forget. His step-sister, Martha, had all the fat in the family; he was as scrawny as a picked pullet, and, with his long neck and hair all tousled, he looked like one.

"Evening, Half," I said. "Little late to come calling, I know, but you'll have to excuse us this time. Mind if we come in?"

He hadn't said a word, just stood there staring, but he mumbled something about being real glad to see us. I said we knew he would be and pushed past him into the house. Dick followed after me and I shut the door. The room was a kind of combination parlor, dining room, and kitchen and was about as neat and tidy as Pound was himself. It smelled of a good many things, especially fish. There was a lamp with a paper shade on the table. I took the shade off. It wasn't often that I was particular about seeing Half's face, but I was then. The expression on it—the face, I mean—was what I was hoping it would be. Mr. Half Pound was worried and, unless I missed my guess, scared besides.

He didn't invite us to sit down, but I pulled up a chair and pulled up another for Dick. There was another chair in the room but Half didn't sit down. He stood there, rubbing his hands and blinking.

"Don't know as you've met Mr. Clarke yet, Half," I

said. "He is staying with me over at the Inn. Dick, this is Mr. Gus Pound. He takes folks out fishing sometimes."

Pound's expression changed a little at that. I judge he thought he saw a reason for our being there.

"Pleased to meet you, Mr.—er—Clarke," he said, pumping up a smile. "Thinking of having a try after the cod, was you? They are hooking on fair to middling good just now."

Before Dick could answer, I took charge again. I don't believe in bullying, as a general thing; but I believed Half Pound was frightened when he saw us at the door, and I wanted him to stay frightened.

"No," said I, "Mr. Clarke isn't thinking of going fishing just now and neither am I. But we are both considerable interested in that fishing cruise you went on with Doctor Grover yesterday. You did take him out, didn't you, Half?"

He looked at me and then at Clarke. The scared expression was coming back fast.

"Why—why sure I did," he stuttered. "What of it? We caught considerable many fish, and he had a good time. He told me he did, too. Certain I took him out. What of it?"

"That's what I want to know. What did you charge him?"

"Eh? Charged him five dollars. Cheap enough, wasn't it?"

"Cheap as dirt. Cheap as dirt on a twenty dollar bill. Ever see a twenty dollar bill with a smudge of black dirt on it, Half? They are kind of unusual. Doctor Grover found one in his pocketbook yesterday afternoon. How do you figure it got there?"

That hit him. He was scared plenty now. I was feeling

happier every second. If the rest of my bluff worked as well as the first part was going, this wild-goose chase of ours was going to bag a bird.

"I—I don't know what you're talking about," he blustered. "What's this about a twenty dollar bill? Who said anything about a twenty dollar bill?"

"I told you. Doctor Grover said it. He says he didn't have that kind of bill when he started out fishing with you, but when he got ashore there was one in his pocketbook. And a couple of tens were missing. He seemed to think that was kind of funny, and he spoke to me about it. I thought 'twas funny, too. What do you think, Half?"

"I—I— What are you talking about? I—I never stole nothing out of his pocketbook. If he says I did he's a liar."

"He didn't say anything was stole. Changing a twenty for a couple of tens isn't stealing, exactly. Only changing them without telling the man the tens belonged to is—well, it's sort of out of the common run, that's all. He says he left the pocketbook in the cabin of your boat and that, after the boat landed, you went into the cabin and fetched the pocketbook to him. I don't know that proves anything. Or does it?"

In the quiet that came after these remarks of mine I could hear Dick Clarke chuckle. Half Pound didn't chuckle.

"Grover came to me, I suppose likely," I went on, "because he knows I am constable here on Sepatonk. It's part of my job to arrest people that meddle with other folks' property. Maybe he won't want to have anybody arrested. Maybe if there was some good explanation for what happened he would be satisfied. I can't swear to it, of course, but I should think he might be."

Half jumped at this bait. Anybody else would have kept still and denied everything, but he didn't have sense enough for that, or sand either. He stammered and stuttered and then out with it. Maybe he had changed the bills around, what of it? It was harder to get a twenty changed at the Sepatonk store than it was a ten, and—and the pocketbook was lying open on the cabin thwart, and he had seen the two tens "kind of sticking out," and he happened to have that twenty with him—and so on. Part lies and part truth. I heard all that was needful and I stepped in.

"Wild goose chase isn't so wild, after all, is it, Dick?" I said. "All right, Half, all right. You own up that you did swap those bills?"

"Well. Well, maybe I did, but I didn't steal nothing. And you can't arrest me for it, either, Ham Ownley. You know you can't. I—"

"That's enough. You've heard him admit it, Mr. Clarke. Now then, Pound, we'll get right down to real business. Where did you get that twenty dollar bill you put in Grover's pocketbook?"

The poor ninny hadn't seen that coming at all. Anybody would have thought he might, but he didn't. He was so anxious to get out of being arrested for swapping the bills that he forgot to notice he was hopping from the frypan into the fire. He turned green. Even by the amount of light that filtered through the dirty lamp chimney I could see him turn.

It would take too long to tell how I kept him on the toast fork and how many wiggles and twists he gave trying to squirm off it. He shifted and lied and lied and shifted, with the water pouring off his forehead. He had got the bill in this place and from this or that person and every yarn was sillier than the one afore it. What smashed him finally was this:

"Half," I said, "I don't enjoy having to lug you off to jail; your sister is a good, respectable woman, and it would be a bad disgrace for her. But to murder a person and then rob him is—"

"Murder!" he finally screeched the word after me.

"Yes," said I, solemn as an owl. "If you can prove to me that you didn't kill poor John Kelly and then steal a watch and pocketbook from his dead body, I shall be glad, for Martha's sake and for yours, too. But if you *can't* prove it—well, you'll have to take your medicine, that's all. You had better come along with me to the lock-up now."

He went all to pieces. He hadn't never hurt anybody; he wouldn't do a thing like that, I ought to know he wouldn't. He had never so much as hit a person in his life. He was an innocent man. Yes, and a poor man that everybody was down on. If he hadn't been poor, if he was rich like some folks, I wouldn't dast talk to him like that. He was crying by this time, and it was hard to keep from pitying him. Pity, though, was something to come afterward; just now I was getting close to truth and I meant to have it.

"There, there!" I ordered. "You can tell all that in court. Pound, you know and Mr. Clarke and I know that that twenty dollar bill was one that John Kelly had in his pocketbook the night he was killed. Doctor Farmer and Martha know it, too, only they don't know yet that it was ever in your possession. You can't lie out of having that bill; fact is you've just owned up that you had it."

"Oh, Mr. Ownley—oh, Judge, I never killed that Kelly man. I never saw him that night, never laid eyes on him.

Didn't even know he was dead till the next morning. That's the honest God's truth, I swear it is."

"Bosh! If you never saw him, how did you get hold of his money? If you've got a decent reason for having that bill, you better come out with it. Now is your last chance."

And then he told us. The yarn was all full of tears and beggings and pleadings for mercy, but, with them sifted out, it amounted to this:

It began about eleven o'clock on the night afore the one when John Kelly-Sanger died. Pound had been down to the poolroom in the village—a pet loafing place of his—had walked home and was just opening the door of his shack when a man stepped out of the bushes and touched him on the shoulder. "Your name is Pound, isn't it?" the man said. "Your sister works for the doctor, doesn't she? Yes, I thought so. Well, I want to talk with you."

Pound was scared; the fellow spoke like a stranger, and Half hadn't the least notion who he could be. He let him into the house, though—too scared to try to keep him out, I presume likely—and lit the lamp. Even in the light he didn't know him, but he wasn't kept guessing long. The fellow told who he was and why he had come there. He was Kelly, the man who had come ashore from the wreck of the *Nellie B.* and who was supposed to be in Doctor Farmer's spare room, too feeble to get out of bed.

He didn't talk nor act particular feeble right then, and Half judged that the heft of his weakness and sickness had been make believe. Seems he had listened at the door between the Farmer dining room and his bedroom and had heard a talk between Half and Martha. The talk was pretty personal—Half was trying to borrow money and Martha was telling him she was sick of his loafing and general no-goodness—but from it Kelly learned that Half had a boat with a kicker in it and gathered that he was the kind who wouldn't ask questions if it paid him to keep still. He got a glimpse of Half through the crack of the door, too, so he would know him again. He didn't say so, but I have no doubt he found out from Martha afterward where her step-brother lived.

Anyhow he had got out of the doctor's room, through the window, probably—and had come to Half with a proposition. He wanted to leave Sepatonk right off, the very next night, and he offered Half twenty-five dollars to take him across to Brandt in his boat. Well, for some reason or other—something to do with Martha, I believe 'twas, but it doesn't make much difference anyhow—Half couldn't leave the Island that next night, but he could the night following. Kelly, according to Half, was broke up about that. He *must* go sooner, he had to. Pound couldn't make it, that's all. So it was finally put off until the second night, although Kelly didn't like it one bit. "I've got to beat it," he kept saying, "I've *got* to."

Then, after doing some walking around the room and thinking, Kelly told Pound he had something else he wanted done. Having to wait this extra night was still troubling him, and he was going to write a letter to a business friend of his. What he said about the letter sounded queer, even to Half, but it was along this line:

"I'll have the letter ready about ten tomorrow evening. It will be sealed and addressed and stamped, and I want you to come to the doctor's house at ten and tap on the window of the room I am in. That window will be open, and I'll hand the letter out to you."

And then came the queerest part. "Don't mail that letter right off," Kelly ordered. "If I meet you at eleven the next night and we get away in your boat, I don't want you to mail it at all. Hand it back to me, that's all. *But,* if I shouldn't show up, it will mean that our getaway deal is off—for then anyhow—and I want you to mail it the very next day. Understand that, do you? And don't you say a word about it to anybody, afore you mail it, or afterward, or any time. If you do—"

Pound didn't tell Dick and me what would happen if he did say anything, but I judged that the Kelly fellow was so ugly that he wouldn't have dared so much as whisper concerning the letter. There was an extra five dollars added for getting and taking care of the letter, anyhow, and Half would promise anything for considerable less than five dollars.

Well, the next night at ten o'clock—that was the night Kelly died, remember—Half was sneaking along the doctor's fence waiting to tap on the spare room window. But when he hove in sight of the window, he was surprised to see that it was wide open and the shade run up to the top just as it was when Clarke and I got there a while later. Pound went up to the window and looked in. The room was empty; no Mr. Kelly there at all. What had become of him Half couldn't think, any more than Dick and I could when we came.

And then was when Half Pound found temptation too strong for him. Kelly's watch was on the bureau with the lamp burning beside it. The sight of that watch made Half remember what Martha had told him about the pocketbook with all that money in it. She had told him, too, how she had put that pocketbook in the top bureau drawer. Was it there now? A hundred and ten dollars with nobody watching it! What couldn't a man like Half Pound do with as much money as that?

How he ever mustered spunk to climb in that window

and take the risk of being caught, I can't understand even yet, but he did. I'll bet he made a hurried job of it. Anyhow, a few minutes later Augustus Half Pound, Esquire, of Sepatonk Island, Massachusetts, was traveling across said Island as if the Old Scratch was after him, and Mr. John Sanger-Kelly's personal property was traveling with him.

The rest of it didn't really need telling; we could have guessed it. Half, when he got safely home with the pocketbook and opened it to look at and gloat over the money, saw the burnt places on the bills. Martha had told him how she scorched them with the iron, but he hadn't paid much attention to her. Now, though, what those marks would mean came to him and knocked the gloat out of him. All his plans for living high, wide, and handsome on his stealings went by the board. He couldn't risk changing one of those bills—not on Sepatonk anyhow. Goodness knew how many other folks Martha had told about burning them. If he could get across to the mainland, he would have a better chance to get rid of them; but even in Brandt it might be dangerous. He carried one of the twenties around with him, but he hadn't dast try to spend it. It wasn't until he went into the cabin of his boat to fetch Doc Grover's pocketbook and saw the tens in that pocketbook that the idea of getting rid of his twenty came to him. So he made the swap, same as he had told us.

"And—and that's all," whined Half, finishing up his long yarn. "I swear to the Lord 'tis, Judge Ownley. I never see Mr. Kelly that night or had any notion of laying a hand on him. I never knew he was dead until somebody told me next day. That's the honest God's truth.

Please believe me, Judge. You believe me, don't you, Mr. Clarke?"

I looked at Dick and he looked at me. I guess likely I looked as happy and excited as he did, for I felt that way. Half Pound was crying like a sprinkling cart. For a desperate lawbreaker he was an example of what crime can do to a person who is part fool to start with.

"You *do* believe me, Judge," he wailed. "You don't think I'm no murderer. Say you don't—say you don't."

"Still waiting for proof, Half," I told him. "Where is that stuff you stole?"

"Eh?...Oh, right here, right here. I never touched a thing of it except that one twenty. Oh, if I hadn't touched that! If I—"

"Be still! Where are your thievings?"

He stumbled over to a corner of the room behind the rusty cookstove and began rummaging there. I looked at Dick Clarke again. He nodded and grinned at me.

"Well done, Sherlock," he whispered. "I'll see that the Knowlton Library sends you a gold medal. Regular cheer for our side. Rah! Rah!"

Half was scrabbling there behind the stove. There was a loose floor board there, and he lifted it up. Then he came back to us, a pocketbook in one hand and a gold watch and chain in the other. He dumped them on the table in front of me.

"There they be," he panted; "right there for you to see. Now you count that money, Judge. Count it afore Mr. Clarke, so's he can bear witness that I am telling the truth. You'll find it all there—every cent but that twenty.... Go ahead! Count it, why don't you?"

I looked at the pocketbook and at the watch. Then I looked at Half.

"The counting can wait," I said, sharp. "Where's the rest of the stuff? Trot it out! Hurry up!"

He stared at me, his mouth hanging open.

"Rest of it?" he stammered. "What do you mean—rest? That's all there is—there ain't no more."

"What! Don't talk like that to me. Pound, do you realize how nigh you are to state's prison this minute? Go get that package, the one done up in oilskin. Go get it!"

"Eh? Package? There ain't no package. I don't know what—"

"Shut up! There was a little oilskin package in that bureau drawer along with this pocketbook. Don't tell me there wasn't, for I know better."

"But there wasn't, Judge. As sure as I'm a living man there wasn't another thing in that bureau drawer but that pocketbook. The watch was on top of the bureau and the pocketbook in the drawer. And that's all! It was all, I tell you! I *ain't* lying! Why should I lie—now?"

He was crying again, and I was beginning to feel like crying, myself. My spirits, which had been way up to the masthead, were sinking down to the keelson. I didn't think he was lying. As he said, why should he—now? I heard Dick say something, but I didn't ask him to say it again. I didn't look at him, either.

Well, we didn't let it go at that, of course. For another ten minutes we took that Half Pound thing apart question by question. We bullied him and threatened him, but we pumped and scared nothing out of him except another hogshead of tears and prayers. He stuck to his story. The Kelly watch and the Kelly pocketbook was all there was in that bureau drawer. The oilskin package with the sixty thousand dollar New England Primer in it looked as far off from us now as it had been that morning.

I gave up, finally, and, just to be doing something, I opened the pocketbook. The rest of the bills, ninety dollars altogether, were there all right. There was something else, too; an envelope with two or three folded sheets of paper inside it. I took the sheets out and looked at them.

"Here you!" I said to the sniveling Pound. "What's this?"

"Eh? I—I don't know, Judge. It was there, along with the money, that's all I know. I kind of thought maybe it might be that letter Mr. Kelly was going to give me, the one he wanted me to mail if he didn't show up to go over to the mainland on my boat. There ain't no address on the envelope, though."

I read the writing on the sheets of paper. Then I turned to Dick Clarke.

"Here," said I, "read that."

He took it and read. Then he handed it back. He was so dreadfully down in the mouth that I doubt if he understood a word of what he had been reading.

"Well," he growled, "what of it?"

I didn't know what of it.

PART IV

Perry Hale Steps In

As Told by
Dickson Clarke

I

I AM afraid I disappointed Ham Ownley by my lack of excitement after reading the letter we found in Kelly's pocketbook. Just then there was no excitement left in me, no belief, and no hope, either. Emotionally I was practically numb, and I think I had reason.

Just let me review my situation for a minute. When I found Doc Payson on the floor of the library strong room, I took out after the man who had put him there, and by bull luck I found him. Did that do me any good? No. All that I got for my trouble was a beautiful knock on the skull. The man was gone and the book was gone. Next came a new lead that brought me down to Sepatonk. I was excited, for it looked as though once more the man and the book were right under my hand. Did that do me any good? No. The man died and the book vanished. Next came the appearance of the marked twenty dollar bill. Once more the trail was hot and I was excited. Did that do me any good? No. We found the wallet and we found the watch, but Doc Payson's Primer was just as much gone as ever. Now we had a letter. Perhaps it was important, and I probably should have been excited, but I wasn't. I had been slapped too often by the hand that pretended to feed me. The Clarke eye now had a definitely jaundiced tinge.

I sulked in my tent while Ownley gave the miserable Half Pound a final going over. Ham said that Half was as fine a hundred and thirty pounds of jail meat as he had ever seen. He said that he would be only half doing his duty if he promptly slapped Half into the Sepatonk clink. Half put up a terrified howl at this, although what else he could have expected I'm sure I don't know. He cried, and begged for mercy, and would have got down on his knees if Ownley had let him. He swore that he "didn't mean no harm," that he wouldn't do it again, that if he were jailed he would "up and die" of the disgrace. Ham let him rave on for a while and then appeared to relent a little. He said that on certain conditions he would leave Half at large for a time while he thought the case over. The conditions were that Half was not to leave the Island and was not to say a single word to anybody about what had happened. Half, of course, agreed. I think he would have kissed us if we had let him.

On our way back to the Inn, Ham explained to me his feelings about Half. He said that he thought Half was not so much crooked as he was feeble-minded. Half had never done anything actually criminal before, and the chances were that he never would again. Half's sister, Martha, moreover, was a good-hearted soul and a hard-working woman. If her brother were to be arrested, she probably wouldn't be able to hold her head up on Sepatonk again. Those things counted, he pointed out, but the thing that counted most was that if he put Half in jail all the circumstances surrounding Kelly would have to become public property. So long as there was still a chance of recovering the Primer, that did not seem wise. Did I agree?

I replied briefly that I agreed, and we completed the rest of our walk in silence. Ham must have noticed my mood, however, for when we walked into the deserted lobby of the Inn he looked at me intently. "Kind of down, ain't you, Dick?" he observed. "Don't know's I blame you. You was pretty nigh certain that when we got back here to-night you'd have the little Primer book in your pocket. Now we're back here and the book is still Lord knows where. Enough to make you feel bad."

"Maybe you're right, Ham. I only know I'm lower than a skunk."

"Don't give up the ship, Dick." He patted me on the shoulder. "Don't haul down the flag yet, by a long shot. We've still got Kelly's letter, you know."

"Damn Kelly's letter," I said. "So far as I can see it is just one crook writing to another crook. What do you and I and poor Payson get out of it?"

"Well, now maybe we may get something out of it. You read that letter kind of careless, I shouldn't wonder. Got some interesting points in it, that letter has."

"Has it? Well, well!" I was quite indifferent.

"Yes. What do you say we go into my office and have a *good* look at it—that is, unless you have something better to do."

"No." I shrugged. "I haven't *anything* to do, unless it's to sleep, and I don't think I could do even that. We'll have a look at your precious Kelly letter, if you like. May as well do that as anything, I suppose."

We went into Ham's office, lit the light, and shut the door. Then we sat down at the desk and carefully read the message that Kelly, or Sanger, or whatever his real name might have been, had left in his wallet. It had been written laboriously in pencil on cheap paper and had been sealed in an unaddressed envelope.

Dear Pal Eddie:

Keep this letter under your hat for a couple of weeks. If before the two weeks are over you get a wire from me saying Okay forget the letter altogether for the wire'll mean I'm in the clear and things are breaking right again. If you don't get that wire you'll know I'm down and out and it's up to you, see? When we had our last spiel together I put you wise to my being onto something good along the old book line and that I was heading east on the job. Since then things have broke bad and I'm laid up on a hunk of sand called Sepatonk Island which is off the Mass coast, and you can spot it on the map if your lamps are good. As you know I started in on the deal with a sidekick—you know who he was. Then I seen a chance to do better for myself by leaving the sidekick out, so I dug in on my own, and gave him the air. See? It was working fine when the hurricane caught me and landed me here. It also landed me in plenty of trouble, because the sidekick is here, too. I've tried to keep out of his way by playing sick, but I don't know. Maybe he's spotted me. And if he *has*—well, he's a tough babe to monkey with, and any old thing may happen.

If he gets me I'm putting it up to you to get square for your old pal and make a lot of jack for yourself, if you handle it right. *Get that.* Now listen, Ed, old pal. If you don't get that wire you'll know the goods will be hid away good, but that, as you will tumble to from what I've wrote already, there will be *others* on the hunt and they are the old gang, see. Give them *all* the double cross. The good old ♯. Them old spiels of Mikes don't ever work. I'd can Windy too and with Hank and Eli's new gags plain tripe and N.G. the end's here, Ed, for I'm keen for man who is just as live at runing down buyers and free spenders as anybody. Sully knows who he is but when you deal with Sully be careful. Of course I'm hoping to send you that Okay wire and clean up myself, but if I don't wire and you take over, step light and be leery all the way. *Look out for that trouble*. It will be hot and *bad*. that's all I can say now. Here's luck to both of us. See you some day, maybe. If not, well, luck anyhow. Get the dough and get square for your old pal

Legs.

Ownley finished reading a few seconds before I did, and when I looked up he was watching me with a little smile. "Some interesting items there, don't you think, Dick? Seems so to me." He nodded his head. "Seems as if Mr. Kelly with the pointed shoes was telling us that most of the guesses we made were right, and seems, too, as if he had hove in some new stuff we hadn't even tried to guess."

"That's so." In spite of my low state of mind I had to admit that the letter opened up lines of thought. I pointed to it. "Look here, Ham. It looks as if this Sanger-Kelly man had a friend working with him on the job of stealing the Primer, and as though he had tried to give his friend a dirty deal. See here? It says—"

"Wait a minute. Lay to and take it easy." Ownley put out a mildly restraining hand. "Let's not skip around. We might miss something that way and we don't want to. Let's go over the thing together sentence by sentence and see what we get. After that we can add it all up and see where it takes us—if anywhere." He reached for a pencil and a sheet of paper. "You read and I'll set down the notes. Now what's the first thing that our Kelly chum has to tell us?"

"Well, for one thing, that he's a book thief," I said, "and not for the first time. He talks here about heading east on a good job in the 'old book line.' "

"Um-hm." Ownley scribbled down some words. "And if stealing books was his regular trade, he probably has been caught by the police two or three times before this. That might help us to get his real name. It couldn't have been Sanger, and I don't believe any self-respecting Kelly ever wore shoes like the ones he had on. All right. What's next?"

I was ready for him. "Kelly had a pal and he double-crossed the pal. He says so in so many words."

"Good." Ham wrote some more. "Nice kind of critter, the late lamented Kelly! Probably when times got dull he fed rat poison to his children just to hear 'em holler."

"He was washed ashore on Sepatonk, which he lists as a piece of bad luck." I was getting really interested by this time.

"Hm. Seems to me as if he ought to have been glad he was washed ashore alive *anywhere,* even if 'twas on dead old Sepatonk. Oh, well, there's no accounting for tastes. But why was he so down on this place in particular?"

"It seems to me that's one of the most important things in this letter. He says that his sidekick—the man he double-crossed—is here; that must mean on Sepatonk Island. And he says that the sidekick may have spotted him; and that, if the sidekick *has* spotted him, his life is in danger!"

"Hm," Ownley scraped his chin with his thumbnail. "Hm. And that *is* interesting."

I had a new thought, and it hit me hard. "Ham!" I was spluttering, "suppose the sidekick—whoever he is— *did* spot him! Why, in that case Kelly's death may not have been accidental at all! Maybe—"

"I know, Dick, I know. Maybe Kelly didn't fall down. Maybe he was helped down with a fist or a club. I've had some thoughts along that line, before this letter turned up. There wasn't anything in Kelly's pockets when we found him, and one of those pockets was half turned inside out, remember. I thought considerable then. Afterward I decided not to think. The doctor called Kelly's death an accident, and that's the way it'll stand. Thinking won't change it, and there isn't any proof."

"What do I care about proof?" I demanded. "I'm not hunting for a murderer—I'm hunting for a book. If the sidekick killed Kelly, and this letter makes me think he might have, then the sidekick bird has the book and has flown with it. And if that's the case," I added bitterly, "then Doc Payson and I are sunk. Completely sunk!"

"Wait a minute, Dick. Let's not heave the tiller overboard and let her steer herself. If I remember rightly, there's more to that letter. Doesn't Kelly say something about hiding the goods?"

By this time I was in the depths again. I had convinced myself that the Primer was hundreds of miles away and gone beyond hope of recovery. I felt tired and slightly sick and not at all interested in the rest of the letter. Still I found the passage Ownley wanted and read it aloud.

"I guess this is what you want. It says here 'If you don't get that wire, the goods will be hid away good.' "

"I thought so." Ham nodded and wrote something down. "I thought it said something like that. Now that may be important. Let's see what else there is. Not much, as I recollect."

There wasn't much. In the event his sins caught up with him, as he evidently feared, Kelly urged his friend, Eddie, to find the book by way of revenge. He heartily endorsed the idea of double-crossing the rest of the unsavory gang, some of whom he named. He warned Eddie to step care-

fully, since there was trouble around which he character-
ized as "hot and bad." He wound up by bestowing his
blessing and by signing himself tastefully as "Legs."

When I had finished, I tossed the letter in Ownley's
general direction and sat staring gloomily at nothing.
Ham carefully read the penciled script once more and then
studied his notes. Finally he spoke. "Well, Dick," he said,
"we've squeezed this as nigh dry as we can. Let's see what
we've got in the way of juice."

"Help yourself," I told him wearily. "I'll take vanilla."

He paid no attention. "We've got quite a lot," he mused,
almost as though talking to himself; "but we've got two
things that are specially important. One of them is that
when Kelly wrote this letter, this sidekick one, the fellow
he double-crossed, was on Sepatonk. That's amazing, if it's
true."

"Amazing is right," I laughed shortly; "but the word
to emphasize is 'was.' Mr. Sidekick knocked Kelly on the
head, took the Primer, and is probably now making merry
under the white lights of Broadway!"

"Think so?" Ownley looked doubtful and scratched his
chin. "Wish you'd tell me, Dick, how the sidekick happened to come to Sepatonk at *all*. To this particular little
island, mind you. He didn't come to see Kelly, that's certain, because the hurricane blew Kelly on here, when,
according to his tell he was bound up the coast. Even his
mother, if he had one, wouldn't have known where to find
him. Did Kelly write his sidekick—the man he's double-
crossed—a postcard giving his address? You bet he
didn't!" He pointed a finger at me. "Dick," he said, im-
pressively, "if there's anything in logic, Mr. Sidekick is a
man who *lives* on Sepatonk—a man we see every day probably. He's got to be."

"But—" I was slightly bewildered. "But—"

"But leave him for now," Ownley went on. "Let's think about the Primer book. From this letter we can be pretty sure one of two things happened to it. Either old Sidekick stole it from Kelly's body, or Kelly hid it before he died."

"Exactly. I said that at the beginning. If Sidekick stole it, it's gone. If Kelly hid it, it's gone. In either case you and I are left out on the end of a long limb. There isn't a thing we can do."

"Think not? I wonder. I'm not so everlasting sure. We might find Sidekick, for one thing. *He* hasn't gone, you can bet on that. He's still on Sepatonk."

"Find him? Still on Sepatonk?" I felt that either Ham or I must be getting feeble-minded. "How on earth can you say that?"

"Because it's true," Ham explained patiently. "It *has* to be true. Admitting that Sidekick must be one of the regular folks on the Island—one we most probably see every day—then we know—I know, anyhow—that nobody of that description has left the Island since Kelly died. If he hasn't gone, he is still here. Who is he? Well, we might try to find out. I've lived here all my life, and I know almost everybody well as I know myself. There aren't such an awful lot of folks to account for. We might check up on who was where about the time Kelly took his last walk. If we can find out who Sidekick is, we might find out where the Primer is—always granting that Sidekick stole the Primer. It's a slim chance, but still it's a chance."

"I suppose you're right." I couldn't be very enthusiastic for it seemed a very slim chance indeed to me. "We might check the alibis of likely people."

"Yes. That's one thing we can do, and unless I'm mistaken it'll keep us busy for a while." He nodded. "We'll start in on that tomorrow, but right now let's think about the other thing that might have happened to your missing Primer. Suppose Kelly hid it—hid it 'good' as he said he was going to in this letter. What can we do about that?"

"Hunt again, I suppose." I made a little gesture of hopelessness. "We have hunted already and had no luck. If he hid it at all cleverly, we haven't a chance. As a matter of fact, we are worse off, really, than if Sidekick stole it."

Ham did not answer. He sat looking at the letter on the desk in front of him and tapping it with a pencil. Then he suddenly asked me a question. "If Kelly hid the Primer, Dick, how do you figure this man, Eddie, was supposed to know where to find it?"

I hadn't thought of that point, and I couldn't see any good answer to it. "I don't know," I said uncertainly. "Not unless Eddie and Kelly had previously arranged where the book was to be hidden."

"I don't think they had." Ham shook his head. "Not from the way this letter reads, and not when you remember that Kelly didn't come here on purpose. No. I think that if 'Eddie old pal' had got this letter, as he was meant to, it would have been the first time he ever heard of Sepatonk, and the first time he had heard anything about the book being hid here."

"Then how," I demanded in exasperation, "could Kelly expect him to find it? He *couldn't* unless he sent him a message saying where it was hidden."

"A message! Why—yes. Maybe that's the ticket, Dick. A message."

"You mean Kelly sent him a telegram, or phoned him, or wrote another letter?"

"No. He had no chance to do that."

"Then how?"

"I'm not sure, Dick, but I've got a tiny little bit of an idea. This letter here kind of tantalizes me. I think I'll kind of puzzle over it, as you might say, for a spell."

I didn't know what he was talking about, and he didn't offer to explain, so after a little while I gave up and went to bed. I left Ham still sitting at his desk with the letter in front of him. He was humming under his breath as he studied it, and seemed surprisingly cheerful.

As for me, I was anything but cheerful. My hopes of recovering the Primer had reached a new all-time low.

II

At ten o'clock the next morning Anne Francis telephoned to say that Perry Hale wanted me to come over for a picnic lunch on the beach in front of his house. "Some of the others are coming from the Inn," she told me, "and Perry just asked me to include you." She paused and then spoke in a low, quick voice as though she did not want to be overheard. "If you aren't busy, how about meeting me in ten minutes somewhere along the path through the pines? There are things to be said. Important, maybe."

On my way out I stopped to tell Ownley where I was going and he approved. "Good idea, Dick. You might ask a few quiet questions up at Hale's. 'Twouldn't do us any harm to know what *those* folks—all of 'em—were doing the night Kelly died. Seems to me Perry Hale and the Folger man are just as likely candidates for jail as Grover or House or Drake, Holley, or my clerk, George Silver."

I agreed, even though I didn't take much stock in what

he said, and I was whistling cheerfully as I walked along
the little path by the shore. The waters of the Atlantic
stretched away deeply blue to the distant horizon and
sparkled under a September sun that was shining in a
cloudless sky. The prospect, I decided, was definitely pleasing, and the sight of Anne waiting for me in a secluded
group of pines failed to make it any less pleasing.

I had no inclination to talk about serious matters, but
Anne gave me no choice. She was just as lovely as ever, if
not more so, and there was a little wrinkle of worry between her eyes and she got down to business without pre-
amble. "See here, Puss Clarke," she said quickly and with
an air of injury, "I'm in a jam. Maybe you're in one, too.
And it's all your fault."

"A jam?" Being slightly intoxicated—by the sea air,
no doubt—I made a carefree gesture. "Always remember,
my dear, that what is jam to the goose is so much sauce
to the gander. By the way, how would you like to be
kissed, just for the hell of it?"

"Don't be a fool!" She stamped her foot. "Ted Folger
had a brainstorm at breakfast this morning and asked me
if you weren't the Clarke who worked for the Knowlton
Library. Said he thought he remembered reading something in the paper about your finding a rare book. How
do you like *them* for apples, Mr. Clarke?"

"Oho!" That news brought me down to earth with a
thump. "So that's the way the land lies! May I ask what
you told him?"

"That's just it," she said, testily. "Just because I'd
promised you something, and with some fool idea of saving your precious skin, I lied. I said you weren't the one. I
said that I doubted very much if you'd so much as read
three books in your entire life."

"Thanks, Anne. Thanks a lot. And did the lie go over?"

"That's just it." She shook her head. "I don't think it did. Ted Folger shook his head and looked doubtful and muttered something about being almost willing to swear that you were the one he'd read about. I tried to change the subject, but I didn't have any luck because Perry suddenly stuck his oar in. For some crazy reason he seemed very much interested. Almost excited. Asked me questions. Was I *positive* you weren't the Library fellow, and so forth? I had to keep on lying, of course, and I don't think they believed me for a minute. Anyhow I stuck to my story, and you, Puss, have got to back me up. If they ask you, you've never been inside the Knowlton Library in your life."

"Of course not, Anne, and I don't think it's much to worry about. They probably won't ask me."

"I'm not so sure of that, and this is why: I left the men for a while after breakfast, and the minute I came back Perry told me to phone and ask you for lunch."

I shrugged. "Anything so strange about that?"

"Of course." She was impatient. "Perry doesn't like you. That's obvious. Then why would he ask you to lunch?"

"I wouldn't know. What's your idea?"

"I think he's still on the trail of the Library business. I think he's going to ask you questions and make a liar out of me."

"I see. Well, don't worry. I'll back you to the limit."

I was interested and definitely puzzled. I could see well enough why Hale might not like me, and I couldn't understand why he should be at all concerned about my past. Then I remembered something Ham Ownley had said to me only a short time before. He had said that Folger and Hale were just as likely to be mixed up in the Primer affair as anybody else on the island. I hadn't taken him very seriously at the time, but this news of Anne's made things different.

"Tell me something," I asked her after I'd taken a moment to collect my thoughts. "Didn't you say that Ted Folger was interested in rare books?"

"Yes. He's always batting on about them. Says it's his hobby. Why?"

"Nothing much. Do you know anything else about Folger?"

"No." She shook her head. "He's a friend of Perry's, from New York. That's all I know."

"I see." I did some more quick thinking. "And how about Perry? Is he interested in rare books, too? Is he a collector, maybe?"

"I wouldn't know." Anne looked doubtful. "He's never said anything about collecting *books*."

"You mean he collects other things? What things?"

"Well, it—it's sort of funny." She hesitated. "I never knew he was interested in any sort of collecting, but the other day when he and I were in his library he opened the safe and showed me."

"Safe?" I was surprised. "Do you mean to say he has a safe in his summer cottage on Sepatonk?"

"Perhaps I shouldn't have said 'safe,' because it isn't really one. I mean it isn't particularly burglar proof. It's just a big steel box set in the library wall back of the book-cases."

"Back of the bookcases?"

"Yes. The center section of the bookcases swings out like a door and the safe is behind. It hasn't any combination. Just a lock, and Perry keeps the key under the clock on top of the bookcase. He says he isn't worried about burglars—just fire."

"I see." I was becoming more and more interested. "And you say he showed you some of the things he keeps in this safe?"

"Yes. He pulled them out one after another like rabbits out of a hat. A queer assortment, too. There was a beautiful piece of porcelain, a tray of semiprecious gems, a portfolio of etchings, and a hunk of carved jade. There was a lot of other stuff, but that will give you the idea. Perry said that they were all museum pieces."

I whistled. "I'd say that Mr. Hale had catholic tastes for a collector."

Anne looked a little bit uncomfortable, I thought. "That is the first thing that would occur to anybody, of course," she admitted. "When I remarked on it Perry just laughed. He said he wasn't an ordinary kind of collector—that as a matter of fact he isn't at all interested in the things he collects—for their own sakes."

"No? Then why on earth does he collect them?"

"He says," she said slowly, "that he gets a big kick out of owning something that nobody else in the world owns. No matter what." Her color suddenly became deeper. "I suppose that isn't what you'd call an admirable trait."

I thought that it was anything but an admirable trait, but I had brains enough not to say so. "I suppose that that feeling is the real basis for all collecting, when you get down to it. Were there any books mixed in along with the other things he showed you?"

"No." She shrugged. "There weren't, but—"

"I think I know what you mean. Being the kind of collector he is, he might have a few rare books just as well as not."

"Yes."

There were a lot of thoughts crowding into my brain just then. They were new thoughts, some of them exciting, and they didn't fall readily into order. I was silent for a time, trying to get myself organized, and for once in my life I almost forgot Anne. She reminded me by speaking.

"If it isn't too much to ask," she said almost plaintively, "I'd very much like to know, Puss, what all this is about."

"About?" I didn't understand her at first. "What do you mean?"

"What are you doing on Sepatonk Island? Why don't you want anybody to know that you have been with the Knowlton Library? Why did you tell me that there had been trouble there and that you had to leave? Why are Perry and Ted Folger so interested in you? Why are you interested in them? Why did you tell me that you came down here to see what was left of your cottage, when a phone call would have told you that only a few shingles were blown off in the hurricane? What's everything all about, anyhow?"

"Call a halt!" I laughed and held up my hand; but I knew that I was in a corner, and I wasn't quite sure what to do about it. "What's got into you, Anne? You're dreaming things. There isn't any mystery. I've told you everything there is to tell, except maybe that my real reason for coming down here was to see you."

"That's not true—and you know it."

She said the words so contemptuously that I felt my cheeks burn. "You're right, Anne," I said abruptly. "That wasn't true, and I don't know why I said it. The truth is, that I'm down here for another and definite purpose, and that I can't tell you what that purpose is. To the contrary,

I've got to throw myself on your mercy and ask you to keep on being quiet about what you know about me."

"I see." I could tell from her tone that she was hurt and I felt more like a mutt than ever. "Is there any particular reason, Puss, considering everything, why I should do what you want?"

"None."

"Is it possible that my keeping quiet about you might work against the interests of my friends, Perry Hale and Ted Folger?"

I felt that I had done all the prevaricating and quibbling to Anne that I wanted to, so I blurted out the truth. "If you'd asked me that question yesterday, I'd have said no. In view of what you've just told me, I don't know. It might."

"I see."

"Look here, Anne." I broke in before she could go further. "How much do you know about Perry Hale? Really *know* about him, I mean?"

"I don't know." She shrugged. "I have been acquainted with him for some time, but—know about him? Not very much, actually, I suppose."

"There's something else." I was in deep water already so I could see nothing to be lost by not going in deeper. "It's none of my business, of course, and you have every right to tell me to jump in the lake, but I wish you'd tell me how you really feel about Perry Hale. Are—are you going to marry him?"

I thought she might flare out at me then, but she did not. She merely shook her head uncertainly. "I don't know. I'm not sure. I—I don't think so."

There was a lot of relief for me in those words, and hope, too, but then was not the time to show it. "In that case," I went on quickly, "I'm asking you to believe in me, and to trust me, for just a little while more. I hope I'll be on firm ground shortly and be able to tell you everything. I'll do it the moment I can. In the meantime I'm in your hands."

She looked at me for a long, thoughtful moment. Then she sighed. "I suppose I'll do what you want. I'm a fool, of course, but I suppose I'll do it."

I tried to thank her, but she would not let me. Neither would she let me walk the rest of the way to Hale's house with her. She said it would be better if it were not known we had talked together. She said that she would go back alone and that I could follow in a few minutes. "You'd better be on your guard, Puss," she warned me, "because I'm sure they are suspicious of you. You'd better make up your mind just what you are going to say."

I agreed with her. I had to make up my mind about that, and about a lot of other things. After she had gone, I sat down in the sun on the warm pine needles and spent some ten minutes in heavy thought.

III

A few minutes of conversation with a pretty girl in a pine grove had certainly changed my outlook in a big way. Twenty minutes before I had been tired and discouraged, and had felt that in spite of all I had done the Primer was gone forever. It seemed as though I were faced with a blank wall—as though there were no more leads left to follow. But that was twenty minutes ago. I had leads now, all right, plenty of them. The question was what did they mean and where would they take me.

Ham Ownley had told me that every single person on Sepatonk Island must come under our suspicious eyes as being a possible partner in crime to the late Mr. Sanger-Kelly. He had specifically included the people at Perry Hale's house in this category, but for some reason I had not taken this very seriously. It did not seem possible that Perry Hale, or any of his friends, for that matter, could be mixed up in a dirty business of theft, and assault, and pocket-picking. But after all—and in the light of what Anne had just told me, I now asked myself the question most earnestly—why *not?*

On Anne's say-so Ted Folger was much interested in rare books. That let him in. Perry Hale was a man who collected everything and anything, just so long as it was valuable and scarce. That let him in, too. More significant still was the fact that both Folger and Hale were oddly concerned in the possibility that I might have some connection with the Knowlton Library. Why that concern? So far as I could see there was absolutely no reason for it, unless the pair were somehow mixed up in the theft of the Primer.

I scratched my chin and contemplated Hale and Folger in roles of criminals. Suppose they were. What then? Well, in that case they were a couple of bad actors. They had connived in the stealing of a very valuable book. They had been silent partners in a brutal assault on an old man, and a similar assault upon a younger man. Their murderous pal had double-crossed them, and then had been delivered by fate into their hands. Where was the pal now? He was dead, and there might even be something strange in the manner of his death. Of course Doctor Farmer was sure it was accidental, but evidently Ham Ownley was not so sure.

All this, it must be granted, was not a pleasant line of reasoning, but there was an element of possibility in it and it opened up further unsavory fields of conjecture.

If Hale and Folger had obtained possession of the little book, where was it now? That did not seem hard to answer. It was probably in the steel box Anne had told me about—the steel box behind the bookcase in Hale's library. They might easily have hid it elsewhere, of course, but probably not since they must have felt themselves entirely safe from pursuit.

And then? Well, then Folger had what Anne called a brainstorm, and remembered seeing a newspaper picture of me in which I was tagged as an employee of the Knowlton museum. That must, if he was a crook, have been a nasty shock to him and his associate Hale, especially since I had denied having any employment and had said that I was on Sepatonk merely to inspect my cottage and recover my hurricane-damaged health. They must now be thinking that I had somehow picked up their trail and was making a quiet investigation.

"And if they think *that*, Puss Clarke," I told myself grimly, "you're in what might be known as one hell of a sweet spot. If those babies *are* that sort, then violence is meat and drink to them; and if you don't tread lightly, you'll wake up some bright morning to find the entire back of your skull bashed in!"

I realized, of course, that all this was pure supposition and that Hale and Folger might eventually turn out to be the eminently respectable citizens they were rated as being. I couldn't, on the other hand, make myself believe that I was barking up the wrong tree altogether. The fabric I had woven in my brain seemed sound somehow. It held together. In any event it demanded the careful testing that I intended to give it.

I got to my feet and walked slowly toward Hale's house accompanied by the uneasy feeling that I might be blood brother to a lamb offering himself meekly to the slaughter. On the other hand, I was forewarned, and, therefore, knew what I should do. First of all I ought to find out something about the activities of the Hale household on the night of Kelly's death. I knew that I'd have to move with extreme caution along that trail. Secondly I had to quell Folger's notion that I had any connection with the Knowlton Library. Anne had tried to help me there, but apparently her story had not been good enough. Mine must be better. If it was not—then I felt that some kind person might very well invade the dark privacy of *my* cranium with a blunt instrument.

IV

I can't say that Hale's stronghold gave any impression of danger and impending evil. It was a big, gray-shingled affair built in the days of broad verandas and many turrets. It stood on a high point of land commanding a wide view of the Atlantic, and on this particular morning, with its many windows sparkling in the sunlight, it seemed cheerful and inviting and friendly.

The wide front door stood open, but the big living room inside was empty. There was no sign of Anne or of anyone else, and I was looking about for a bell to ring when I heard the boom of Perry Hale's laughter from an adjoining room. The door to that was open, too, and I walked in, uninvited, to find myself in the library Anne had talked about. Books lined the walls everywhere, and in two big chairs by the window sat Perry Hale and Ted Folger with a backgammon board between them.

I did not like Perry Hale—Anne was undoubtedly the reason for that—but I had to admit that he was pleasant to see. He was a broad-shouldered, burly man with jet black hair and black eyes that went well with his deep coat of tan. His teeth flashed white when he smiled, which he did often, and which he did this time when he saw me. He did not rise, but greeted me with a show of friendliness. Ted Folger also raised a languid hand in salute. Folger was a tall, gangling individual with extremely blond hair and the sort of pallor that no amount of sun seems to change.

"The front door was open," I explained, "and there wasn't anybody in the living room, so I just barged in. Hope you don't mind."

"Certainly not." Perry Hale was emphatic. "This place has always been informal and always will be if I have anything to say about it. That front door is seldom shut and never locked. As a matter of fact, I don't know where the key is—if there is one."

"Isn't that rather inviting to burglars, Perry?" Ted Folger asked the question in a tired voice, his eyes resting contemplatively on me.

"No burglars on Sepatonk." Perry laughed. "Even if there were, there isn't anything to steal in this place—not anything they could find, anyhow."

I thought about the steel box behind the bookcase and wondered if that was why he had so much confidence. Aloud I said, "Don't let me interrupt your game, please. I know it's an indecent hour for me to get here in response to a luncheon invitation, but I went out for a walk and just sort of ended up here."

"Nonsense! Glad you came," said Perry heartily. "This game of Ted's and mine won't take very long. It's just a matter of routine, anyhow. We play a couple of games every morning after breakfast and I win a few dollars. It gets me in a good humor and puts Ted in his proper place. Roll 'em out, Folger, and be careful about doubles."

The dice rattled hollowly in the box but Ted Folger did not roll them. He spoke to me, instead. "Do you know, Clarke," he said thoughtfully, "I have a strange obsession about you. I could swear that I saw your picture in one of the papers as an assistant curator of the Knowlton Library at Bainbridge University. The recollection is so clear that I'm beginning to think I'm getting feeble-minded. Anne says you aren't anything of the kind—and she surely ought to know."

There it was. Folger was looking at me, and Hale was looking at me, and for some silly reason I felt a little chill of fear. I went into my act, at once, however, and felt that I didn't do it badly. "I'm afraid that Anne is right," I said with a laugh. "What I don't know about curators and libraries and books is a great deal. I'm totally ignorant about them. My business is farming."

"Funny thing." Folger shook his blond head. "You're right, of course, and yet I could almost swear—"

"Butternuts!" Hale interrupted impatiently. "Don't be a fool, Ted. If the man says he isn't a curator, he isn't a curator. Who ought to know better than he? What difference, anyhow? Roll the dice, will you?" He turned to me with a smile. "Don't mind Ted, Clarke. He may not have all his buttons at times, but he's harmless. We'll be through here in a few minutes, and in the meantime there are some fairly new magazines on that table over there. Look them over, if you like."

Ted Folger muttered something about "extraordinary," and rolled the dice. I gladly accepted Hale's invitation and strolled across the room to a table that was littered with newspapers and magazines.

For what happened almost immediately after that I have practically no excuse. I've been ridden about it enough, heaven knows. I've been kidded so much, as a matter of fact, that I'm just a little bit sensitive on the subject, and would give a good deal to be able to think up an alibi that might hold water. The thing is, I can't. At the time I had just faced a crisis of sorts, and was feeling that I had weathered it rather well. I was relieved, and relaxed, and as defenseless as a babe. In the lingo of the prize ring I was a complete sucker for the left hook that immediately came my way.

This is what happened:

The table, as I have said, was littered with reading matter, and through this I shuffled as I stood with my back to the backgammon table. I wasn't reading anything, and I wasn't even looking at the pictures. I was merely going through the motions while I congratulated myself on being a deft deceiver. It was in this frame of mind that I picked up a small, board-bound copy of Cooper's *Last of the Mohicans* that was lying carelessly in the midst of the rest of the junk.

I picked it up and noted its title without conscious thought. My leafing through it and my glance at the title page were entirely automatic. Automatic, too, was what I did next. "My gosh!" I exclaimed, spinning half around with the book in my hands. "Why, this—!"

That tore things, of course. If ever a poor fish had risen

for a dangling piece of bait, I was that fish. The book had been planted there by Hale and Folger, and it was such an obvious and valuable rarity that even a beginner in the study of old American books, like myself, could not have failed to spot it.

I did not fail. Oh, no! Being a good pupil of Doc Payson, I recognized it at once; and, being a prize candidate for a half-wits' home, I failed to keep my mouth shut. Without stopping to think, I gargled my excitement aloud, which was almost more than Messers Hale and Folger could have hoped that I would be moronic enough to do.

The backgammon game stopped instantly. "Why, Mr. Clarke!" Perry Hale's voice was so smooth it sounded as though it had been oiled. It also oozed sarcasm. "Why, what's the matter? You haven't come across a piece of bad news from home, I trust?"

"Oh, no!" I could feel the blood burning in my cheeks, and I could have wept from the shame of having been such a gullible jackass. "It's nothing at all. I—"

"Let's see." My trying to hide the book under some newspapers didn't do any good, for Hale popped out of his chair and came over to pick it up again. "Why, no, there couldn't be any bad news in this." He shook his head in mock astonishment. "It's just a frowzy old copy of *The Last of the Mohicans!*"

"Really?" Ted Folger was enjoying himself immensely, but he pretended to be puzzled. "Perhaps it's a first edition and Mr. Clarke spotted it. But no." He shook his head sadly. "That can't be. Mr. Clarke doesn't *know* anything about books and libraries, or such things. Oh, no! His line is farming!"

"The book hasn't anything to do with it!" I blurted the words. "It's just that—"

"Perhaps he has a pain," said Folger soberly. "Perhaps Mr. Clarke knows so little about books that he has a pain in his stomach!"

"Appendicitis! That must be it! Does it hurt, Mr. Clarke?" Perry poked me gently in the midsection. "Here?"

How long the bear-baiting would have continued I'm sure I don't know. Folger and Hale were enjoying themselves thoroughly and probably would have carried on for some time, if Anne hadn't burst in just then and demanded my services as a partner at tennis.

That saved me, for my tormentors, unaccountably, seemed content to let me go. They said nothing to Anne about the way they had trapped me, and sent us away with their blessings. As I was walking down the veranda, however, I heard them laughing in chorus. They sounded happy, and I don't know that they were to be blamed. The joke, if it could be called a joke, was certainly on me.

I shall pass over the rest of that unhappy morning as rapidly as possible. I was deeply disgusted with myself for being so incredibly stupid, and was also alarmed about the possible consequences. Anne's disgust when she heard the story was even greater than my own, and she did not hesitate to express it. "I dislike dumb people," she said acidly, "and I particularly dislike them when their dumbness results in my being shown up as an out-and-out liar!"

There wasn't anything I could say to that, and there wasn't anything that I could do, either. Given my choice, I would have gone off somewhere to hide, but instead I was forced to stay and face the music. I played tennis with Anne and got back to the house just in time to welcome the gang from the Inn who had come over for the picnic. Included were House, Drake, Grover, and Holley, so that

Anne and Mrs. Folger were the only girls in a party of nine.

Perhaps the rest of them enjoyed the proceedings which followed even if I did not. We lay around on the beach and watched Hale's man cook steaks over a charcoal fire. Then we ate them and all the things that went with them, and I had to admit that Hale made a good host. His food was good, and he was pleasant to everybody. He and Folger were even decent enough to leave me alone. Momentarily I expected to have my job at the library flung in my face, but nothing happened. It was not until the meal was over and everybody was in a more or less somnolent condition that the blow fell, for then Perry came over to me and asked quietly if we could have a few words together in his library.

Meekly I agreed and meekly I followed him to the place where I had made a fool of myself only a few hours before. There, with the door closed behind us, we sat ourselves down in big chairs and came immediately to business.

"See here, Clarke," said Hale by way of opening what was to be an almost incredible conversation. "Let's you and I do some plain talking. We're alone, and we don't have to be too awfully careful." He eyed me closely. "That was a mean trick Ted Folger and I played on you this morning—the one about the book, I mean."

I knew what he was talking about, all right, but I took refuge behind a blank look. "I'm afraid I don't understand."

"Nonsense." He scowled impatiently. "Don't take that line with me. It won't wash. You fell for that *Last of the Mohicans* trick like a ton of bricks. First you told us that you didn't know a thing about rare books, and two minutes later you proved that you knew a lot. What *I* want to know, Clarke, is why you tried to bluff."

"I'm not admitting any bluff," I told him as coolly as I could, "and I'm asking you a question in return. Why, Mr. Hale, are you so interested in my supposed knowledge of rare books? What affair is it of yours?"

"*Touché!*" Hale put back his head and laughed with entire good humor. "An eye for an eye, and tit for tat! A question for a question. Fair enough. The point is, however, who's going to come out in the open first?"

I shrugged, though I felt a thrill of excitement. "It seems to me that you were the one who asked for this conversation."

"True." He pondered for a moment and then said: "I suppose it's up to me, and I don't really know why I shouldn't talk, anyhow. You'll get what I mean even if I don't call a spade a spade. I'll answer your question. Your knowledge of rare books interests me, Clarke, because in the light of recent, and not generally known, events, I'm not surprised to find somebody like you camped on my trail. Is that plain?"

Plain! It was so plain that for a few moments I could hardly credit my ears. Hale had the Primer! He had just admitted it to me—or what amounted to that—and had even admitted that he wasn't surprised to find somebody from the Library close on his heels. A dozen things flashed through my mind. Hale had the Primer, and it was a cinch bet it was in that steel box of his, right at that minute. *He* was the "sidekick" referred to in the Kelly letter. He was the "mean trouble" to be wary of. He, Perry Hale! Even then, as I faced him in that library of his, with all the evidence of wealth and luxury about him, the idea that he could be a thief and the partner of a blackjacker, a fellow who would stop at nothing to get hold of some treasure he craved, seemed ridiculously unbelievable, but it must be true. Payson had told me stories of collectors to whom collecting had become a mania. There were such people, and he was one of them.

I don't know what I showed in my face, but it must have been something, for Hale laughed—grimly this time. "I guess I've answered my question, all right. And just to save time I'll answer yours. You kept your knowledge of rare books quiet because you didn't want anybody on the Island to know why you were down here. Am I correct?"

"Yes." I nodded weakly. "You're quite right."

"Very well, then. Let's quit stalling and talk business. You aren't above talking business, are you?"

Business? What business? Once more I was out of my depth, so once more I stalled. "I—I imagine not."

"Good. That being the case you might as well give me the bad news right away. What's this little matter going to cost me?"

Again I was floundering. Cost him?

"Well," he snapped impatiently, "come on. Would twenty thousand interest you?"

And then, at last, I thought I saw it. Bribery! He realized that I knew he had the Primer and was ready to pay twenty thousand dollars to me as my price for leaving it in his possession and keeping my mouth shut. He was to keep poor Payson's treasure and I, Payson's friend and employee, was to betray that trust and put the money in my own pocket. He really thought I was that kind of worm.

I looked at him. Perry Hale will probably never be nearer being socked on the nose than he was just then. I choked—and glared, I guess, for he spoke again.

"Come, come!" he snapped. "Don't haggle. I'll make it twenty-five, cold cash on the barrelhead, but no more. Not another cent."

"You're a cool proposition, Hale," I told him with slow wonder. "You've got a magnificent nerve!"

That seemed to amuse him, for he grinned. "Not so much," he observed. "There aren't any dictaphones around, you know. We're alone, Clarke. We can talk plain English. Well, how about it? Twenty-five thousand dollars is a lot of money, you know."

I was struggling with the situation. He was right when he said we were alone. No witnesses, no listeners, merely his word against mine. He could deny having said one compromising word, and I could prove nothing. The louse! And this was Anne's playmate, the man she thought she might marry.

Well, I must be careful. I couldn't afford to tell him even a little of what I thought of him—yet. I must lead him on. He spoke once more. "Well?"

I drew a long breath. "It's a lot of money, all right."

"I'll say so. Especially for a shrimp of a book that may have sold for a shilling when it was new. But that's neither here nor there. I—"

There was an interruption then. Hale suddenly jumped to the door and flung it open. The living room was empty, but I could hear the voices of the rest of the party from the veranda, where they had presumably retired out of the warm sun. The booming voice I heard was that of Holley, and the quiet reply might have come from any of the other men.

"Funny thing." Hale was muttering as he closed the door again. "Three or four times I've thought I heard somebody moving around quietly in the living room. Must have been wrong. Never mind. What do you say to my proposition?"

The interval had given me the time I needed. After all, I had not got my hands on the Primer yet. Ways and means must be devised.

"Why—er—" I faltered, "will you give me twenty-four hours to decide?"

"All right. Twenty-four hours." He shrugged and then looked at me hard. "But don't try any tricks in the meantime. I'm good natured enough as a rule, but when I really get mad I'm apt to be a tough customer."

"I can believe it, Mr. Hale," I told him fervently. "I can readily believe it!"

That was the end of our conversation, and it almost seems as though it might have been enough for one day. It was not, though, for very late that same night I sneaked into Hale's house with intent to steal.

V

It may seem fantastic that a hitherto completely law-abiding citizen should suddenly set forth upon a deliberately planned burglary. I have been told often enough that it not only seemed, but *was* fantastic; that I must have been out of my head at the time. I do not agree, and I do not intend to defend myself, except briefly, here or in the future. No matter how it worked out, the act seemed perfectly logical in the light of the certainties that I carried away with me after my talk with Hale.

The first and most important of those certainties was that Perry Hale was in possession of the Knowlton Library's New England Primer. He, himself, had as much as told me that. All right, then. My only, and all-important problem was the one of getting the Primer back. How was I to do that?

I considered the various possibilities as I walked back to the Inn that pleasant September afternoon. The obvious thing to do was to get a warrant to search Hale's house. But where, and upon what grounds, could I obtain such a warrant? I had no evidence whatsoever. Hale had implied that to me more than once, and he was right. There had been no witnesses to our conversation, so legally my hands were tied.

The only thing left, as I saw it, was burglary. If I could walk into Hale's house that night, and walk out again with the Primer, it would be tit for tat. He had stolen the book—or assisted in its stealing—from us, and we had stolen it back again. The case would be closed. I determined, then and there, so to close it, if I could. I also decided that Ownley must be kept entirely out of the picture, since I could hardly ask a Justice of the Peace to help break the law he was sworn to uphold.

I was alone, therefore, when I stood in the jet blackness of Perry Hale's living room some time late that night. There were sneakers on my feet, a small flashlight in my hand, and a weakness in my knees that was not the result of a long sickness. The library door stood ajar before me.

My luck so far had held, for the door from the veranda had been unlocked—something Perry Hale said that morning had led me to hope for that—and I had been able to get in that way by merely turning the knob. My progress across the living room had been as silent as the floorboards would permit, although their creakings had, to me, sounded loud enough to wake the dead. Now I was only a few steps from my objective; and if Lady Luck would only favor me twice more, the thing would soon be done. First the key to the safe must be under the clock on the bookcase where Anne had said it was kept. Second, the New England Primer must be in the safe.

I said a little prayer and had reached out my hand to push the library door open, when I heard a sound that froze me in my tracks. What kind of a sound it was I did not know, but it was quite loud and came from the room I was about to enter. I stood absolutely motionless and held my breath, listening, but the noise was not repeated.

I am not ashamed to admit that I was badly frightened. Given half a chance I would have quit right there, and cried uncle, and gone home to bed; but I had no such chance. Having come so far, I knew I had to go into that library in spite of any number of strange noises, and finally I made myself do so.

It was very quiet in the room, and I felt a breath of air as though the French window there were open. I could see nothing, however, and after a long moment of intense listening I pushed the button of my flashlight. In its glow the rows of books that lined the walls became visible. Two dark blurs at one side were the chairs facing the backgammon board. The larger blur in the center was Perry Hale's big desk. The beam of light fell on the desk, jerked, and came to a full stop. Seated there, with his back to an open French window, was Perry Hale.

I must have exclaimed aloud, but Perry did not hear. He was slumped forward with his head on the blotter and was quite unconscious.

I'm a little uncertain just what I did after that. I know I forgot all about being an intruder and the necessity for being quiet. I ran over, shook the limp shoulder, and spoke Perry's name, but I got no response. With my flashlight

I found the switch on the wall and turned on the overhead lights.

There was an ugly bruise on the back of Hale's head, and the hair about it looked matted. I touched the place gently with my fingers, and they came away wet with bright red blood. I was staring at them stupidly when a sound behind me made me spin about.

Anne Francis was standing in the doorway. She was in a negligee and her hand was at her throat. She stared first at me and then at Hale, her eyes widening with horror. Then she took a half step forward.

"Dick! My God!" Her voice was low and choked. "Dick! What awful thing have you done?"

PART V

The Clambake

Told by
Dickson Clarke

I

Wʜᴀᴛ awful thing have you done?"

Those were the first words that Anne said when she saw me standing at the library desk beside the awkwardly sprawled figure of Perry Hale, and nobody can possibly blame her for saying them. It was late at night, and I was wearing sneakers and an old black sweater. I was carrying a flashlight. Perry and I were alone, and Perry was unconscious. There was even blood on my hands. I certainly must have looked the picture of guilt.

"It's Perry Hale!" I babbled inanely. "He's been hurt! Looks as though he'd been hit on the head."

Anne shivered. "Is—is he dead?"

"No. You can hear him breathe. He's just been knocked out. It may not even be bad. I—"

"Lay him on the floor. Quickly! I'll get a pillow."

Perry was a heavy man, and his limpness made him difficult to handle; but I managed to slide him out of the chair and onto the carpet. Anne had a cushion ready, and we placed his head on it. "Loosen his necktie," she ordered. "Open his shirt!"

My fingers were fumbling to obey when she spoke again.

"Dick!" she said in a strange, choked voice. "Why did you do this terrible thing? Are you crazy?"

It took a moment for the meaning of her words to sink into my confused brain, but when it did I stopped jerking at Perry's necktie in sheer surprise. "I? I do this? You don't honestly think that I slugged him, do you? You can't!"

"Who did, if you didn't?" Her eyes blazed anger. "Do you think I'm an idiot? Of course you hit him! Never mind that now. Get water, quickly! There's a place right over there."

I ran into the lavatory that opened off both the library and the living room and got a glass of water. Anne splashed some of it in Hale's face, causing him to moan a little. He even tried to turn his head.

"I didn't hit him," I said with all the conviction I could put into my voice. "It wasn't I, I tell you. He was this way when I came into the room. Someone else did it."

"Yes?" She did not take her eyes from Perry's face, and her voice had a flat weary note of total disbelief. "What are you doing here at all—at this hour?"

The question made me realize, for the first time, my exact position. I could not answer it truthfully without confessing myself to be a burglar, and if I refused to answer it at all, I stood self-convicted of assault.

"Look at the French window," I said quickly. "It's open! Whoever hit Perry must have gone out that way. For all we know he may still be close by."

Anne's cold contemptuous voice stopped me before I had taken more than one step toward the French window. "Quit bluffing, Dick Clarke. It's no go. I'm not exactly a child. If you didn't hit Perry, what are you doing here at all?"

"I—I—"

"You see? You're not even a good liar." Perry groaned loudly then, and she bent over him. "He's coming to in a minute," she said quickly. "Get out of here, Dick. Get out fast while there's still time."

"Get out? Why? What do you mean?"

"Just what I say. For the last time in my life I'm going to be a fool about you. Get out of here before it's too late, and I won't say anything about having seen you. I'll cover up for you. That's a promise, if you'll only get out! Get out of the house and get off the Island. Get out of my life, because I never want to see you again. Only get out!"

"No." I shook my head stubbornly. "There's no reason why I should get out. I had nothing to do with this."

"Have it your own way." She shrugged and sat back on her heels. "If you won't take your only chance, when I'm fool enough to give it to you, it certainly isn't any concern of mine. Why should I worry? I'm going to yell for help, now. Ted Folger, probably, will be the one to hear me and come down. And where, Mr. Clarke, will you be, then?"

"I?" I said lamely. "I'll be right here."

She laughed, without amusement. "You'll be right here until Ted has you slapped into the jail, and that won't take him long, I can promise you. He won't be a soft, sentimental fool like me. He is Perry's friend and isn't apt to love somebody who has done what you've done."

"I haven't done anything." I was dogged. "I'll tell him so."

"Do you think he'll believe what you tell him, any more than I do? Of course not! What are you doing here in the dead of night? Why are you wearing a sweater and sneakers? What's the flashlight for? Why is Perry unconscious? Why have you blood on your hands?"

Before I could answer any of those questions, Perry moved his arms; and that settled the question so far as Anne was concerned. She put back her head and screamed at the top of a very healthy pair of lungs:

"Help! Help! Ted Folger! Ted! Help!"

There was silence for a moment after that while we both listened. Then, from overhead, there was a confused thumping and the sound of a door opening. "Who is it? What is it?" Folger's voice sounded as though he were still half asleep but thoroughly alarmed. "What's the matter?"

Instead of answering him, Anne turned to me. "He'll be down here in a second," she said with swift urgency. "Do you want to go to jail? I won't say anything, I promise. I'll even ask Perry to hush it up for my sake. Please go!"

I was in a pretty spot then, if ever I was in one. Ted Folger was bellowing again, and in a few moments he would be down in the library. Would he accept my word that I hadn't hit Perry, any more than Anne had accepted it? Probably not. When Perry came to he might be able to clear me, if he had seen the man who hit him. But even so, what explanation could I give for being in the house at all?

It was a bad situation, all right, and there was no time for weighing the pros and cons. I hesitated, and Anne saw that I was weakening.

"Get out!" she said. "Quickly! He's coming!"

"I didn't do this, Anne," I said miserably. "I swear I didn't do it."

Then I turned from her look of contemptuous disbelief and sneaked out that French window like a dog with his tail between his legs.

II

I don't think it would be very hard for anyone to guess the frame of mind I was in, or how I spent the rest of that night. I· dragged myself back to the Ownley Inn, slunk up to my room, and locked the door. Then I flung myself, fully dressed, on my bed and contemplated a situation, which, I felt, took all the bronze medals for unpleasant features. It also seemed to me that as a hard luck king I had few equals.

It is easy enough now, of course, for me to be flippant about the thing, but at the time it was pretty grim. All that I could think about was Anne: about Anne's face as she saw me standing over Hale's unconscious body with blood on my hands; the horror in her voice as she asked me what I had done; her contemptuous disbelief when I told her I hadn't done anything; the weary disgust with which she had offered to protect me and with which she had shoved me out of the room before Folger arrived.

I realized very clearly indeed what a pretty picture Anne must have of me in her mind at that very moment, and the realization was maddening. Telling myself that she no longer meant anything in my life didn't help matters either. I still loved her—engaged to her or not—and she thought I was the kind of a rat that went sneaking around in the night socking people over the head with a lead pipe!

Neither was she to be blamed for the thought. If the evidence of her eyes was trustworthy, she couldn't very well think anything else. Blood on my hands, sneakers on my feet, and guilt written all over me! And to cap the whole thing, I had, at the showdown, run like a rabbit.

The more I thought about that running away the worse I felt about it. I might just as well have signed a type-written confession and put it in Anne's hands as do a thing like that. Why had I done it? Why hadn't I stuck to my guns and let Ted Folger do his worst? When Perry Hale revived he would have cleared me of the assault charge—he would have, that is, if he had seen who attacked him. Anyhow, I would have proved myself a man and not a yellow dog.

The trouble was that there hadn't been time to think. I had had to make a snap judgment in a matter of seconds, and with the knowledge that I was in the house for a reason I couldn't hope to explain. After all, if I had faced the music, I would have had to admit an attempted burglary; and while that was undoubtedly better than assault, it would have been nothing to brag about.

On second thought, except for the wrong impression it gave Anne, running away had probably been the smart thing to do. It had eliminated awkward explanations and left me free to continue my hunt for the Primer.

The Primer! I realized then, suddenly and for the first time, that I had been so wrapped up in my own predicament that I had forgotten all about that precious and confounded little book. Where was the Primer now? Was it still in Perry Hale's safe? Had it been stolen after Perry was knocked out? Was the Primer the reason he had been knocked out? If so, and even if not, who had done the slugging?

Those and a thousand and one other questions crowded into my head at that point and made it throb. All of the questions were new. Most of them I could not answer at all. The elaborate jigsaw puzzle that only a few hours before I had thought fitted together so neatly was now knocked into a cocked hat. Nothing fitted any more, and nothing added up.

Well, I paced the floor for long hours that night, but with little result. Somebody had sandbagged Perry Hale, but who that somebody might be I had no way of knowing. Ted Folger leaped forward at once as a likely candidate, but so did plenty of objections to his election. In my book Folger was Hale's partner. Why, then, would Folger swing a blackjack? Why would it have been necessary? How could he hope to get away with such a thing? If it wasn't Folger, who was it? Where was the Primer now? Was it, for the nth time, lost again?

The dawn brought me no enlightenment and only an elementary plan of action. I was determined to go, just as soon as I could, to Perry Hale's house, and to thrash the thing out with him. If he was well enough to talk, and *would* talk, dictaphones being absent, I might discover some of the things I had to know. I was determined, also, to talk with Anne. Somehow I must convince her that I was not what she thought. I would make her change her opinion of me, I promised myself, if it was the last thing I ever did.

My face must have shown something of the way I was feeling that next morning, for Holley took occasion to comment on my appearance while four or five of us were waiting in the lobby for the breakfast bell to ring.

"Whew!" he whistled loudly. "What in the name of time have you been doing with yourself, Clarke? Your eyes look like a couple of holes burnt in a blanket! If this weren't Sepatonk Island, I'd say that you had been on a bend that was a complete loop!"

Drake put his oar in before I could think up an answer. "Mustn't question these young bloods too closely, Pete," he said with a wink. "Who's to blame a young man if he comes in late when there's a girl as good-looking as that Anne Francis living only a mile or so away? Only fair to warn you, though, Clarke. There's no use trying to keep the hour you come home to roost a secret around here. Not the way the Ownley Inn's built. You may have tried to be quiet when you came in last night but the floorboards made so much noise you might just as well have had a brass band."

"Oh," said Grover with a little smile. "So that was Clarke who came in late last night. I must have been mistaken. I'd have sworn those footsteps went to *your* room, Drake."

Grover was only kidding him, of course, but for some reason Drake was nettled. "Poppycock!" he snapped, his color rising. "I was in bed at ten o'clock. What are you talking about, Grover?"

"No offense," Dr. Grover was still smiling. "I just thought it was you, that's all. Why not? There have *been* nights, you know, when you've come in quite late, indeed."

"What of it?" Drake was glaring now. "Who's business is it but mine when I come in at night? You attend to your affairs, Oscar Grover, and I'll attend to mine!"

It looked like the beginning of a slight unpleasantness, but the breakfast gong intervened. As we trooped into the dining room, pompous old House winked elaborately at Grover, and I thought the Doctor's eyelid flickered in return.

After breakfast I stopped in at Ham's office with the idea of having a talk with him. My twenty-four hours of independent investigation had not been exactly a howling success, and I felt that I could do very well with the advice of an older and unquestionably wiser man. Ham greeted me cheerfully enough, but he did not invite me to sit down.

"Don't ever be a hotel man, Dick," he advised me, slipping into his jacket and cramming a battered felt hat on the back of his head. "In the hotel business it's either one thing or another, and if it isn't another it's something else. Today it's that everlasting annual clambake. I always give one free gratis for nothing a couple of nights before the Inn closes, and tonight's the night. Don't know why I ever started the habit, but, now that I have, I can't drop it. The guests kind of look for it, the way they do for mistakes in their bills."

"Oh, yes," I nodded. "I'd heard something about the clambake. Down at the cove, isn't it?"

"That's right. It's right on the beach so you can have the regular allowance of sand on your lobster. And work! Talk about work. I've got to see that the clams are dug and ready, build fires, heat rocks, gather up rockweed, cart about fifteen tons of grub from here down to the cove, and Almighty knows what else. And all so Old Souse can complain about having dyspepsy tomorrow! I'm afraid you'll have to excuse me, Dick. Time seems to be the thing I have the least of, today—for a change. Anything particular on your mind? Find out anything up at Hale's yesterday?"

I hesitated. Ham was in a hurry, and the talk that he and I must have would take time. Perhaps it had better wait, anyhow. I was on my way to Hale's house and when I came back I was sure to know more than I knew then. "A little," I admitted. "Do you suppose you could give me half an hour some time later on today? There are things I want to discuss with you."

We made a tentative appointment for the afternoon and then parted; Ham to make arrangements for the clambake and I to walk once more the pine-bordered path that I had used four times the day before.

It seemed to me as I crossed the broad lawn toward Hale's house that there were, surprisingly enough, no outward signs of the excitement that had so recently taken place there. I felt almost as though there should be a uniformed policeman standing guard at the door or at least an ambulance waiting in the drive, but neither was in evidence. Everything seemed entirely normal and undisturbed by human activity of any kind. Then I heard a woman's voice calling my name, and turned to see that I was being summoned by someone lying in a brightly striped deck chair that had been set out in the sun facing the sea.

I hurried across, and instead of Anne, as I had hoped, I found Betty Folger. She was smiling and looking at me out of wide black eyes with frank interest. "Good morning, Mr. Clarke," she said brightly. "Won't you park yourself for a few minutes? I find at this point that I desire conversation—most particularly conversation with you."

Well, the desire was not mutual, for I was on anything but intimate terms with Betty Folger. If I had been conscious of her at all in the past, it was simply as a well-turned out, highly decorative young female with jet black eyes and hair to match, who formed part of the Hale background. She talked very little, as I remembered, and had hardly so much as addressed a remark to me. Now she was demanding my attention, and I supposed I would have to be nominally polite. I returned her greeting and reluctantly sat down on the grass beside her.

"Mr. Clarke," said Betty Folger rapidly, "I am going to pour out my soul to you—like it or not. Can you take it? Good! I am going to confess that I never should have married Ted Folger." She held out a quick hand to forestall the remark I had no intention of making. "Please don't reproach me. For once I'm telling the truth, and I'm heaving no brickbat at Ted. It is just that stolid domesticity is not for me. I decided this morning that I was born to be a gangster's moll!"

Oh, well. Some women are like that and you have to humor them. "A gangster's moll?" I repeated. "A noble ambition, of course, but surely not beyond the hope of attaining."

"You think not? Wonderful! You make me so very 'appy." She smiled dreamily. "I like to think of myself with my man, Bloodshot Dick, the Bronx Torpedo, in our combination love nest and arsenal. There I shall be waiting when he comes home from work. There I shall banish his petty worries, such as having murdered an old lady for a net gain of only three dollars and eighteen cents. There I shall be waiting when the press brings me the news that the pardon came too late." She sighed. "I shall be wearing a simple black Bergdorf model, at the time, and shall cross my shapely limbs. 'Gentlemen,' I shall whisper huskily for publication, 'Bloodshot may have been the enemy of society, but to the bambino and me he was just a right guy. Yes, gentlemen, a right guy!'"

I laughed politely. "Since you feel so strongly about the desirability of the underworld life, you had better take steps."

"Take steps?" She spread her hands in supplication to an imaginary audience. "I give the man everything but a typewritten proposition, and he tells me to take steps! Ah, me. Never mind. Love will find a way. Skip it." She lowered her voice. "Did you wipe the gore off the sandbag? Have you contacted a mouthpiece? Why aren't you on the lam?"

I frowned then, because back of all the gibberish I thought I detected a hint of meaning. "Just what are you driving at?" I inquired rather coldly.

She shrugged. "He's sewn a button on his lip. He won't talk. Just hand me that section of rubber hose, will you, Mike?" She turned to me and made a plaintive little face. "Don't be this way with me, big boy. Don't you realize that I'm your Public with a great big capital P? Don't you see that it's perfectly safe for you to come clean to mother?"

"Come clean? In what way, Mrs. Folger?"

She sighed again. "Just tell me about last night. Tell me how, why, when, and for how much you smacked Perry Hale on the back of the skull with a weighty object."

Whew! That was something, was it not? I walk into the midst of the Hale stronghold with the utmost confidence that nobody but Anne and I knew that I had even been in the vicinity the night before, and the next thing I know Betty Folger calmly tells me that I am the one who assaulted her host. The only possible answer to the thing was that Anne had broken her promise to keep me out of it.

"Are you surprised, darling?" Betty asked solicitously. "Did you think that you got away with it without anybody knowing? Too bad, because something must have slipped. All is known. I know, Ted knows, Anne knows, and Perry knows. Here's a tip, by the way. I wouldn't get too close to Perry just now. He doesn't love you at the moment, and even in his weakened condition he might be able to do you personal injury."

"Wait a minute." I knew from Betty's tone that a denial would not do me the slightest bit of good. She was entirely convinced of my guilt, and, according to her, so were her husband and Hale. I thought I knew why, but I had to be sure. "If I understand correctly, you think that I attacked Perry Hale some time last night. Let's let that pass for the moment. I'm wondering if you'll be willing to tell me, from your own point of view, exactly what happened here last night."

"Eyewitness account? But of course! It'll be excellent practice for my future appearances in court. Let me see." She pursed her lips in thought for a moment and then began to talk rapidly. "It was some time in the dark watches of the night. Mrs. F. was busily knitting up the raveled sleave of care. That means I was asleep, darling. Sudden alarums and excursions. Mrs. F. wakes. Friend husband is bellowing out of bedroom door. Female voice is shrieking from downstairs. Change of scene to library beneath. Group hovering over Perry Hale. Perry not dead; merely blotto from blow at base of skull. Perry dragged up to his bedroom. Mrs. F., being generally useless, is shooed away. Gets story later from her husband, said story being to wit and as follows: Anne, hearing noise, went down to find Perry. Perry on coming to, mentions the name of Mr. Dick Clarke. Indicates that he would like to strew the interior mechanism of Mr. Clarke from Dan to West Orange, N. J. It is gathered that Perry objects to being smacked on the head. Anne mentions doctor for Perry. Perry has tantrum. Won't have doctor. Will take care of himself, and having taken care of himself will take care of Mr. Clarke. The last is his solemn promise. This morning Perry is in darkened room with splitting headache. Wants to see Clarke, but in return for no doctor will wait until tomorrow morning. Ted Folger puzzled, angry, and wants to call in the law. Perry won't let him. Anne wan and distrait, which is understandable. Betty Folger *was* bored, but is bored no more. Is definitely thrilled. Has determined to become gangster's moll. That is all."

"I see. Thanks." The thing was becoming increasingly clear to me, although it seemed almost impossible. "Then you didn't *hear* Perry Hale say that I hit him on the head?"

"Hear him? No, but of course he said it."

"Really?" I inquired. "What makes you think so?"

"Because—" She stopped in bewilderment. "But this doesn't make any sense."

"Perhaps it does," I said grimly. "Perhaps Perry didn't say anything about me. Perhaps the words were put in his mouth."

"But—but—"

I looked up then to see Anne coming toward us across the lawn. Betty saw her, too, and characteristically lost the thread of our talk. She motioned triumphantly in my direction and said to Anne, "You see? He's here, in person! The only trouble is that I'm afraid he's losing his grip. We've been talking for ten minutes, and he hasn't once offered to cut my throat!"

"Go away, will you, Betty?" Anne did not look at me. "I want to talk to Dick."

"All right." Betty got out of the chair with a great show of reluctance. "I'll go. I don't like it, but I'll go. Perhaps I'll see Mr. Clarke at the clambake tonight. We're going, aren't we, Anne?"

"I guess so. Perry wants us all to go so that no one will think there is anything wrong up here."

"Good. You'll be there won't you, Bloodshot?"

I shrugged. "I imagine so."

"Good. At the clambake then, and later. Call me up some time when you're not busy. We can get together and raise a check. If not that, we can just spend a quiet, homicidal evening!"

She went away then, and Anne and I looked at each other.

"Betty apparently thinks it's all a joke," said Anne. She was very pale and looked tired and listless. "I'm glad for her that her sense of humor is still working. I'm afraid I've lost mine. I don't think it's a joke at all. What are you doing down here, Dick? What are you doing on the Island at all?"

"I never," I told her coldly, "had the slightest idea of leaving the Island. Not, anyhow, on account of anything that happened last night."

"I see." She looked at me with a sort of wonder. "You thought that, because of the promise I was silly and weak enough to give you last night, you would be safe here. You thought I'd protect you. Well, I suppose your reasoning was sound, but I'm afraid you are out of luck. As it happens, you are *not* safe here. Perry knows, you see, that you are the one who hit him."

"So I gather." I put plenty of sarcasm into the words. "Perry knows, Betty Folger knows, Ted Folger knows. I wouldn't be at all surprised if there were an item to that effect in this morning's *New York Times!*"

"I don't think you need worry about that." She shrugged. "For some reason Perry wants to keep the whole thing a secret. He says that he'll deal with you himself."

"That suits me, and we'll talk about it later. Right now let's stick to the point. Would you mind telling me why you gave me that promise last night? It wasn't necessary, you know. I didn't ask for it."

"I've been wondering about that myself." She shook her head. "Ever since it happened I've been asking myself why I did such a thing. It must be that there's a streak of weakness in me somewhere. When I found you in the library with Perry, I should have called Ted and had you arrested. But no. I let you go. Maybe I did it out of gratitude for having found out about you before I made the horrible mistake of marrying you. Maybe my false pride objected to having my former fiancé listed as a jailbird. I don't know. Anyhow I did it."

"Thanks." I laughed without mirth. "Your intentions were undoubtedly of the best. It's just too bad you couldn't stick to them."

"What do you mean?" She frowned and then suddenly the color flooded her cheeks. That was a warning sign, as I very well knew, but just then I did not care. "Just what are you trying to imply, Mr. Puss Clarke? It sounds as though you had the supreme nerve to accuse me of breaking my promise!"

"Does it?" I inquired sweetly. "Well, is that so very strange, in view of the fact that Perry and the Folgers all name me as the man who did the slugging? How could they think it—unless you had broken your promise and talked?"

"Oh! Why, you—!" She was furiously angry now, but she finally managed to control her voice. "I don't know why I lower myself and waste my breath talking to you. You're cowardly enough in the first place to try to hide behind my skirts, and then you have the nerve to accuse me of breaking my promise!"

"Well, Anne, you broke it, didn't you?"

"I did nothing of the kind." She was suddenly icy cold

and heavily contemptuous. "I'm not in the habit of break-ing promises. I have not said a single word to a living soul about finding you in the library at midnight last night. Even if I had wanted to break my promise, it would not have been necessary. When Perry came to, the first thing he did was babble about you. He called you by name, and he cursed you up and down. I don't blame him."

"Thanks." With every word that she said I was getting on surer ground. I led her on. "Did he say anything defi-nite about me? Did he make any specific accusations?"

"He did. He said that he had an appointment with you last night and that you kept it! He said that you came into the room and knocked him over the head! Those were his words, and how do you like it, Mr. Clarke?"

The whole thing was clear enough to me, of course. When I had left the library the night before after getting her promise, Anne had been sure that I was the one who hit Hale. She had regretted her promise and had welched on it, telling Hale what she thought to be the truth. Now she was trying to save face with me by denying that she had told him. If I *had* been guilty, I might have believed her story about the things Hale was supposed to have said. Being innocent, I knew better.

"I'm sorry, Anne." I shook my head. "It's no good. That's not the truth."

She would have liked to strike me then, I am sure. "Are you calling me a liar, Dick Clarke?"

I answered the question indirectly, feeling almost sorry for her. "Perry Hale could not have said the things you claim, for two reasons. First, I had *no* appointment with him last night. Second, I did *not* come into the room and hit him on the head. Is that quite clear?"

Anne looked at me as though she were sure that either she, or I, or perhaps both of us had gone quite mad. Then she laughed in a way that was slightly hysterical. "Do you really expect me to believe you?"

"I don't know what to expect. I only know that I'm telling the truth."

"Wait just a minute." She shook her head and spoke very patiently, as though to a child. "Just let me outline the situation to you once more and then see if you still want to stick to your story. I found you in Perry Hale's library after midnight last night. You were dressed like a burglar and had a flashlight in your hand. Perry had been knocked out, and there was blood on your hands. Was I logical in assuming you had hit him?"

"Entirely. But I didn't do it, just the same."

"So you said at the time and, fishy as it all sounded, I wanted to believe you. Even when you jumped at my promise to protect you and ran away from Ted Folger, I still *wanted* to believe you—heaven knows why."

"That part looked bad," I admitted; "but it could be explained."

"Just a minute. Let's get the whole picture. The next thing that happened was that Perry Hale, on coming to, flatly said that you kept an appointment with him and that you hit him on the head." She drew an unsteady breath. "You might possibly be able to explain all the rest, Dick Clarke, but you never can explain that."

The situation had to be faced, so I determined to face it at once. "I suggest," I said slowly, "that Perry never made any such statements. In the light of the facts—he *couldn't* have!"

"Then why would I say that he had?"

"It looks to me, Anne, as though you were trying to cover up the fact of having broken your promise."

"I see." She nodded brightly. "I'm a person who breaks promises, and a liar into the bargain!"

"Is that any worse," I asked her, "than what you think of me? You're willing to believe that I'm the kind of a man who would hit Perry Hale on the head. When I tell you that I did not, you say that I'm not telling the truth. I wouldn't say that your opinion of me was exactly complimentary."

"You're right. We're just standing here like a couple of children and saying 'you're another.' But all the same—" She stamped her foot and made a weary gesture of dismissal. "What are the odds, anyhow? You and I aren't engaged any more. What does it matter what we think of each other? It doesn't matter a bit. Let's be civilized and quit bickering. You go your way and I'll go mine."

"That sounds sensible." I was so very tired and numb that I felt hardly any pain at the time. "First, though, there's business. I want to see Hale. When can I do that?"

"He wants to see you just as badly, but he's in no shape to see anybody today. He has promised to stay in bed, on the condition that I won't get him the doctor he needs."

"How about tomorrow at nine o'clock?"

"I imagine that will be all right. I'll tell him." She held out her hand. "Good-by, Mr. Clarke. If I'm ever up the river I'll drop in. Perhaps the warden will let me see you."

"Good-by." I shook her hand. "When you're calling on me in Sing Sing, why don't you say hello to your rich husband, Mr. Perry Hale? He might have the next cell to mine. Who knows?"

III

"Hello, there!" Ham Ownley looked up from the serious business of making an open-air dining table by placing long boards on the tops of empty wooden boxes set at intervals on the sandy beach, and smiled at me. "You again so soon? I had you all ticketed as being up at Perry's house having a nice long confab with a nice girl."

"I had a chat with one," I told him grimly, "but it wasn't so long and it wasn't very nice. That's why I'm here."

I did not want to be there. If I had followed my inclination after my cozy little interview with Anne, I would have promptly crawled into some secluded nook and have quietly choked myself to death with a handful of clamshells. It is easy enough, and customary, to laugh at the sufferings of some other person in love; but when you have the disease yourself, it isn't half so funny. I know that I never felt mentally worse than I did that morning when I left Anne and wandered away into the pines bound for no place in particular.

I was deeply disgusted with myself for having been so stupid in the beginning as to barge into a situation that made me look like a thug, and a yellow thug at that. I was badly hurt that Anne could believe me to be such a person, no matter how conclusive the evidence might seem. I was worse hurt that she did not believe me when I told her the truth about it. I was disappointed and angry that she should have broken a promise to me, and then deny having broken it. All those things were bad enough, but the hardest thing of all to contemplate was the knowledge that, after all the long road we had come, Anne and I had at last reached what must be a final parting of the ways.

It is true that our engagement had already been broken for some time, but somehow I had never made myself believe that the rift was final. Anne's talk with me in the library just before the Primer was stolen had led me to hope for things to come. Her attitude toward me on Sepatonk had made me think that matters between us might yet be patched up. Now, however, I had no such hopes or thoughts. Love might be a tough bird, and able to survive a lot of hard knocks such as quarrels and adverse circumstances, but I was certain it could never stand mutual suspicion and distrust. No, the little romance between Anne and me was now a thing to be spoken of only in the past tense.

Well, what next? There was no sense, I lectured myself sharply as I walked away from the Hale house, in brooding about what might have been. If I had to continue the business of living, I might just as well keep myself as fully occupied as possible. That was why I had hunted up Ham Ownley at the clambake beach, and why I was determined he must listen to my story no matter how busy he might be.

"So!" My opening remarks must have interested him. He did not pick up the plank he was bending over, but straightened, instead, and came over to my side. "Trouble, eh? I thought you looked kind of down in the mouth when I saw you this morning, but I was so everlasting fussed-up about this fool clambake I didn't seem to have time for anything else. Well, I have time, now. If I haven't, I'll make it! Heave ahead, boy. What's troubling you?"

"There's plenty to be told, Ham," I said; "and when

I've told it, you'll probably think I'm the craziest fool that ever lived."

"Maybe so, maybe not." He pulled out his pipe and fished about in his pocket for tobacco. "Anyhow, let's hear the yarn."

I told it to him, and as the thing spun itself out I was surprised at how much had happened in the small number of hours that had gone by since he and I read Kelly's letter together in the Inn office. I was also surprised to realize how much I had taken upon my lone, unadvised, and slightly reckless self. Ham, always a good listener, did not interrupt me once, though some of my more lurid disclosures caused him to grunt with astonishment.

When I had finished, I said gloomily, "And so there we are—wherever that is. I hope you can tell me."

Ham was silent for a little time. Then he said, quietly: "I can tell you one thing. I'm sorry that you and Anne Francis had to squabble over this business. Course I don't know Anne very well, but what little I've seen of her I like first rate. It's too bad that you and she—"

"Let's skip it, shall we?" I was not in the mood to discuss Anne with anyone. "I admit that it's too bad, but let's not let my personal troubles get mixed up with the other thing. Let's worry about the Primer. What I want to know is, where is it now and how are we going to get our hands on it?"

"Steady as she is, Dick," Ham held out a restraining hand. "If you don't mind, I'd like to have time to get my bearings, sort of. All this business may be as clear as blue sky to you, don't doubt it is, but it's middling foggy to me. It's all new, and there's a lot of it. Some of it ain't any plainer to see than a stone on the bottom of a riled-up mud puddle. Godfreys mighty, how things do keep on happening around old Sepatonk! It strikes me you've had a rough cruise all by your lonesome in the past thirty-six hours."

"I know," I admitted ruefully. "I've been a jackass, of course. I should have consulted you. I've known that all along, but somehow things just seemed to happen before I had time to think. I should have talked to you when I came back from Hale's yesterday, before I even considered breaking in there and trying to steal the Primer. I should have—"

"There, there. Don't blame yourself, Dick. Maybe it would have done some good to have had a chin with me before you decided to sneak into Perry's house. Maybe not. After all, with any luck, you *might* have come home with the Primer, you know."

"I know. That's what I thought, but I didn't. I didn't come back with anything but a bad scare and the same kind of reputation."

"I know, I know." I could see that Ham was thinking hard. "Mind if I run over your story again, out loud, so's I can see if I've got the business parts straight? Let's see. You met Anne yesterday morning on the path, and she warned you that Perry and Folger suspected you of working at the Knowlton Library. Also and moreover, she told you some things that made *you* suspect them—Hale and Folger—of being mixed up in the Primer mess. A little bit later the pair worked a pretty slick trick on you that showed you knew full as much about books as you did about farming. Later on still you and Perry had a confab in his library, and that confab is the part I can't make myself believe—even though I know it's the gospel truth!"

"Exactly." I nodded. "I couldn't believe it, either, but there it lies."

"Perry Hale!" Ham shook his head wonderingly. "Perry Hale a common, low-down book thief! Perry Hale a man who hits people on the head and picks pockets! It just don't seem possible, that's all."

"I know."

"Can you remember any of the *words* he used when he talked to you, Dick? For instance, did he say anything like, 'I stole the Primer,' or 'I hit Professor Payson on the head'?"

"It's hard to remember," I frowned. "He didn't say anything so out and out as either of those things, of course. But when I asked him why my knowledge of rare books was any concern of his, he answered: 'Because, on account of things that have happened lately, things not generally known, I'm not surprised to find somebody from the Library on my trail.' I think those were almost exactly his words. Conclusive enough, aren't they?"

"It seems so. I do declare it seems so." Ham shook his head again. "And yet— He tried to bribe you, you say? Did he use the word, 'bribe,' right straight out?"

"Of course not. But he asked me if I was ready to do business—asked what it was going to cost him. Offered me a flat twenty thousand cash, and then upped it five. He was bribing me, all right, even if he didn't use the word. What difference does it make, anyhow, what words he used?"

"I don't know, Dick. It's just that I can't make myself believe Perry Hale is such an out-and-out crook as he must be, from what you say. I'm trying to see if maybe you could have twisted his words in your mind so that they sounded different to you from the way he meant them to."

"No chance of that, Ham." I was a little impatient. "He talked about no witnesses and no dictaphones and things like that. The man is a low-down crook, you can take my word for it."

"All right. Let's let it go at that for now and finish up your story. You walked into Perry's house late that night, and instead of the Primer you found Perry Hale—hit over the head. Now then, who hit him and why?"

"The answer to both those questions," I said wearily, "is that I haven't a notion! Unless maybe Ted Folger hit him so that he could steal the bribe money Perry was going to pay me. But don't ask me to justify that little accusation. I can't."

"Hum. Might not be so terribly foolish a notion at that. Another thing, Dick. When Perry came to his right mind, after you left the house last night, why did he say you were the one who hit him?"

I shrugged. "I don't think he said it at all. Anne caught me in the library and jumped to the natural conclusion I had slugged Perry. When he recovered, she told him I was the one who had done it. She put the words in his mouth."

"What makes you think, Dick, that Anne did a thing like that, after promising you she wouldn't?"

"What other explanation is there? I didn't hit him, you'll grant that. Then how could he say I did, unprompted?"

Ham did not answer the question. "Perry is supposed to have said that you had an appointment with him that night, ain't he? Did Anne snip that out of whole cloth, too? If she did, why?"

"Just the icing for the cake," I said with some bitterness. "When people lie they often can't resist throwing in an extra lie just for good measure. That must be the answer here."

Ham stirred the sand around with the toe of his old sneaker for a moment. Then he looked at me with a smile. "Something tells me, Dick, that, in about ten seconds, you're going to think I'm feeble-minded."

"Why should I think that?"

"Because I'm going to tell you that I think you're all wrong about Anne. I don't think she lied at all. I think she told you the truth this morning."

I stared. "You mean?"

"I mean I think that Anne kept her promise and never mentioned your name to anybody last night. I think that when Hale came to he said that you and he had had an appointment—that when that appointment was kept, you hit him."

"Am I goofy, Ham Ownley, or are you?"

"Wait a minute, Dick, before you call the wagon and have me hauled off to the crazy asylum. Let me do a little guessing and supposing, first. You and Hale had agreed to meet in twenty-four hours, hadn't you? Well, suppose later that same day Perry got a note signed with your name and saying that you would come to his house that night and to have the money ready."

"But I sent no such note!"

"I know. I'm just supposing. I'm supposing that somebody else sent such a note and signed your name to it. Let me go on. Suppose Perry was fooled by the note and waited for you at his desk with the French door open behind him. Suppose that the man who sent the note came in then, and, before he was seen, hit Perry over the head. Suppose all those things were true. In that case what would Perry have said when he came to? Why, that you and he had had a date and that you had knocked him over the head with a sandbag!"

I really did think, now, that Ham was being a little childish. "Why all this elaborate build-up, Ham, when there's a much more logical explanation right at hand?"

"Maybe I'm doddering, but I still don't think the explanation you're talking about *is* logical, as you call it. Reason number one is Anne Francis. I don't know her very well, but well enough. She's a nice girl. She wouldn't break a promise to you, and she wouldn't lie about it if she did."

I sighed. "It must be swell to believe in Santa Claus, Ham. I wish I thought you were right. I'll admit I used to think those same sweet things about Anne, but—"

"Reason number two," said Ham imperturbably, "is the frosting on the cake. By that I mean the business about the appointment. That would have been such an out-and-out dumb fool lie, that it can't be anything but the truth! Nobody would have thought it up—or used it if they had."

"Dream on," I told him kindly. "Don't let me interfere with your childish pleasures. Pretty soon you'll be saying that Perry Hale is a pillar of the church."

"No," Ham grinned, "I don't think I'll come to that. "All the same, I think you're wrong in some of the things you suspicion about Perry. I don't know how you can be wrong, but I'll bet on it just the same. I know Perry Hale pretty well, and I'm betting he doesn't steal books or pick pockets. He might have an extra ace up his sleeve in a poker game, or forge a check, but he wouldn't pick a pocket!... There, there! You don't need the strait jacket, Dick. I'll go peaceable."

I groaned. "I'm the one that's going to need the strait jacket if this keeps up. Lay off, will you? Be sensible and tell me what happens next in this squirrel cage. What do you think we ought to do now?"

"Well, according to my way of looking at it there isn't but one thing *to* do. That's to see Perry Hale and have a talk with him. That ought to clear up a lot of things."

"I have an appointment with the admirable Hale," I said grimly, "for tomorrow morning at nine. He professes the desire to tear me limb from limb. The desire is mutual."

"Mind if I come along, Dick? I've liked fireworks ever since I was a young one."

"If," I told him, not altogether facetiously, "you can stand the sight of blood, come along by all means. I'm only warning you that the gutters are apt to run red. I only wish it could be this minute, though. What on earth am I going to do with myself until tomorrow morning?"

"If you haven't anything better," said Ham, getting up from the heap of sand he was decorating, "you can help me with the bake. I could use an extra hand. There's plenty to do getting ready for the gang that will be here tonight. Nigh as I can see, every white man, woman, and child on the Island is going to be on deck for the Ownley Inn's free grub. Even the high and mighty Hale party have sent word they're coming."

"Really?" My long talk with Ham had served to take my mind off my troubles for a time, but the thought of Anne at the clambake brought them all back again. "Well, in that case, here's one hungry mouth you won't have to feed. I'll have a pressing engagement somewhere else."

"Don't say that, Dick." Ham was serious. "I know how you feel, and I don't blame you, but I wish you'd come to the bake. For one thing I'm kind of proud of my bakes, and I'd like to have you see what one's like. That's one reason, but it isn't the main one. The main one is that nigh everybody will be here. Maybe the Primer thief will be among 'em."

"The Primer thief," I said stubbornly, "is Perry Hale."

"All right, Dick, I won't argue. Then maybe somebody else will be here—maybe the man who hit Hale on the head. What is that man's name, by the way? Can you tell me? You've probably talked to him often enough. Is it Grover, Holley, Folger, House, Drake?"

"Grover? Drake?" I was startled. "Why—"

"I know." Ham nodded. "Putting a name to him sort of brings it close to home, don't it? The name of somebody you know. Well, he has a name, you can bet, and he'll bring the name to the clambake. If both of us watch close, he may give himself away. Come, come. You won't turn me down, will you?"

"No, Ham, I'll come if you think it's necessary." I sighed. "By the way, I might as well tell you *my* real name. It's 'Bloodshot.' "

"Your real name? It's—what?"

"Bloodshot Dick—known from coast to coast as the Bronx Torpedo. I mow 'em down, laddie, and leave 'em kicking! Give me a sniff of snow and I'm a thousand roaring lions. Indiscriminate slaughter is my dish. I'd rather shoot your child than kiss it. What is more, Ham Ownley, I'm just plain hell on brunettes. When Bloodshot whistles the brunettes whinny!"

It was only a fair exchange. This time it was Ham who thought that *I* was crazy.

IV

I have called this particular section of our story "The Clambake," and it occurs to me that the title might, with some justification, be likened to the glue in the conundrum. The glue in the conundrum, you will remember, was "just put in for a sticker."

The clambake was just a clambake, after all; I'll be able to tell about it in very few words, and at it, so far as anyone knew at the time, nothing at all exciting happened. In spite of those things, I'll keep to my title, for the clambake was essentially the crisis in our affairs. It touched off a fuse that exploded the fireworks. Before it, things seemed to go uphill with tedious slowness; after it, the descent to the finish line was a breathless rush. If anyone asked me to indicate the turning point in the saga of our Primer, I should unhesitatingly say, "the clambake."

It began, innocently enough, about six o'clock on the afternoon of as beautiful a September day as anyone could possibly have hoped for. It was comfortably warm; there wasn't a cloud in the sky, a ripple on the wide water. Nature was peaceful, and so was the scene on the beach as the guests began to gather. Ham, his work practically done, was sitting on an upended nailkeg smoking his pipe and contemplating a large dome of sand from which occasionally escaped a lazy curl of white vapor. Having been recently initiated, I knew that in the deep wide hole underneath that dome, the contents of the bake were steamily baking. Quantities of small rocks, previously heated almost white hot, were the cooking agent, and the amount of foodstuffs they were cooking seemed to me enough to feed an army. For that matter, the eaters when fully assembled represented just about as large an army as Sepatonk could hope to muster.

All of the guests of the Inn were there, and all of its employees, headed by a bustling and tremendously important Hettie Bassett. She issued totally unnecessary orders with machine-gun rapidity. Her chief victim seemed to be the hotel clerk, George Silver, who was kept frantically hunting for things which Hettie tragically declared had been "left behind," but which never had. The island physician, Dr. Farmer, was there, and his housekeeper, Martha Pound, and the lighthouse keeper's family, and a lot of others. I even noticed that desperate criminal, Half Pound, stationed at a point strategically near the food supply but suitable for a quick getaway in case of need. Last in order of arrival, but most important in the social order, were the crew from Hale's. The Baron Perry, himself, didn't come, of course, but Anne and the Folgers honored us with their presence.

Anne contrived not to see me, which was difficult since she nearly tripped over my feet on her way to greet Ham, but the Folgers spotted me fast enough. Ted fixed me with a lazy and arrogant eye and said, "Ah, there, Clarke. You still in evidence?" He seemed about to enlarge on this brilliant opening, but his wife gave him no chance. "Go away, worm," she told him shortly, "and leave me with my vision of paradise!" To me she said carelessly, "Allo, bebe. 'Ave you slit your daily throat? Which reminds me—when do we eat?"

We ate very shortly, and how we ate! There are those poor ignorant beings, I suppose, who think that a clambake consists exclusively of clams, but they have much to learn. Ham Ownley's bake included quantities of steamed clams, of course; but also whole lobsters, half chickens neatly sewn up in white cheesecloth bags, corn on the cob, sweet potatoes in their jackets, and rosy red frankfurters. All those came from the cavern in the sands. From Hettie Bassett's department came hot biscuits and beachplum jelly, coffee, and finally great slabs of watermelon for those incapable of deep dish apple pie.

The range of choice was wide, the aroma tantalizing, the taste delicious, the quantity unlimited. The result was just what might have been expected. We forgot our figures, diets, chronic ailments, sense of proportions, and self-restraint. We ate, in other words, until we could eat no more—at which point we collapsed in our tracks.

When dusk finally shrouded the stricken field, I found myself staring at the faintly appearing stars with a feeling of complete satiety, relaxation, and lassitude. I was even mildly surprised when the corpse strewn next to mine —it was that of Doc Grover—heaved itself up to a sitting, and finally a standing, position. I remember lazily contemplating asking him what rash thing he did, but before I could find the strength to speak he was gone. "Vanished," I told myself sleepily. "Gone into the night, and who knows where—or who cares?"

It was then that I remembered Ham's solemn admonition to keep careful watch over each and every one of the clambake guests, in the hope of picking up some clue that would help in the Primer mystery. My conscience pricked me, and I sat up to look about. A fire had been lighted, more for sociability than from necessity for warmth, and in its flickering I could make out the dim outlines of many forms. Some were prone, some sitting up, but none recognizable. Cigarettes or cigars gleamed here and there. There was a low murmur of mingled voices.

I told myself that detective work under such conditions was practically impossible, and was about to lie down once more, when I heard Anne's laugh. Instantly I was miserable. I had tried to thrust her altogether out of my thoughts, but the thing was hard to do. In spite of myself I could not forget Ham's defense of her that morning. Could it be possible that I had been wrong and that she had kept her promise to me, after all? Would she be decent to me if I went to her now and once more tried to get the thing straightened out?

The end of that line of thinking was, of course, inevitable. Almost without volition I threaded my way among the people on the beach until I had found Anne and sat down beside her. Once there I immediately realized that I had made a bad mistake.

Anne had no intention of being friendly. She spoke my name and introduced me to the girl she was talking with, but that was all. The other girl—I learned that her name was Barbara Taylor and that she was the daughter of the Sepatonk lighthousekeeper—was forced to carry the conversational load alone. Anne spoke not a word. She just sat there like a sphinx, silent and motionless in the dusk, until I felt an almost overpowering urge to lay violent hands upon her. But I did nothing of the sort, naturally enough. I just sat there and traded inanities with Barbara Taylor until I could stand it no longer. Then I went away.

I don't mean that I merely took myself away from Anne's side. I mean that I felt so horribly lonely and miserable that I altogether forgot my duties as a sleuth and my obligations as a guest. Without saying a word to anybody I dragged myself out of the circle of firelight and walked back to the Ownley Inn.

What would have happened if I had stayed? I've often wondered, but I don't know. Would I have been able to prevent what happened? Would I have been lucky or vigilant enough to have been present when I was most needed? Or would I, like all the rest, have blandly gone home in due time, totally unaware that anything awful had happened? Once more I don't know. I wasn't there at the time. I was in my room, and in bed.

V

Even the next morning everything was still tranquil when, promptly at nine o'clock, Ham Ownley and I kept my appointment with Perry Hale in his library. A sofa had been put in there, and on it, with a silk robe over his shirt and trousers, lay Perry. He was not swathed in bandages as I had rather expected, but merely had a square of white adhesive tape on the back of his head. He was in an evil mood, and showed it the moment we appeared.

"Ah, I might have known it." He glared at Ham and then turned to me with a contemptuous scowl. "I wondered, Clarke, how you had the nerve to show your face here this morning. Now I see. Brought your bodyguard along with you, eh? Probably a good thing for your health that you did."

Since I was about four inches taller than Perry, quite a bit huskier, and many years younger, the insult was entirely gratuitous. I should have ignored it; but my nerves were on edge, and I was spoiling for trouble. "That's dangerous talk, Hale. I might forget you are half sick, and smack you!"

"I'd love to see you try!" His black eyes gleamed. "Half sick or not, I think I could handle anybody that's yellow enough to slug a man from behind!"

I took a half step toward him. "When I hit you," I promised, "it won't be from behind."

"Why not?" He sneered. "Want variety? Getting tired of hitting me from behind?"

This wasn't getting anywhere. I tried to control myself and contribute something reasonable. "I haven't yet," I told him slowly, "had the pleasure of hitting you at all. Yet."

"No?" He laughed nastily. "Not man enough to admit it, eh? Well, that's what I thought. Yellow clean through."

I don't know what might have happened then except for Ham, who stepped swiftly into the picture. "Just a minute, Perry. You, too, Dick. Don't you think it might be better if you both acted like a couple of grown-up men instead of school young-ones with chips on your shoulders?"

"Look here, Ham Ownley." Perry turned his fire on Ham. "You and I have always got along fine in the past. We'll keep on that way if you don't interfere with my handling of this fellow, Clarke. He has probably fooled you the way he has some others. You probably think he's all right."

"I do," said Ham promptly. "I like him first rate."

"So does Anne Francis, but she's just as wrong as you are. I've already sent the maid for Anne. When Anne gets here, I'll show you both what kind of a bird this Clarke creature really is!"

I could not take any more. "And just what kind of a bird am I, Mr. Hale?" I inquired as gently as though I were asking about his sick mother. "I'd like to know."

"And I'd like to tell you! You're a yellow, murderous crook!"

The patch of adhesive tape on the back of Hale's head saved me then, and maybe him. If it hadn't been for that, I'd have taken a poke at him without wasting any more time. As it was I had to use words. "Thanks. You'll eat those remarks, every one of them, the minute you get into shape so that I can make a hospital case out of you with a clear conscience! In the meantime let me say that if I'm a crook, I'm keeping bad company. You, Mr. Hale, are about as contemptible a crook as I've yet to meet! As for being yellow and murderous—those words apply to you if they ever applied to anybody! You're even so darn yellow that you have to *hire* thugs to do your darn blackjacking for you!"

When that blast hit Mr. Hale and sank in, I thought for a moment he was going to have a stroke. He choked, and his face turned brick red. Then he half slid and half rolled off the couch and got to his feet. "I've stood all I'm going to stand from you, Clarke! I'm going to knock the tar out of you!"

We were just starting for each other when there was an interruption. "Mr. Hale!" A uniformed maid was standing in the doorway and her voice sounded frightened. "Mr. Hale, I can't find Miss Francis!"

"What?" Perry dropped his hands and glared at the poor girl. "You can't find her?"

"No, sir. She's not in her room."

"Then hunt for her! Don't stand there gaping at me. Look around the house, the grounds, the beach."

"I already have, Mr. Hale. She isn't anywhere about. I—I don't think she was here last night at all."

We all turned to look at her then, but it was Hale who

spoke. "Nonsense!" he snapped. "What rubbish are you talking?"

"It's Miss Francis' bed, sir. I turned it down last night and put out her night things. When I went to her room just now, they hadn't been touched."

My mouth suddenly felt dry and I licked my lips. "You mean?"

"I mean that Miss Francis couldn't have been here at all last night. On account of her bed, sir." The maid looked at us as though begging us to believe. "The bed," she repeated. "It hasn't been slept in!"

PART VI

The Gold Penknife

Told by
Seth Hammond Ownley

I

I DON'T think any of us got the full meaning of what that maid said when she came into the Hale library and made her proclamation. I am sure I didn't. The past few minutes had been lively ones. For a spell there it had looked as if the only thing that could head off a fight between Hale and Clarke was the fact that Perry was too badly used up to get off the sofa, although I had been on pins and needles for fear he would try. When he sent for the Francis girl, I breathed a little mite easier. What the newspapers call "hostilities" wouldn't break out till she got there, anyhow. So when the maid came back and said Anne wasn't in her room, all I could think was: "Oh, Lord! now it will start all over again."

It was Hale who first got a real hold on what the maid had told us. He raised himself on one elbow and glared at her.

"What?" he sang out. "*What!* Say that again."

The maid was scared; her boss looked as if he was going to eat her, and maybe she had doctor's orders not to be eaten between meals. She fussed with her apron and made two or three false starts, but finally she stammered out her story. Miss Anne was not in her room, her night things were lying on the bed just where the maid had left them, and, furthermore, that bed had not been slept in.

"You are sure of that?" Hale wanted to know.

Yes sir, she was certain sure. Perry looked at Clarke and me and we looked at him. "That's darned funny, if you ask me," he said. "Where the devil is she?"

Dick jumped out of his chair. What he was going to say or do I don't know, for just then the maid had an idea. It was pretty late in making port, but I judged most of her notions came by slow freight.

"Excuse me, sir," she says, "but I shouldn't wonder if Miss Anne had went to spend the night with Miss Taylor over at the lighthouse. She was telling me the other day that she was going to do it some time. She likes Miss Taylor and she thought it would be fun to see how a light-keeper's family lived. Anyhow, that's what she said."

I fetched a breath of relief. I don't know what I had been thinking, but the past week on Sepatonk Island had been so het up and feverish that I was liable to think 'most anything. Barbara Taylor is a nice girl, and she and Anne had struck up quite a friendship. Yes, and Barbara had been at the clambake.

"That's it, of course," I said. "Seems to me I saw her and Barbara walking off together just as the bake party broke up. She's down to the light, that's where she is."

Dick sat down again. Perry Hale began to look less like a hyena. He turned to the maid.

"There is a telephone at the light," he said. "Go and phone the Taylors and ask Miss Francis if she won't please come over here for a few minutes. Tell her I say it is important. Tell her I will send the car for her, and it can take her back if she wants to go."

The maid went out. Nobody said anything for a spell, but Dick and Perry were looking at each other sideways, the way a couple of dogs eye one another before the rough-and-tumble begins; and I thought it was high time the innocent bystander stepped in between. Of course I knew well enough what the innocent bystander usually gets when he steps that way, but the queer doings on Sepatonk had to be cleared up somehow, and pretty soon, or the mainland police must be sent for. I didn't want that, not yet anyhow. It would be advertising of a kind, but it wouldn't do the Ownley Inn any good.

"Look here, lodge brothers and fellow citizens," I said; "I have been sitting here listening to the well-chosen remarks of the speakers so far—meaning you, Dick, and you, Mr. Hale—and it does seem to me that it is just about time this meeting was called to order. Considerable hints and some left-handed compliments have passed back and forth, but neither of you has said anything yet that the other could answer with a yes or no. Why not speak plain for a change?"

Dick caught my meaning, I guess, but all he did was scowl and look doubtful. Hale scowled, too.

"Just what do you mean by that?" he wanted to know.

"What I said. Stop hinting and come out with the testimony for both sides. That sometimes fetches out the truth in a court case and it might do it here. Mr. Hale, I judge from your chatty remarks so far that you think Dick Clarke cracked you over the head night before last. Well, *I* think you're wrong—he didn't."

Hale fairly bounced on the sofa. "The hell he didn't!" he sung out. "I *know* he did. Yes, and I know why, too."

"No, you don't. . . . Hush, Dick, you'll have your turn in a minute. . . . You don't know, Hale, you only think you know. And Dick here thinks he knows things about you. Maybe you are both wrong. Instead of backing and filling and bluffing why not put all the cards on the table? That would save time and at least cut out whatever misunderstandings there might be. Sounds sensible, wouldn't you say?"

Hale glowered at me; he wasn't too tickled with the proposition, I judged. Dick said nothing right off. Then he asked: "Do you mean tell him everything, Ham? The whole of it?"

"Certain. The whole yarn from the beginning to now. Why not?"

"We-ll, considering how careful we have been and—there is Doctor Payson, you know."

"What the Doctor wants is his book. It is what you want, too. If Mr. Hale knows something about that book, then why not find out what he knows?"

Dick hitched his shoulders. "If he has the nerve to tell it," he mumbled, pretty sarcastic.

It was Hale's turn. "Nerve!" he snorted. "You talk to me about nerve! Ham, do you suppose this—this thug is going to tell us any more than he wants to tell? Bosh? I dare him to."

"All right. I'll guarantee he tells as much as he knows, and I know what that is because he and I have been working together ever since he landed on the Island. . . . Well, Dick, do you take up the dare? I would if I was you."

Dick considered some more. "All right," he said. "I'll tell my part if he'll tell his. Suppose he does his telling first."

Hale sneered. "And then you will welch, of course. Why should I tell anything? To him or to you either, Ownley? My business is my business, isn't it?"

"Yes, but considerable of your business may be ours, you can't tell. If you are innocent of any of this skull-duggery that's been going on around here, I don't see why you should be afraid. Of course, if you are guilty, if you have got something to hide and *are* afraid, why—"

"That's enough! I am ashamed of nothing and afraid of nothing. I— Yes, what is it? Where's Miss Francis?"

The maid had come in to tell us that all this time she had been trying to get the Taylor house on the phone and hadn't been able to get any answer. The wire was broke in the hurricane and hadn't been fixed yet, she guessed likely. Hale snapped at her like a muskrat trap. "Tell somebody to take the car and go down there and bring her back in a hurry. Good heavens, can't *any*body around here think for themselves? Ask Folger; he'll be glad to go. Hurry up!"

The maid stammered something about Mr. and Mrs. Folger having gone out for a walk down to the post-office. "I saw Mr. Folger before he went, though," she said. "Miss Anne did go to the lighthouse place last night; she told Mr. Folger she was going. That's why him and Mrs. Folger came home from the clambake alone."

Hale barked at her to get somebody else to drive the car, the chauffeur or the gardener or anybody. "Only move, you—you Statue of Liberty!" Between his weakness and his row with Clarke his temper was all shredded to rags.

After the maid cleared out, he looked at us for a minute. Then he nodded.

"Cards on the table it is to be then," he said. "*I* have got nothing up my sleeve. Go ahead, Clarke, your deal."

Dick looked at me. I nodded. "Somebody's got to start," I said.

Dick began with what happened at the Knowlton Library. He told about the assault on Payson, of the Primer's turning up missing, of his chase after the Sanger one, of his own knockout and trip to the hospital. Perry Hale didn't cut in on him once; only when the New England Primer was first mentioned I noticed him start and open his mouth as if he was going to speak. He shut it again, though, and Dick went right on.

He told about his telephone talk with me and how the news of the *Nellie B.*'s wreck and the saving of her passenger brought him to Sepatonk. He went on with our trying to see Kelly and our finding him dead in the woods. He told it all, except that he didn't say anything about the twenty dollar bill business or Half Pound. Hale, like all hands on Sepatonk except Farmer and Clarke and me, believed Kelly's watch and pocketbook had been in the Inn safe all the time since he died and they might as well keep on thinking so.

And then it came to the place where Dick had to tell of his grand scheme to sneak into Hale's house in the middle of the night and have a try at getting the Primer.

"I didn't know, of course, just where the book was, but I thought the most probable place was that—" He pulled up short, as if he had caught himself just in time. "Well —er—what I mean to say," he went on, kind of hurried, "is that I thought it would be in this room somewhere. So—"

"Here, here, hold on!" Hale was speaking for the first time. "You thought that Primer would be in this room? You thought *I* was the crook who stole it?"

I hitched forward on my chair, ready for real trouble; but Dick didn't answer the way I was afraid he might.

"I didn't say you actually stole it," he said. "The

Sanger-Kelly guy did that, of course. All I knew was that you had it now."

"Indeed!" Perry Hale was holding himself in by main strength. "You knew I had it, eh? How did you know?"

"How? Why, because you told me so, yourself. When you and I had our talk in this room the day before yesterday."

"*I* told you that? Why, you infernal liar, I didn't tell you anything of the kind. You told me that you——"

I got out of my chair then. "Steady, steady!" I said. "Handsomely does it. Better not, either of you, take too much for granted. Seems to me I recollect saying there might be misunderstandings somewhere. Never mind what each of you told the other; forget that for the minute. Finish your yarn, Dick."

Dick was pretty white and mad but he nodded.

"Isn't much more to tell," he growled. "The front door was unlocked and I came in through the living room. When I got to the library I found you lying across this desk unconscious, and with that bruise on your head. I was stooping over you when Anne came in and found me. She——" he hesitated; it was pretty hard for him to say, I guess—"well, she thought I had knocked you out. I don't blame her; it must have looked that way. I tried to explain, but she wouldn't listen and ordered me off. Like a fool I went. I should have stayed, but—well, I was pretty badly shaken up myself and I lost my nerve, I suppose. I didn't hit you, though, Hale. Believe it or not, I didn't."

"Oh, yeah? Then, if you didn't, who the devil did?"

I answered that. "The same fellow that had been doing a lot of other nice sociable things around here lately," I said. "Who he is we don't know.... Now let's get back to that talk you two had in here day before yesterday.

Dick says you told him you had the Primer. You say you didn't tell him anything of the kind."

"Sure I didn't! When he says I did, he—"

"Yes, yes. Shh! Well, Dick?"

Dick Clarke leaned forward. "You offered me twenty-five thousand dollars in cash, Hale. Do you deny that?"

"No."

"And you offered it because you figured I knew you had the book and the money was a bribe for me to keep my mouth shut about it. To go away and say nothing. Do you deny *that?*"

"Of course I deny it. Why, blast your hide—"

I held up both my hands. "Hush!" I ordered. "Hold on! Hold everything, the two of you. This calling names don't do any good. There's a snarl here and we've got to pick it loose. You offered Clarke twenty-five thousand for something, Mr. Hale. You just said you did. You say it wasn't a bribe. What was it, then?"

The question was plain enough and called for a plain answer, but Hale didn't give that answer right off. He seemed to be thinking what to say and, while he was thinking, I tried again.

"Dick has told me about that talk you and he had," I went on. "What you said to him and what he said to you. You were talking about rare books, wasn't you?"

"I was talking about *a* rare book—yes. He had a book I wanted, or I thought he had. He wanted to sell it, and, if it was what he said it was, of the date and in the condition his letter said it was, I wanted to buy it."

Dick was on his feet. "Letter!" he sung out. "What letter?"

Again I had to do some hand waving.

"Hush, hush, *hush!*" I begged. "Be still, Dick! Sounds as if we might be getting somewheres now. Go on, Perry. This book somebody wrote you about was a New England Primer, wasn't it?"

"According to the letter it was *the* New England Primer, or pretty near it. He wrote me that he had picked up, he didn't say where, a New England Primer of a date earlier than 1750. He knew, so the letter said, that I was interested in early Americana and maybe I might be interested in this item. I was decidedly interested. I have been trying to get hold of a Primer for a long while; but when I add anything to my collection, it has to be more than just good, it must be mighty close to the best of its kind or I don't want it. What that letter said about this particular Primer sounded promising, so I wrote him to bring the book to me here, on Sepatonk Island, and let me see it. We could talk price then, I said. So—"

But Dick couldn't hold in any longer. "Where is that letter?" he shouted. "Have you got it now? Show it to me."

Hale grunted. "Sure I've got it," he said. "Right here in this desk. But why do you want to see it? You wrote it, didn't you?"

"*I?* I never wrote that letter, or any other letter to you, in my life."

Oh well, it takes too long to set down all the talk and powwow that followed after this. Hale got out the letter, finally, and showed it to us. It was type-wrote and the name signed at the bottom was Albert P. Brown. The answer was to be sent to General Delivery, Buffalo, New York, and the date at the top was July second, a full six weeks afore the Knowlton Library Primer was stole. The signature was no more like Dick Clarke's handwriting than mine is, and that's as far as the West Indies is from the North Pole. Even Perry Hale had to admit that much.

He—Hale, I mean—had heard nothing from Brown since he sent his answer, but he had been expecting to hear ever since. He had been waiting, too, for Brown to show up on Sepatonk. Hale knew nothing about the Knowlton Primer being stolen; nobody did except Clarke and Payson and the Library trustees—and me—for it had been kept out of the papers. Dick, when he heard this, grinned.

"What's the joke?" Perry Hale asked, pretty brisk and snappish. "I tell you I didn't know. If you think I did—"

I poured on some more oil. "No, no, course you didn't," I put in. "Clarke knows you didn't. Nobody knew, except a few insiders."

And *he* hadn't known, until we told him, no doubt of that. But he must have guessed there was something fishy about the book the Brown fellow was trying to sell him. The way he talked with Dick about "no dictaphones" and the like of that proved he was smelling rat; he didn't want to see the critter, that's all. He wouldn't have bought a book he *knew* was stolen, I am sure; but I am about as sure that he wouldn't be too fussy about finding out how the person he bought it of got hold of it. Perry Hale was a hard-boiled collector, and some collectors' consciences are easy satisfied. So Dick Clarke tells me, anyhow.

Hale, as I say, had been waiting for Brown to show up on Sepatonk and he kept a weather eye on newcomers. When Folger spotted Dick as a clerk—or whatever you call it—in the Knowlton Library and when they tricked him with the Cooper book into showing he was a rare book man, then Perry guessed he was Brown. Their talk together settled it, in Hale's mind.

"So when you phoned me," said Hale, "telling me to have the twenty-five thousand in cash ready when you called at twelve o'clock that night I—"

Both Dick and I jumped clear of our chairs then and we both hollered together.

"Telephoned you?"

"Dick telephoned?"

"Eh? What's all this? You phoned me, making the appointment. Certainly you did."

"Certainly I didn't! I never telephoned you—at any time."

And then, while the three of us were staring at each other—with our mouths open, I shouldn't wonder—there was a knock at the door, and the maid came in once more. She was looking queer, too.

"Mr. Hale," she said, "the car has just come back. Miss Anne isn't at the lighthouse place. She wasn't there last night, either. Miss Taylor says she didn't come home with her from the clambake. She was going to, but she changed her mind at the last minute. They don't know where she is and—and nobody does. Oh dear, I'm afraid something has happened to her. I—I—"

She began to cry.

II

That put an end to the "cards on the table" business. There were still plenty of points to clear up, including who had telephoned, if Dick didn't, and three or four more besides; but the maid's news shoved everything else out of our heads for the time. Anne hadn't been at the Taylors' at all. She hadn't gone home with Barbara, nor with the

Folgers. I knew she hadn't rode back in the Inn station wagon. She hadn't been in her own room or her own bed all night long. Where on earth had she been and where was she now? Considering what had been going on on Sepatonk Island for the past week or so, I own up I didn't hardly dare to guess.

There was no time for guessing either. She must be located, and located right off. I was almost as excited and frightened as Dick was, himself, although I tried not to show it while the maid was there. Perry Hale was the coolest of us all, but he didn't have quite the inside information we had. *He* didn't know about the Kelly letter, you see. He didn't know there was a "Sidekick" loose on Sepatonk.

He ordered the maid to stop her sniveling. "Did the Taylor girl say anything more?" he asked her. "Why Anne changed her mind about going with her?"

"No. No, Miss Barbara took it for granted she was going with Mr. and Mrs. Folger. That's what Jerry said she said; it was Jerry drove the car down to get her, Mr. Hale."

Hale might have asked more questions, but I hushed him up. "It's all right," I told the maid. "She's up at the Inn, most likely or—er—well, she's all right anyhow. Look here, don't you say anything about this to anybody. We don't want the whole Island stirred up when there is no need of it. You run along, there's a good girl, and remember to keep mum. Miss Francis will be here in a little while, all safe and sound, don't you worry."

That is what I said, but I was a long ways from believing it. Dick was as white as a Sunday tablecloth and pacing up and down like a second mate on watch. The maid was hardly outside the door when he swung 'round to me.

"Come on, Ownley!" he ordered. "Come on! What are, you waiting for? We've got to find her. God knows what he may have done to her. Come *on!*"

I caught him by the arm. "We'll find her," I told him. "Now, Mr. Hale—"

But Hale, of course, had heard what Dick just said, and he was trying to sit up on the sofa. "Stop!" he roared. "Stop, I tell you! What's all this? Who may have done something to Anne? What 'he' are you talking about, Clarke?"

Dick was on his way to the door. I waited just a jiffy. "Hale," I said, "I can't tell you more now, haven't got time. *Some*body hit you over the head and it wasn't Dick Clarke. That same somebody—and we don't know who he is any more than you do—may be responsible for Anne's being missing, though why he should get after *her* I swear I can't see. We'll find her, though; I promise you that. You stay right here and—"

He was off the sofa, trying to stand up and making a tottery job of it. "Stay here nothing!" he raved. "Do you suppose I am going to—"

"Yes, that's just what I suppose. You want to help, don't you? Well, the biggest help you can be, in the shape you are in, is by staying here, pacifying all hands that ask questions, telling nobody, not even the Folger folks, that there is any trouble and keeping that maid's tongue from running loose. I won't have a general alarm rung in, with all that would mean, until it is needful, which I hope it won't be. Sepatonk's a little place, and I know every foot of it. She's all right and we'll be fetching her here to you in a little while. Get back on that sofa and try to act serene and natural; that's your job just now."

He would have said more, a lot more, if I'd given him

the chance, which I didn't. I ran out of the house and caught up with Dick who was heading off somewheres in the general direction of the clambake beach. I caught hold of him and held him tight.

"Time! Time is the thing," I told him. "We want to save time and walking takes too long. You could drive Hale's auto if you had the chance, couldn't you? . . . Of course. Fine! . . . Then we'll get that car."

The car was standing in the back driveway where the chauffeur had left it. I didn't wait to ask permission; we jumped in, and Dick got her under way. Inside of fifteen minutes we were alongside the place where the clambake party was the night before. We jumped out and began our hunt.

We walked over every yard of that beach for half a mile back and forth. We went into every one of the scallop shanties. Nothing in them but hoes and dredges and rakes and old oilskins and smell—plenty of smell. There was no sign or trace of Anne Francis anywhere. Lots of footmarks in the sand, but all huddled and stamped together. Old Sherlock himself couldn't have picked hers out from that mix-up, not with two or three Doctor Watsons to help him.

"She isn't here, that's certain sure," I said.

Dick didn't answer. He was looking at the surf rolling in. I didn't ask what he was thinking, I didn't like the looks of that surf any better than he did. There is a lot of water around Sepatonk Island and water can cover up things so complete and so easy.

He turned to me. "I am going down to see Barbara Taylor," he declared. "Maybe Anne told her more than she told the chauffeur. Perhaps she said something that might give us an idea where—"

He broke the sentence in the middle and looked at the surf again. I said going to the light was a good notion. He could drop me at the Inn and I would do a little asking and nosing around there. "Don't scare the Taylors," I warned him. "And don't let them see you're scared, either. Brace up, boy. She's safe and all right, I feel it in my bones."

Which sounded a whole lot more confident than I felt. I was beginning to get really scared.

He left me at the Inn and went whizzing off towards the lighthouse point. I went inside and to that little office of mine, always a sort of safety harbor for me when there is thinking to be done. I couldn't spare time for much thinking, but I wanted to do a little bit. To begin with, I wanted to run over what had happened at the break-up of the clambake party and see if I could remember anything that, in the light of Anne Francis's disappearing, looked the least bit out of the common.

I couldn't think of one single thing of that kind. I hadn't paid any attention to Anne, of course, for I had taken it for granted she was going home with the Folgers in the Hale car, which was the way she had come to the bake. I drove my station wagon down and back. Now who had come back with me?

The regular crowd. Holley and the Hunter girl and the Fay one; Mr. and Mrs. Foster; Commodore House; Doc Grover and Charlie Drake— Eh? No, I was wrong there. Drake hadn't come back in the station wagon. He wasn't on hand when we started, and somebody—Grace Hunter, seemed to me it was—said Mr. Drake had left the bake quite a spell afore we broke up. As nigh as I could recollect, she said Drake had told her he had had all the tough clams sprinkled with sand and indigestion he wanted and he was going for a walk. I remembered her saying it was just like him, going off by himself like that. Anyhow, I hadn't waited for him; he could walk and be darned far as I was concerned. Those clams wasn't tough; they were the youngest and tenderest I had et for a long time; and there wasn't any sand in them, either, for I superintended that bake myself.

That was all the attention I paid to Charlie Drake the night afore. Now, though, I was commencing to pay considerable. So far as I could reckon he was the only Inner not present and accounted for when the station wagon left the bake place. I wanted to see that man Drake.

I didn't see him then, though. He hadn't been around the Inn since after breakfast, so George Silver said; went out about nine and hadn't been back since. Well, where he was now could wait; what I wanted to know was what time he came in the night afore. Obed Silver ought to know that. I would go and see Obed.

Seems to me I haven't mentioned Obed Silver up to now in this yarn of mine. He was the new addition to the hired help at the Ownley Inn, and he had been added on only for a few days. I had never had a night watchman at the Inn, never calculated one was necessary. I generally attended to the locking up at night, and, when I didn't, Hettie Bassett did. But after I found those insurance policies in my safe mixed up—or suspicioned I did—I got uneasy and hired Obed. He was a cousin of George Silver, my bookkeeper, and he was glad of the chance to earn a few extra dollars for a week or so. He came on duty about eleven at night and was supposed to spend his time walking around the lobby and corridors and keeping guard, as you might say, till morning.

I never told anybody why I hired Obed, not even Hettie

nor George nor Dick Clarke. I never mentioned a word to a soul about my suspicions concerning the safe. It all sounded so—well, ridiculous, the notion that a person would break into a safe and steal nothing, not even money, that I was sort of ashamed to tell it. My excuse for getting a night watchman so late in the season was that Hettie and I were both tired and wanted freedom to go to bed early if we felt like it.

Obed Silver lived in a little house down the hill toward the Cove and boat landing. He would be asleep now, but I was going to roust him out. There was a bare chance that he might have seen or heard something of the Francis girl, and, anyhow, he ought to know what time Drake came in.

Afore I started in his direction, though, I went into the kitchen to see Hettie Bassett. She was flying around, shooing the kitchen help ahead of her like a hen driving chickens. "Don't you bother me now, Ham Ownley," she snapped. "I've got dinner to see to."

"Heave ahead and see to it then," I told her. "When you are bristled up like this, Hettie, I wouldn't bother you if they offered me a farm Down East with a pig on it. I just wanted to know if Miss Francis has been in this morning. Haven't seen her, have you?"

She flounced around at me, with her wet hands wrapped up in her apron.

"Miss Francis?" she wanted to know. "Oh, that's the city girl over at the Hale place. No, if she's been here I ain't seen her. I've got something else to do besides keep track of girls."

"All right, Hettie. I wanted to see her, that's all. So long."

She took a look at me. Then she got between me and the

door. "Oh, you want to see her, do you?" she said. "Well, well, I want to know! What for?"

One of Hettie's pet bugaboos, along with her premonitions and signs and trance medium notions, is the idea that some woman is going to get hold of me some day and lug me off to the minister by main strength. No use telling her that a fellow as old as I am, who has trotted single harness all these years, is a pretty safe bet to keep on trotting that way till he fetches up at the cemetery. She just sniffs and says those are the worst kind.

"What do you want to see that Francis girl for?" she asked again.

I slid past her and got a hand on the door knob. "Well, I tell you, Hettie," I said; "she and I are fixing to elope on the next boat, and I wanted to ask her if she thinks I ought to take along that new nightshirt, the one with my initials on it, you gave me Christmas."

She said: "Ugh!" and slammed back to the stove. I cleared out. By the time I got to the front door, I had changed my mind again. I wouldn't bother to see Obed now. I could learn about Drake's coming in some other time. Just now I must find Anne. I was really scared by this time, and I won't write down some of the thoughts that were in my mind. I don't want to think them again, and I am only too glad to forget them. I started toward the boat landing, then turned and went back through the village. I met three or four folks all told, and I asked each one of them, careless as I could, if they had happened to see Miss Francis that morning. They hadn't, nary one of them.

At the last house on the main road, the one just beyond the church, old Mrs. Sarah Wixon was leaning over her front gate. I asked her the same question. No, she hadn't seen the Francis girl. She was calculating to go down to the store, though, pretty soon and if she met Anne anywhere she would tell her I was looking for her.

"Speaking of seeing folks," she went on—she's a great talker if you give her the chance; "I see somebody a few nights ago, and he acted so kind of funny that I have been wondering ever since who it could be. It was the night that poor Mr. Kelly—the wreck man, you know—was found dead up in the woods. I thought afterward it might have been him, but it don't seem as if it could. I was up late with my dyspepsy that night—I have it awful nowadays, regular spells, and the doctor can't seem to do nothing for it. Well, anyhow, I was up and looking out of my upstairs front window there and I see this person, whoever it was, come out of that path yonder and go past my front gate, running as if the Old Harry was after him."

I hadn't paid much attention to her gabble until she said that about Kelly. Then I pricked up my ears. The path was the one Dick Clarke and I had took when we went over to spy in at the Kelly window and found him gone. It was nigh that path, close to the other end of it, by the big pine, that Dick and I came across Kelly's body.

"You say this man, the running one, came out of that path on to the road?" I asked.

"Yes, that's where he came from. He was running hard, but he didn't make much noise. Trod awful soft, almost as if he had rubbers on or something. He went right past the gate here. Where he went after that I couldn't see, 'twas too dark. Now who do you suppose likely 'twas, Ham? Wasn't any of the neighbors, 'cause I have asked them."

"What time was this, Sarah?"

"Around eleven or so, nigh's I can guess. My clock ain't

keeping time the way it ought to, but I have been so pestered with them dyspepsy spells that I haven't bothered to get it fixed."

She was still rattling on about her dyspepsia when I left her. What she had told me was interesting; mighty interesting, but just then I didn't give it much thought. All I could think of was Anne Francis and some of the things that might have happened to her.

I had intended following along the road, but Sarah's reminding me of the path made me decide to take that. From it, a little way this side of the big pine place, another path joins on and that path—the second one—comes out on a section of rough road that ends at the beach close to where we had the bake. The two paths and the eighth of a mile or so of rough road make the quickest cut-off to that part of the beach for a person walking and in a hurry. My idea was to give the clambake ground one more looking over. If I found nothing this time, my next move would have been to go back to Hale's and see if any news had been reported there. If it hadn't, and if Dick had had no luck on his trip to the lighthouse, I would be about ready to send out a general alarm and start the whole Island hunting. I hated to think of doing that and stirring up all the talk and hurrah it would mean, but desperate diseases call for desperate remedies, as the saying is. I couldn't imagine any profit the Sidekick scamp could gain by hurting Anne Francis, but he was in my mind along with other cheerful possibilities.

The stretch of rough road, when I came to it, was just a cart track all grown over with briars and huckleberry bushes. No wagons or cars ever went over it now nor hadn't for a long spell. There was an old tumbledown house by the side of it; but nobody had lived there since old Erastus

Phipps's time, and he had been dead years and years. From abreast the house I could see the beach and the water beyond and there was the Hale car standing by one of the scallop shanties. Dick must have come back and was looking for me, probably. Maybe Anne had been found, or had come home or something. I picked up my feet and began to run, something I hadn't done for one while, I can tell you.

I hadn't run more than two steps when I saw something else, something that fetched me up short, with all brakes on. The flash of it happened to catch my eye as I went past a bunch of bayberry bushes on the right hand side of the cart track. I went over, reached down through the bush, and picked it up. It was one of those little fancy handbags such as women and girls nowadays carry with them wherever they go. My grandmother would have called it a reticule, I presume likely. The handle was broken off at one end.

The bag was open, and some of the things that had been in it were spilled out on the ground under the bush. I picked them up, too. There was a handkerchief and a little purse and one of those contraptions with a powder puff and lipstick in it. The handkerchief had the initials A.F. worked on one corner. The purse had A.F. on the metal part at the top. Yes, and the silver rim of the bag itself—it was what I had seen flash when the sun struck it—was engraved with the name "Anne Francis."

So she had been here, along this road. The bag was wet where the dew had gathered on it, so it must have laid where it was the bigger part of the night. I opened the purse; there was a few dollars in bills in it and some silver.

My first feeling, as I stood there with the bag and things in my hand, was to yell and keep on running till I got to the Hale car and Dick Clarke. Then I had another thought, and I started scratching around under the bayberry bush again. I didn't find anything more, though. The things I had already found was all there was. The bush twigs wasn't broken, and the grass underneath wasn't trampled nor mussed up. The bayberry clump was five or six feet from the edge of the track so it didn't seem hardly possible that the bag had been dropped there. It looked to me as if somebody had thrown it where it was.

I looked all around me. A lonesome sort of place. The woods—pines and scrub oaks—were thick just there; and, although the road, if you could call it that, was clear enough to walk on without trouble, the bushes and briars and weeds were a tangle on each side of it. The old tumbledown Phipps house was the only sign of humanity, and that looked as dead as old Erastus was now, himself. I looked at the house, and then I noticed that the front door of it was standing wide open.

The next minute I was standing by that doorway looking in. A narrow little hall with a narrow flight of stairs, straight up and down as a ladder, leading to the second story. That was all I had time to see for I heard somebody talking. The talk came from inside and sounded kind of muffled. I went in on tiptoe. At the back end of the hall, under the stairs, was another door, and it was open, too. I got as far as this door and put my head past the jamb. Then I heard a voice—Dick Clarke's voice—saying: "Anne! Anne, darling! Are you all right? Are you *sure* you are not hurt?"

And then another voice, the voice I had been hoping to hear for a couple of hundred years as I had been reckoning time that forenoon, said, kind of half laughing and half crying:

"Oh, Dick! Dick, dear! I am *so* glad it is you! I think I was never so glad to see anybody in all my life."

Maybe I ought to have sung out, or knocked or something. I didn't though. I forgot all my manners and bolted pellmell down as rickety a flight of steps as ever I traveled. At the bottom of those steps was a dirty, damp, dark little cellar with a brick wall and a cement floor. And on that floor was Dick Clarke, down on his knees, with both his arms around Anne Francis and her head on his shoulder.

"Glory to God!" I said. Sounds as if I thought I was in prayer meeting, doesn't it? Well, I was—in a way of speaking.

III

The first thing we did, after the praise service was over, was to get Anne out of that cellar. She said she was all right and perfectly able to walk, but Dick wouldn't hear to that; he picked her up and carried her up the steps and out into the sunshine. She was pretty white and shaky, not to mention rumpled and dirty, but she didn't seem to be hurt at all.

"Put me down, Dick," she said. "Yes, do please. I want to—to rest and—and breathe again. Oh, this light is so good! It was horrible down there in the dark, and I was so afraid he might come back. I— No, don't ask me anything just yet. Just—just let me be, please."

She was close to hysterics, and no wonder; but she was a game sport, if ever I saw one, and she didn't give way; bit her lip and held on. Dick was about as upset as she was. I asked him how he came to find her. It was more by good luck than anything else. He had learned nothing new at

the Taylors' and so had driven the car back to the cove
by the scallop shanties; and there, just as I had been planning to do, he decided to have another hunt. When we were
there before we hadn't been along the old road, never
once thought she could have gone that way. Now, though,
he had come along it as far as the Phipps house, noticed
the door being open, and went in. He looked about the
lower floor rooms, and then, in desperation sort of, he called
her name. She knew his voice and answered. The cellar
door was shut and locked. There was an old rusty bolt in
it and that had been pushed into the socket. All this was
only a few minutes afore I got there.

Anne put in a word at the end. "I didn't dare call at
first," she said. "I heard you tramping about up there;
but of course I didn't know it was you, and I was afraid
it might be—the other one."

I had a dozen questions I was dying to ask but I managed to hold them in. "There, there," I said, "don't try to
tell us about it now. You ought to be got home quick as
possible. Dick, you go and fetch the car."

She kept saying she was all right and could tell her
story well as not, but we wouldn't have it. Dick galloped
off, to where he had left the Hale auto, and he was back
with it in a jump less than no time. We got her in and
started, Dick at the wheel and I on the back seat with her.
She leaned back on the cushions and drew a long breath.

"Oh, this is wonderful," she vowed; "but I do think it
is mean of you not to let me talk. Just think, I haven't
had anyone to talk to all night long—except the rats.
There were rats in that awful cellar, big ones. I could hear
them."

She shivered all over. The rats were more liable to have
been field mice or red squirrels, and I told her so. "Oh,

don't spoil my adventure," she said. "They were rats, I am sure of it. I could almost smell the dreadful things."

We made time on that trip to the Hale place. The maid saw us coming and was at the door to meet us. Perry Hale, plastered head and all, was there, too, and there was a jubilee convention. The maid took charge of Anne and got her upstairs to her room. Dick and Perry and I went into the library, and there we told Hale our story. He was full of excitement and swearing mad to think of her being locked in that cellar all night and part of a day. The Folgers hadn't got back yet, so we had the place to ourselves.

"What in the devil does it all mean?" Hale wanted to know. "How did she get there? In that God-forsaken hole, with the door bolted?"

He knew as much about that as we did.

We knew more in a little while, though, for the maid came to say Miss Francis wanted to see us and wouldn't we please come up to her room. You couldn't have held Dick back with a chain cable, so he followed the maid and I followed him, with Perry Hale trailing along behind, growling because his head hurt him, but tagging on just the same.

Anne was propped up in a big chair with a tray on a little table beside her. Judging by the empty cup and plates on the tray, I figured that her adventure, as she called it, hadn't spoiled her appetite. She looked well, too. Her color had come back and her eyes were shining.

"*Now* I am going to talk," she made proclamation, "and I should like to see anyone try to stop me."

Her yarn took quite a while to tell, but you can bet that no one of her listeners lost interest. Seems, so she told us, that she had intended to go home with Barbara Taylor after the clambake and stay at the light over night. She told the Folgers she was going to do that. Why did she change her mind? Well, she wasn't very clear about that. She kept glancing at Dick every once in a while, and I was inclined to the notion that he, or something to do with him, was mixed up in it some way.

"I just didn't feel like going anywhere," she said, and we let it go at that.

The Folgers had gone; and, although there was plenty of room in the Inn station wagon and I should have been glad to go around the Hale way and leave her, she didn't want that either. "It was a nice night," she said, "and I— well, I was not feeling sociable, so I decided to walk back alone. It wasn't very far, and I knew every inch of the way. I had walked it dozens of times."

So, after telling Barbara she wasn't going with her and saying nothing to me or the others who were busy packing the picnic stuff into the station wagon, she started off by herself.

"Wait a minute," I cut in. "Were all hands of the Inn crowd there when you left?"

"Why, yes, I think so. Dick wasn't, of course. And— no, Mr. Drake had gone early, too; at least I seem to remember hearing someone say that he had. The others were all there, with you, Mr. Ownley. I don't remember exactly, but I am almost sure they were."

She took the shortest way home, which was along the rough road and path through the woods; it is considerable shorter than the regular road along the beach. No, she wasn't the least bit afraid. What was there to be afraid of—on Sepatonk Island?

She was about opposite the old Phipps house when that question was answered. She heard a rustle behind her, but, before she could turn, a hand was put over her mouth and an arm around her waist. For a second she was so startled and scared that she couldn't do anything, but then she fought and fought hard. She tried to scream, but the hand over her mouth was so tight that she could hardly breathe. She was half carried and half dragged off the road, up the steps of the old house and inside, into the little hall. All this time, the man who had hold of her hadn't spoken a word. He didn't now, but he took the hand from her mouth and grabbed one of her wrists. She had her handbag with her, and, during the tussle she was still holding it. The handle strap was around her hand, she said, and she couldn't have dropped it if she wanted to.

His hand moved down until it reached the bag and jerked at it. He twisted and yanked until the strap broke and he had the bag. She was screaming now, and she judged he didn't like it, for she heard him swear. He dragged her further along the hall. Then he gave her a push. She felt herself falling down a flight of stairs— and that was the end, for a while.

When she came to she was lying on that cellar floor in the pitch dark. There was a little window high up in the cellar wall, but it was so dirty she couldn't see out of it, even after the daylight came, and there were hours and hours and hours before it did come. When it was light enough to see at all, she climbed the steps she had fallen down; but the door at the top was locked. She pounded on it, but nobody came. She called for help once in a while, but no one heard her. And then, at last, she heard Dick's step overhead and—well, that was all.

It was something of a story; and to hear her tell it and to see her sitting there, bright-eyed and excited, even joking once in a while—as full of grit as a peck of wet spinach, after all she had been through—well, she can have my vote any time she wants it. Then and there I swore to myself I would get the skunk that manhandled her that way if it took my last dollar and my last breath.

I looked at Dick Clarke, and, although he didn't say anything, it was plain he was swearing the same thing. As for Perry Hale, he was not only thinking it, but saying it. Anne certainly had her congregation with her, if that was any satisfaction.

We all wanted to know, of course, if she had been able to see the rascal; if she had any idea what he looked like. She hadn't. The whole tussle, from the time he first grabbed her till he shoved her downstairs, hadn't lasted but a few minutes. The only glimpse she caught of his head made her pretty certain that his face was covered with something like a handkerchief. "If I could only have torn it off," she said, "but I couldn't. He didn't give me a chance."

Perry Hale was for phoning the police at Brandt. What kind of a dash-to-blank constable was I to let such things happen on Sepatonk Island? I held up my hand.

"About the kind you think I am, I'm afraid," I said; "but we can argue about that later. Just now I want to have the floor. Anne, is this the bag the fellow took away from you?"

I handed her the reticule I had found under the bayberry bush. She took it from me.

"Yes," she said. "Yes, it is mine. It has my name on it. And the handle is broken—see?"

"I noticed it was. I picked it up outside there, where the scamp threw it, I guess. Just look and see if there is anything missing from what you had in it, will you, please?"

She looked at the things I had put back in the bag, the handkerchief, the purse, and the powder puff thing. She counted the money in the purse.

"Why, it is all here—the money, I mean," she said. "It was my bag he was after, it must have been. Why didn't he take the money?"

I couldn't answer that, but I wasn't quite satisfied. "Are you sure there is nothing missing?" I asked, earnest.

"Yes. . . . No—oh no! The knife! The knife isn't here."

"Knife? . . . Hush, Dick! Both of you fellows keep still for a jiffy, won't you? . . . What knife do you mean, Anne?"

"Why, the gold penknife—the watch chain knife. I had it in my bag with the other things, and now it isn't here. Perhaps you didn't pick up everything when you found the bag, Mr. Ownley."

I had, though; there was no knife under that bayberry bush. It didn't seem to mean anything, though. What had a gold knife got to do with all this? Anne went right on, missing that knife seemed to mean considerable—to her.

"I had it at the clambake," she declared. "I brought it on purpose to give to him. I meant to give it to him—but I didn't. He went away so early."

"Who did?"

"Why, Dick, of course. It was his knife."

Hale and I both looked at Dick Clarke. I don't know which of the three looked the most surprised or puzzled. Dick spoke first.

"I don't understand," he said. "You mean you thought you had my knife in your bag, Anne?"

She turned toward him, and her eyes began to snap.

"Thought!" she said. "Oh, don't be absurd. Can't you be honest—even *now?* I *know* it was yours. I found it on the floor, that night when you— Oh, stop pretending! You know where I found it. I didn't tell anyone I found it, not even Perry, because—oh, because I was a sentimental idiot, I suppose. I—"

I jumped in then. "Wait, Anne!" I ordered. "Be still, Dick! Let's get this straight. Suppose you tell *me* about this knife business, Anne. How do you know it was Dick's?"

"Whose else could it be? He wears it on his watch chain; I have seen it a hundred times. And who else was there—that night?"

"Where? What night?" It was Dick who asked. She looked at him as if he was some kind of poison.

"Do you *want* me to tell? Very well, then I will. I found it on the floor under the corner of Perry's desk that night when I came into the library and found him lying there and you standing over him. You had gone and I was with him, and I saw something glitter on the floor by the corner of the desk. I picked it up and knew, of course, it was yours. I didn't tell Perry, I didn't tell anyone. I kept it— like a fool. I meant to give it to you the next time we met, but—"

"*Stop!*" Dick sung it out like the captain of a ship. "And you say you have had it ever since. You had it, last night?"

"Certainly! It was in my bag. It isn't there now, but—"

"Hush!" Dick took his watch and chain from his pockets. On one end of the chain, the opposite end from the watch, was a little gold knife, maybe a couple of inches long. "Anne," he said, solemn, "as sure as you and I are here this minute, this knife of mine has never been off this chain, or out of my possession, for more than three years. I have never lost it. Why ... look here, Ownley, I sharpened a pencil with it at your desk in your private office yesterday morning, before we went up to Hale's. You saw me do it. Don't you remember?"

And I did remember. I said so.

Anne caught her breath. "But it *must* have been yours," she stammered. "Whose else could it have been—in that room—that night—at that time?"

I squared my shoulders. "When we know that," I said, "we'll know a lot of things. What we know now, though, is why you were choked and locked up in that cellar. The knife is the answer—the knife you picked up in Perry's library. Whoever the fellow was that dropped it there, he must have known you found it and that, the minute you showed it around, somebody was liable to recognize it and blurt out who it belonged to. And *that* would lead right straight to who knocked out Perry Hale. No wonder he was nervous. No wonder he was willing to take any kind of desperate risk to get that knife back.

"And," I shook my head, "blast his miserable skin, he did take that risk and now he *has* got it back."

PART VII

The Letter

Told by
Seth Hammond Ownley

I

THAT was it, of course—it had to be. To get back that gold watch-chain knife was the reason for the attack on Anne Francis. That was what had brought her into the tangle. Sooner or later she was bound to show that knife to Dick Clarke and to have him tell her that it wasn't his. Then it would be shown to other folks, and, again sooner or later, somebody was bound to know the name of its owner. And, considering when and where it had been picked up, that owner would have had some tough explaining to do.

If only she had shown it to Dick when they had their talk the day after Hale was knocked out. She was going to, she said, but their talk had been pretty peppery, and she hadn't done it. She fetched it to the clambake on purpose to give to him—and again she hadn't. As nigh as that. And now—well, Mr. Sidekick, whoever he was, had the luck of the devil, no doubt of that. And he had spunk, too, plenty of it. No risk was too great for him to take, and, as happens often enough, the risk had paid. Godfreys mighty, it was aggravating! I don't know as I ever was madder in my born days.

I wasn't any madder than the rest of them, though.

Dick Clarke's face was paper white and his eyes were snapping fire. Perry Hale's face was red as a fireman's shirt, and his promises about what he would do when he got hold of the rascal were brimstone blue. Anne Francis made the first practical speech.

"Look here," she said, "I suppose you all know what you are talking about, but I don't. For quite a while, ever since you came to Sepatonk, Puss Clarke, I have been wondering why you were here and what you really came for. It was plain enough that something was going on and that you and Mr. Ownley were mixed up in it. Then Perry was pounded on the head, and, of course, Dick was mixed up in that, too. Now I have had *my* share of the fun. All right, only, so long as I am in the game, don't you think I am entitled to know what kind of game it is? *I* do—and I mean to know. Now who is going to tell me?"

Dick looked at me, and I nodded.

"Dick will tell you," I said. "Go on, Dick. This is experience meeting, so speak out."

He did, he told her the whole yarn, just as he had spun it to Hale. He went a little further this time, though, telling about the twenty dollar bill and Grover and Half Pound and everything. When he finished, she turned to me.

"Is that all, Mr. Ownley?" she asked.

"All there is according to the latest bulletins," I told her. "Of course, the way things are moving these days— and nights—there may have been somebody else knocked in the head or shoved down cellar since we left the Inn; but that's the news as reported to date. Now you know as much as we three do. Nice spell of weather we're having on Sepatonk, don't you think? No wonder folks come here for a rest."

She took a long breath. "Why, it is wonderful!" she vowed. "I never heard anything so exciting in my life. . . . Thank you, Dick. I understand now."

She looked at Dick when she said that. If I had been Perry Hale, I shouldn't have liked that look—much.

"And now what are we going to *do?*" she wanted to know.

I won't undertake to write down all the talk that followed along after that. There was so many points to be run over and guessed about afore we could so much as consider doing anything. There were some stickers, too—questions without any answers. How did Sidekick—taking for granted that it was Sidekick who locked her in the old Phipps' house—know she had his gold knife? She might—though she couldn't remember that she had—have said some things at the clambake to put him on the track, and of course he knew somebody from the Hale house must have it. But that answer didn't satisfy me—I couldn't help feeling he knew more than that. Only *how* did he come to know it?

And again: If it was Sidekick—which of course it was —who hit Hale that night, why did he come there and for what? For the Primer? Why should he think Perry Hale had the Primer? If he was the Kelly-Sanger sidekick one he might be after the Primer, of course, but—

Dick cut in here. "It looks as if he *never* has had the Primer," he said. "You and I haven't been certain of that, Ham. Now we can be, I should say."

"Um-hm. Well, I have been middling certain all along. You see, unless he took it from Kelly's body that night in the woods he couldn't have got it. According to Half Pound, it wasn't with the pocketbook and watch in the bureau drawer. And, *if* he had it, he would have cleared out from the Island—which he hasn't done. This getting after Perry here is proof that he is still here and trying."

Hale spoke up. "But if he hasn't got the darned thing," he snorted, "who has? Where is it?"

"Now you are asking something. It looks more and more to me as if Kelly hid it somewhere."

"Yes; he or your Half Pound friend."

"That's possible, of course. I'm going to see Half again. I don't think he knows anything about it, though. He was too scared the night Dick and I got after him about the twenty dollar bill to hold back."

Which brought us round in a circle to the stickiest sticker again. Why, and for what, was Hale knocked out?

"Let's consider that telephone message you got, Perry," I said. "You thought it was Clarke phoning you. Did he say he was Clarke?"

"Yes."

"Did his voice, as you remember it, sound like Dick's?"

"I don't know. I didn't pay any attention to the voice. Of course it was Clarke, it had to be."

"I know—but it wasn't. What time did he phone you?"

"Quarter past three in the afternoon. I know because I looked at the clock on my desk."

I nodded. "Maybe we could find out who was phoning and from where at a quarter past, but I doubt it. There's a public phone at the post office and another at the steamboat landing and a dozen private ones that might have been used. Tracing that call would be a pretty big order, in the time we've got. The Inn is shutting up day after tomorrow, you recollect."

Hale grunted. "And the dog that phoned may not be an Inn guest at all," he said.

"That's possible, too." I was thinking of Folger when I said it.

"What did you say when he told you to have the twenty-five thousand ready, Perry?" I asked.

"Said I would have it, of course."

"That wasn't true, was it?"

"Of course not; but I would have got it later, if he had the goods to deliver."

Anne asked a question then, one that had been in the back of my head—and Dick's too, I shouldn't wonder.

"But, Perry," she said, "if this man came to see you, wouldn't you have asked where he got the Primer? He was so secret about it all that you must have thought there was something queer."

For the first time Perry Hale acted a little bit fussed, I thought. "No business of mine where he got it," he growled. "In this collecting game you can't be too nosey. Not if you want to get good stuff, you can't. I should have asked a few questions, of course; but—well, confound it, Anne, if that book was what he said it was, I *wanted* it."

Anne said, "Oh, I see." She didn't say any more, but that would have been enough for the average person. Hale didn't look too happy, I thought. Dick spoke next.

"What I can't get," he said, "is how this fellow knew what you and I were talking about that afternoon in your library. As you say, he must have known or he wouldn't have phoned, pretending to be me, and saying he accepted your offer. How *could* he have known? You and I were alone."

No answer from anybody. "Who else was in this house at the time?" I asked.

Hale answered. "Nobody," he said. "They were all down at the beach, finishing up my picnic. . . . No, wait a minute. Part of the picnic bunch, some of the men, must have come up to the house while we were talking, because they were out on the porch when Clarke and I came out of the library. They were having an extra smoke and a drink there. You remember that, Clarke, don't you?"

Dick said he remembered.

"Um-hm. Now let's think who they were. Holley, and that queer bird Drake, and the old guy with the pointed mustaches and the face like a three alarm fire—"

"Souse. . . . House, I mean," I said.

"Eh? Ho, ho! Don't edit it, Ham. 'Souse' fills the bill, I'd say; you couldn't improve it. And that prim, precise professor—what's his name—Grover; he is so darned proper he gives me a pain. And—well, that's all, isn't it? Except Ted Folger, of course; he was handing 'round the drinks."

"But they were on the piazza, not *in* the house. And that piazza is a long ways from the library—the whole length of the living room from it. Nobody out there could hear what you two said, could they, Perry?"

"With the door shut? Not on your life. Besides, who in that bunch can you see going around beaning people with a blackjack? I'd bet five to one that not one of them knows a rare book from a Sears-Roebuck catalogue."

"Except Folger." I said that, and I said it afore I thought. It disturbed Perry Hale, too, that was plain.

"Yes," he agreed, after a second or two. "Yes, Folger does, that's right. But if you mean to tell me that Ted Folger is a double-crosser and a thug, I'll bet you are wrong. He would go a long way to get hold of an item he wanted—but not that far, no sir!"

Folger was his friend, or supposed to be, so I didn't press the point. "And, anyhow," I said, "Folger was out on that porch with the others, so he couldn't have heard any more than they could."

Dick had thought of something. "Hale," he said, "do you remember, along toward the end of our talk, you jumped up and opened the door. You said you thought you heard somebody moving in the living room. Remember that?"

Hale thumped his knee with his fist. "By the Lord," he sung out, "I did do that, didn't I! And I had thought I heard someone moving quietly out there. Yes, I had thought that—and more than once. But there wasn't anybody in sight. They were on the veranda, I heard them talking."

"Where were the servants?" I asked.

"Eh? I don't know. Down at the beach, cleaning up the picnic stuff, I suppose—some of them, at least." He scowled. "The servants, eh?" he muttered. "Humph! I hadn't thought of them."

And just then one of the servants knocked at the door. It was the maid who had been looking out for Anne, and, when Hale ordered her to come in, she was looking troubled.

"I hope you'll excuse me, Mr. Hale," she said, "but I— I thought maybe Miss Anne might be needing me. She was so tired and—and weak—that I thought—I was afraid—"

She was right, too, and we all knew it, I guess. Of course Anne vowed and declared she was fine and didn't need anybody or anything, but her looks belied her. She was tired and nervous, and we had no business to be pestering her any longer just then. It was high time, too, that Hale got back to that sofa of his. I had one word of advice to hand out afore the meeting broke up.

"Perry," I said, after the maid had gone out again, "if you and Anne don't mind, I think it would be better if you and she kept at home, here in the house, for the rest of the day and maybe tomorrow."

Well, of course there was a howl from both of them. Keep in that house? They guessed *not*! Perry was for taking his motor boat and starting headfirst for Brandt or New Bedford or Boston or Fall River or somewhere and getting an army or two of policemen and detectives, and one thing or 'nother, to find out who this blankety dashed gangster and thief was and hauling him off to jail where he belonged. That was what ought to have been done in the first place.

"Oh, I know you've done your best, Ownley," he said; "I'm not blaming you. This thing is too big for you, that's all. It takes trained minds, used to catching crooks, to handle a job like this one. What do you know about fingerprints and making casts of foot marks and stuff like that?"

"Nothing," I agreed. "And I never wrote any books about cigar ashes, either. I don't pretend to know a thing about detective work. I do know Sepatonk Island, though, and the folks on it; know more about them than a whole lot of outsiders could learn in a month, to say nothing of a day and a half—which is all the time we've got afore the Inn closes. If Dick and I had called in the police in the beginning, it might have been better—maybe—but we didn't call then and now it is too late."

"Huh! So you are going to sit down and fold your hands and let this son of a gun get away with it? Is that the program?"

"Don't know as it is. Unless we're away off in our reckoning, it looks as if he hadn't got away with the Primer yet, which is what he must be after. We haven't one single mite of proof who he is; and, if we call in a whole mess of strangers and set them snooping, we never will have—in a day and a half. Do you realize how many folks are leaving Sepatonk by day after tomorrow's steamer? Eight that I can count offhand. I don't say ary one is Sidekick; I just say he might be."

Hale growled something about not letting them leave. I shook my head. "We would have some real trouble on our hands if we tried that," I told him. "I'm keeping hotel and these folks are my friends so far. They pay their bills regular, and most of them say they are coming back next year. If we had the least scrap of evidence that one of them was mixed up in all this deviltry, I'd stop his leaving quick enough; but we have no real evidence against anybody. Which is what I said afore."

Perry wasn't satisfied, even yet. He began on Dick now.

"It's Clarke's fault really," he vowed. "If he hadn't been so tight-mouthed at the beginning, we might have nailed the blackguard before this. Just so that old Payson relic could keep his job in the Knowlton Library, he—"

Dick was bristling up and he broke in now.

"If you hadn't been so anxious to get hold of a book you must have known was—" he began. Anne cut him short, and I was thankful she did. He and Hale loved each other like Kilkenny cats anyhow, and she, being the reason why, realized it, of course.

"Hush, Dick!" she ordered. "Be still, Perry! Mr. Ownley, why do you think Perry and I should stay in the house here?"

I told her, best I could. My notion was that the less Sidekick knew of the real state of affairs the better. He had knocked Hale out, but he didn't know how bad he might have hurt him. He had locked Anne up in the

Phipps' cellar, but the chances were he didn't know Dick and I had got her out of there. Stay out of sight and tell nobody anything, that was my advice. "He's been expecting a couple of big sensations and a lot of talk. If there aren't any sensations and no talk at all, he is going to be uneasy. He may go somewhere or ask some questions that *might*—it's a big 'might'—give us the hint we're hoping for. See what I mean, don't you?"

Anne said she supposed she saw. Perry Hale said it looked like a darned slim chance to him. They gave in, however, that, all things considered, it looked like the only chance we had. So it was settled that they was to tell nobody anything about what happened in Hale's library or about Anne's "adventure." The Hale servants were to be warned to keep quiet, and not even the Folgers were to be told of Anne's kidnaping.

That ended the long talk, so far as I was concerned. We helped Perry downstairs to his sofa, and I guess it looked good to him, by the way he flopped down on it. By the front door, though, the maid came down from Anne's room with a message. Could Mr. Clarke come up again? Miss Francis wanted to see him for just a second.

He could and he did. It was a long second afore he joined me outside the house, but, when he did, he was stepping high, wide, and handsome. I didn't ask him why; it wasn't my business anyhow.

II

Dick and I didn't talk much on the way to the Inn. We were both thinking hard, though not the same things, I shouldn't wonder. He went up to his room to get ready for luncheon, and I, after a general look around, went to my hideaway, the little back office. I wanted to do some planning if I could. What sort of planning, or even how to begin to plan, I had no idea as yet. I must do something, or, if I couldn't, I must try to get hold of those who could.

Perry Hale's remarks about calling in detectives from the mainland, and about not calling them at the beginning, bothered me a whole lot more than I pretended. Of course, if I had had any notion of what was going to happen I should have sent for the regular police folks that night when the Kelly-Sanger man died. Dick Clarke didn't want me to; he wanted to keep the news of the Primer stealing out of the newspapers for Payson's sake. If his objections had been all, though, I should have sent for them anyway; I wouldn't have taken all this responsibility on my own shoulders.

But I didn't know, couldn't foresee—we couldn't either of us have foreseen—what was coming. It wasn't until we found the letter in Kelly's pocketbook in Half Pound's possession that we had had the least suspicion that another person on Sepatonk Island knew about the forty thousand dollar Primer book. And even then it was only a suspicion, nothing definite about it. The other things— Dick's finding out that Hale was mixed up in it somehow and the knocking out of Hale and Anne's being assaulted —all those had happened within the last couple of days and nights, one thing crowding right on top of the other.

Notwithstanding, though, I couldn't get over the feeling that I was part way responsible. I should have called in outside help—yes, I should. And now, as I said to Perry and the rest, it was too late. The Ownley Inn was shutting up for the season, and by the time any mainland detectives got here a whole lot of the folks they would be certain sure to want to question and find out about would have gone. No, if anything was to be done in that little length of time, it was up to me to do it. Up to Dick Clarke too, but not so much. The heft of it was on my shoulders.

There was one thing I had done which nobody but me knew about. I hadn't told Dick about it any more than I had told him about my suspicions as to the Inn safe having been opened. I did it the day after that suspicion came to me and I had kept it quiet because, to tell the truth, I was a little bit ashamed of it. It seemed kind of like playing traitor to people that were my friends, folks that trusted me and that I was supposed to trust.

That morning of the safe business I wrote a letter to a man I knew in Boston. He had spent a month at the Inn a couple of years before, and he and I got to be quite chummy. He was high up in the Boston Police Department, and so I wrote telling him there was some queer doings on Sepatonk and that I had a sort of halfway notion some one of the Inn crowd might be mixed up in it. I didn't give him any particulars, but I sent, along with the letter, a parcel of snapshot photographs. The Hunter schoolmarm had taken the snapshots and they were of the Inn with bunches of the men and women boarders standing or sitting around. Some groups were of half a dozen, some were of two or three. I was in most of them myself. The likenesses were pretty good because the Hunter female was handy with a camera.

I asked my Police Department friend to look them over and see if he, or any of his mates in the Department, recognized anybody in the pictures. "I don't expect you will," I wrote; "but, as I say, there have been some queer doings here lately, and I send these things on a chance. For the

Lord sakes don't tell who sent them and hurry them back when you get through with them."

I had a note from him saying he had received the snapshots and would have them checked up. It was plain enough he took the whole thing as a big joke; wanted to know if there was a clamhoe missing on Sepatonk or if I suspected one of my boarders of having an affair with Mrs. Bassett. I hadn't heard from him since, and my wish that I hadn't sent the photographs was stronger than ever. He was a good fellow but an awful hand to tease, and, if he ever came to Sepatonk again, he would make life miserable for me, I knew that.

In spite of which I had a half mind to telephone him, tell him just the scrape we were in, and ask his advice as a practical policeman. I sat there, at my desk, trying to make up my mind whether to do this or not, when Dick came hurrying in to tell me that somebody had been in his room since he left it that morning and had been rummaging through his things.

I was getting sort of callous, as you might say, by this time, and I took the news in my stride, as the magazine stories tell about. I didn't even get up out of my chair.

"Well, well," I said. "And isn't that nice!"

He looked at me as if he calculated I was crazy. "Don't you understand?" he said. "I say someone has searched my room?"

"I heard you. What did he find?"

"Nothing, I guess. At any rate nothing seems to be missing."

"That's a comfort—or seems to me it ought to be.... Dear, dear! Well, suppose I go up with you and we have another look."

His room, when we got to it, didn't look mussed up.

The things in the dresser drawers were a little bit stirred around; but I was young once myself, and I could remember when I had to hunt through a whole bureau to locate the other half of a pair of socks. I was pretty much inclined to think his imagination was running away with him.

"All this head-banging and girl-stealing have got you going, Dick," I told him. "You are seeing things."

He wouldn't have it that way. Somebody *had* been in that room, he was sure of it.

"But why? If there is nothing missing—"

I stopped in the middle of the sentence. I remembered my suspicion about the Inn safe. There had been nothing taken from that, either.

He was moving about the room, and now I heard him mumbling to himself.

"What is it?" I asked.

He didn't answer right off; he was pawing over the things on the top of the table he used as a writing desk. "Yes," he said. "Yes, it isn't here. It's gone."

"What's gone?"

"The letter. The letter I was writing to Doctor Payson. I hadn't finished it, and I left it in the portfolio here on the table. I saw it this morning before we went up to Hale's. It isn't here now."

It wasn't either. It wasn't in his portfolio writing case nor on or about the table; it wasn't in the room anywhere.

"What in the 'nation would anybody steal a letter for?" I wanted to know. "What was in it?"

Nothing out of the common, according to him. He had been in the habit, since he landed on Sepatonk, of writing a few words to his Payson friend every other day or so.

Telling him he was still on the hunt for the Primer, that he was more sure than ever that it was on the Island somewhere, and begging Payson and the Knowlton trustees to be patient and give him just a little more time.

"Of course I haven't given the doctor any details of the mysterious happenings here," he said. "I haven't wanted him to notify the police, you understand. I was partially responsible for the loss of that book, and I— well, darn it, I hoped to be responsible—with you, of course, Ham—for its recovery. See, don't you?"

I saw, but I had a new thought. "Just what did you say in this particular letter?" I asked. "The one you didn't finish. Did you tell Payson once more that you hadn't been able to get hold of the Primer?"

"Yes. I told him just that."

Then, for the first time, I really began to believe that somebody might have been hunting through that room. And I could see why, after he found and read that letter, he hadn't bothered to hunt any more thorough. In one way I was more disturbed and madder than ever, but in another I was easier in my mind. I told Dick so.

"I have been scared half to death," I said, "that you would be the next one to be knocked halfway to glory. Why you haven't been before this I can't see even yet. It is plain that Sidekick knows you are a rare book man, just as he knows Perry Hale is another. He—"

"But *how* does he know? Nobody knows that but Hale, himself, and you, of course, and Anne, and—well, yes, Folger."

"I can't tell you how he knows, but know he does, that's certain. Why he didn't bludgeon you before he did Hale I'm not sure, but I can make a guess. Anyhow, his finding and reading this letter of yours, Dick, ought to make you safe for a spell, anyhow. Afore he read it, you must have been a leading candidate on his list; you might have the Primer. Now he *knows* you haven't got it, and he'll let you alone. He don't waste powder when there's nothing to be gained by it, old Sidekick doesn't."

Dick wanted to know what my guess was about Hale's being tackled first instead of him.

"Because Hale was a double chance for profit and you was only a single one, that's how I figure it. Somehow or other Sidekick heard or learned of what you and Perry were talking about in the Hale library. How he heard—well, we'll forget that riddle because we can't, either of us, think of a good answer. He did hear and, when he phoned Perry, Perry told him the twenty-five thousand in cash was waiting for him then in that room at a given hour that night. *If* Hale had the Primer, he would get it; if he didn't have it there was the twenty-five thousand. According to his calculations he was playing two hands, and, either one—or maybe both—was a winner. Smart boy, our Sidekick chummie; I give him that much credit even while I am hoping he chokes."

Dick was hours late for luncheon—"dinner" we call it at the Ownley Inn—and, although he vowed he didn't have any appetite, I knew they were saving something for him and I made him go and eat it—pretend to, anyhow. As for me, I had Hettie fetch me a couple of sandwiches and some coffee to the little office. I never wanted to be alone more than I did then. It was getting nigh the end of the campaign, and so far the law and order army had been licked all along the line. And I, as constable, was supposed to be the General commanding the Law and Orderers. A darned fine General I had made out to be up to date!

First thing I did was drink a whole cup of strong coffee. Then I took a piece of paper and penciled down a few items. All questions, they was, and the answers opposite them were mainly minus with nothing to carry over.

No. 1.—Who was the person Dick heard in the woods that night when he and I went up to spy on Kelly-Sanger?

Answer—Don't know. Probably the fellow who turned Kelly's pockets inside out. But who was he?

No. 2.—Who was the man Sarah Wixon saw go by her house late that same night?

Answer—Don't know. Most likely the bushes rustler and the pocket picker. But so what?

No. 3.—Did Half Pound tell *all* he knew that night when Dick Clarke and I scared him into giving up the Kelly letter?

Answer—I think so, but it might be well to get after Half again.

No. 4.—Was the man who locked Anne in the Phipps house cellar somebody who had been at the clambake?

Answer—Probably so. Don't see how it could have been anybody else—anybody else who would have known about the gold knife, I mean.

No. 5.—Was it that knife he was after?

Answer—Yes. Almost certain—yes.

No. 6—Who, amongst the clambake crowd, could have got away unnoticed and unbeknownst; manhandle Anne, get back the knife, and then, still unnoticed and unbeknownst, get back to the clambake place again?

Answer—Hard to say. I was busy and so was all the Inn help. Nobody was checking up on the people around. Almost anybody could have done it, if he was quick and careful.

No. 7.—Who had left the clambake before Anne did?

Answer—Barbara Taylor, the Folgers, and Charlie Drake. Those sure—and some of the town folks more than likely. But the town folks, I was almost ready to swear, wasn't, any of them, the kind of critter Sidekick must be. I had known them all, most of them since they and I were children. I counted them out. Sidekick wasn't an all-the-year Sepatonker. There was Half Pound, of course, but he hadn't got spunk enough to hit a ground-mole over the head, to say nothing of a man.

No. 8.—How did Sidekick know what Hale and Clarke talked about in the Hale house the afternoon of the Hale picnic?

Answer—We've asked this a dozen times afore and the answer is just plain "Don't know."

No. 9.—What do I know, or does Dick know, about Folger and his wife?

Answer—Mighty little, and I shouldn't wonder if we ought to know more.

No. 10.—Who, amongst the Inn folks and the Hale crowd, was in the habit of wearing a gold knife at the other end of his watch chain?

Answer—Dick, of course, but his has never been lost. Who else? Don't know, but I ought to try and find out.

No. 11.—Who has been in the Inn this forenoon while Dick and I were out hunting for Anne and while Dick's room was searched and the letter taken—always provided it was taken and not lost or mislaid?

Answer—Don't know yet, but I must hurry up and find out.

Nice little lot of conundrums I had set down on that paper, hadn't I? Eleven of them altogether and only one with anything like a satisfying answer tagged to it. My appetite for puzzles was beginning to fail on me. I used to think I was pretty smart when I was picking out the guilty party in a library detective yarn, and, more than once, I had halfway wished I could have a chance at a mystery in real life. Well, I wasn't wishing it now; I was wishing that Holmes and Philo Vance and Doc Thorndike and Ellery Queen and a half dozen more were in that office at that minute so I could hand that slip of paper to them and walk outdoor and breathe easy.

But they wasn't there and I was, and somebody had to do something—make a try, anyhow. We were up against a clever bird, no doubt of that, one that was ready to take any chance no matter how dangerous and one that didn't have the word "quit" in his dictionary. That was what worried me as much as anything. *If* he was one of those booked to leave on the day after tomorrow's steamer he had only one day and two nights left to work in. Who would be the next one he would pick out to work on? I didn't know, but, for Dick's sake, I really hoped that Sidekick *had* taken the Payson letter and read it. If that was the case, at least Dick's head wouldn't get another knock.

The last two questions seemed the likeliest to give results in a hurry, so I decided to start working on them, beginning, like the ambitious boy in the Sunday School book, at the bottom and working my way up. Who had been in and around the Ownley Inn that forenoon?

I went out and asked George Silver some casual questions. Nigh as I could learn from him almost everybody had been in and out that morning. House, Grover, Drake, Holley, the Fosters, and Grace Hunter and Maizie Fay—they had all been there. Folger? Yes, he and his wife had both been in. She had gone out after a little while, but he had stayed on longer. No, George didn't know whether he had gone upstairs or not, hadn't noticed. Wasn't likely he had, was it? What would Mr. Folger want to go upstairs for?

I might have guessed an answer for that, but I didn't. I went out to talk with Hettie Bassett. She had a lot to say, same as she always has, but nothing within half a mile of the target. I asked the Dolan girl, who took care of the rooms on Dick's corridor, if any of the roomers had come in while she was working. No, she hadn't seen anybody. Some folks had gone along the hall while she was doing the rooms, but she hadn't noticed who they were. She had a notion, though, that Mr. Clarke was one of them. She kind of thought she had heard him in his room while she was making Mr. Holley's bed. That was all she could tell me.

Whoever was in that room at that time it wasn't Dick, but that didn't help me much. Somebody had been there, but I was fairly sure of that afore.

Question number 10, that about the knife, sounded *so* promising. If I could only answer that; but how could I? Cruising around and asking all and sundry to let me see the after end of their watch chains wouldn't get me anywhere. They would all ask what I wanted to know for, and that was exactly what I mustn't tell them. How could I find out without making all hands suspicious? That stumped me. Sherlock or Philo would have known how, of course, but they lived in books, not on Sepatonk Island.

Only thing I could think of was to keep my eyes peeled and watch the men when they looked to see what time it was. But then they would be looking at the other end of the chain; you don't tell time by looking at a knife.

Dick had gone out somewheres; I had a suspicion his port of call wouldn't be far from where Anne Francis was located. I wandered around the lobby, talking weather and such to the boarders who happened to be there, but nobody looked at his watch and nobody acted as if he had a wicked secret hid in his bosom. Old Souse's breath was perfumed up, as usual, and Pete Holley was trying to coax Grover to go down to the poolroom and have a game of billiards. Drake wasn't around. It came across me, as it had so many times, that he hardly ever was around. I wondered if now wasn't as good a time as any to try and dig up something about Charlie Drake. He was the last one you would pick out to be a villain, but I might ask a few questions around the village. Somebody might have seen him somewhere at an interesting time.

Before I started out to do that, though, I went back to my office and took another look at my list of questions. I had already decided it was no use to pay attention to where people were the night Kelly died. As far as I had been able to learn, every boarder, except Drake, had been in his room and in bed. Clarke and I were out on the prowl but all the other Inn-mates were in, according to Hettie and the maids. So much for that night.

But the night of the sandbagging at Perry Hale's I hadn't really checked up on, hadn't had time. And the checking there would be a lot easier. Obed Silver, the night watchman, had been hired afore then; and he was on duty, in the lobby and up and down the halls, from eleven o'clock on. I would go and see Obed and ask him if he had let anyone of the regulars in or out after he came on watch.

I went over in my mind, how much *I* knew about the doings of that particular night. I had stayed downstairs until Obed reported, eleven o'clock, and then I went up to my room. The Hunter-Fay combination had been out for their usual walk, but they came in early and went aloft about half past ten. Doctor Grover had gone up early—to read a little before he turned in, he said; I heard him say it, myself, and I saw him go. The Fosters went up about ten. Commodore Souse went aloft about the same time. Drake, I knew, was out and hadn't come in when Obed showed up. Pete Holley? I couldn't remember.

I told George, at the desk, that I was going out for a little spell, and I started for Obed's little house. He was sound asleep when I got there, but I pounded on the door and rousted him out. He was half dressed and half awake, and his temper was pretty crossgrained; but he sweetened up a little as our talk went on, and he answered my questions clear enough.

According to him, Holley had been out that night, and he—Obed—had let him in at the front door about half past eleven. It was nigher to half past one when Dick Clarke showed up.

"I asked him what kept him out all hours like that," said Obed, "but he didn't scarcely answer me at all. Scowling, he was, and just stomped off upstairs. Don't know what ailed him, Ham, but that's how he acted, anyhow."

I knew all about Dick and what ailed him, of course. A fellow who had just heard his girl accuse him of being a sneak and a murderer isn't liable to come back from it on the broad grin. I asked about Charlie Drake and what time *he* arrived.

And now it was Obed who grinned.

"Oh, he got in about quarter to one," he said. "I looked at him, and you never see anybody look more foolish and sheepish than he did. Ho, ho! I knew where *he'd* been, and he knew I knew, I bet you."

"What are you talking about, Obed?" I asked.

And then he told me. Seems that Sylvanus Baker, who lives away down at the far end of the Island, the opposite end from the lighthouse, has a daughter named Mabel who works in the Fall River city hall—some kind of a secretary job she has got up there. She is a real nice-looking young woman, Mabel Baker is, about thirty year old or so. She hadn't been well first part of the summer, and so they had given her a three months lay-off; and she had been spending it on Sepatonk with her folks. How and when Drake got acquainted with her I don't know, but, according to Obed, he hadn't let the acquaintanceship slack off any. "He's down there to Baker's practically every night in the week and most of some of the day times. He and Mabel are going to get married this fall. Don't many folks know this yet, but *I* know it. Sylvanus told me so himself. He, he, he! That's where old Drakie boy had been that night you are asking about, and that's why he looked so silly when I winked at him. He, he!"

This was news, and it was odd I hadn't heard about it afore. If it was winter time, I would have heard, of course, but in summer I don't hear much of the Island tittle-tattle, having other things to attend to. And, if it was true, all the mysteriousness about Drake was knocked galley west. He hadn't been around with the Inn crowd much, having better company to attend up to. I would have to check Obed's yarn, of course, but it did look as if one of the candidates for the Sidekick nomination could be wiped off the slate. No wonder Drake didn't stay long at the clambake. His girl wasn't there and he went where she was. Kind of disappointing in one way, but pleasant in another. I always sort of liked Charlie Drake, in spite of his queerness.

I asked Obed if anybody had gone *out* of the Inn while he was on duty the night of the Hale rumpus. No, not a soul. Not a one had come downstairs after he got there. He would have seen them if they had, for all the doors were locked tight and the keys put on the bunch hanging in my private office. Obed had his own key to the front door, and he had let Dick and Holley and Drake in with that.

"Sure all the regular keys were on that bunch in my office?" I asked.

"Um-hm. They are there—now. Of course, that time when—"

He stopped and looked a little mite bothered, seemed to me. As if he had started to say something he hadn't meant to say at all. "What time?" I asked, sharp. "What's all this, Obed? Come! Out with it."

He hemmed and hawed, but I kept after him, and, finally, he told me. Seems one of the maids—the Dolan girl—had told him and he had promised to keep it dark. One of the keys to one of the upstairs rooms had been missing for a day and a night and Maggie Dolan had been kind of worried about it; but it had turned up again later, so it was all right.

"What key was this?" I wanted to know.

Well, it was just the key to the little trunkroom at the end of the long bedroom corridor on the second floor. "Nothing in there but trunks and bags and stuff like that," said Obed, "so it wasn't very important, anyhow. The Dolan girl was kind of fussed about it because she had left that key in the door by mistake one time, and, when she thought of it next and went there, the key was gone. She found it, the next afternoon though, on the floor in a corner. It had fell out of the keyhole, I presume likely."

That trunkroom doesn't open into any other room so it didn't seem to me that its doorkey being missing could be any part of our answer to one of my conundrums. However, when I got back to the Inn, I took my bunch of keys from the hook, went upstairs, and opened up the trunkroom.

It isn't more than ten by eight and pretty well crowded with trunks and boxes. There is a full-sized window in it opening out over the back of the hotel at the end where the ell sticks out beyond the kitchen. That corner is pretty well shaded by a couple of big spruces, and there is a wooden trellis, that used to have rambler roses on it, coming up from the ground and ending just beneath the sill of this trunkroom window.

I opened the window and looked out. At any other time I shouldn't have paid any attention to the trellis, but now I was in the state of mind where I paid attention to everything. I looked down at that trellis—a good strong heavy-made one it was—and I noticed, or thought I did, that the two upper crossways slats were kind of blackened up. Yes, and the second one down from the top had a splinter broke off it; the raw wood showed yellow under the white paint.

I bolted out of that trunkroom and downstairs and outside and around the back corner of the Inn. The two big spruces were thick, and they hid the trellis almost altogether. I stepped in back of them and got close to the lower end of it. Yes, there wasn't hardly a doubt. The slats—rungs you might call them—were stained and splintered just as they would be if somebody had been using them to climb up and down to and from that trunkroom window. I looked at the ground below and it seemed to me to be tramped down here and there.

I all but groaned out loud. That key had been missing one whole night and part of a day. It was the simplest kind of a key, too; anybody with any gumption could make one like it in half an hour out of any other of the bedroom keys with a jackknife file. Could make one good enough to open *that* worn old lock out of a button hook. And, having made it, all he would have to do would be to go along that hallway, as if he was going to the bathroom, get into that trunkroom, lock the door after him, climb down the trellis, and be off and away, no matter what time of night it might be.

When he had finished his outdoor business—whatever it was—all he would have to do was climb up the trellis, get in the window, shut it and lock it behind him, unlock the door with the key he had made, lock that behind him, and tiptoe back to his room and to bed.

And, if he was careful to make sure where the night watchman was when he made his trips along the hall, that night watchman would be willing to swear that nobody had left the Ownley Inn that night because nobody had used the front door. Which was exactly what Obed Silver had sworn to me less than an hour ago.

And—this being so—all the nice, ironclad alibis of the boarders at the Ownley Inn for the night of the sandbagging of Perry Hale were not worth a pinch of sawdust.

So far as those alibis were concerned any one of them could have been Mr. Kelly-Sanger's Sidekick. Any one of them!

III

Everybody knows the old saying about its always being darkest just afore morning strikes on, or whatever it is. It is one of those nice free bits of consolation that we are all so fond of handing out to a person in trouble and that generally has the effect of making him mad enough to want to throw the one who hands it out into the creek. There are all sorts of variations to it. Old Captain Noah Sampson, who was pretty nigh the richest man on Sepatonk thirty year ago and by long odds the stingiest, always put it like this: "Now, now, my friend, don't give up. It does look bad to you now, I don't doubt; but remember that when the tide is the farthest out is just when it turns and begins to come in." He would say that and then explain how it was that he couldn't lend the poor fellow a cent.

Captain Noah has been dead a long spell, and he hasn't anything to do with this yarn of Dick Clarke's and mine; but if his ghost had come to me when I got back to my office after discovering that way out through the trunk-room and down the trellis—if his ghost had come and started preaching to me about the tide turning—well, it would have been a mighty uncomfortable spook when I got through with it, that is all. I was sunk—sunk without a plank to hang on to.

Just think for a minute. Here it was, five o'clock in the afternoon of the next to the last day of the Ownley Inn's summer season. The morning after tomorrow morning all my boarders, except Dick Clarke, would be leaving Sepatonk Island. One of them might be—*could* be, any-how—this Sidekick crook and blackguard, and yet I was further from finding out whether he was or not than I had been in the beginning. The alibis I had counted on wasn't alibis at all. I didn't know where anyone of the Inn regulars were the night of the Hale trouble. They might *all* have been out that night for what I knew to the contrary.

The Folgers would be staying on at Hale's—yes. And there was always the chance that Ted Folger, with his wife in the plot with him, might have been the one who hit Perry. I didn't hardly believe it, though. I could see Folger as wanting to get hold of the Primer book, but I couldn't see him as Sidekick, the ex-partner of a professional crook like the Kelly-Sanger man. Perry Hale had known Folger for a good while, they were friends. Was it likely that— No, no, of course it wasn't.

Sunk—that is what I was—sunk. And Dick and poor old Payson were sunk with me. I might try and comfort myself with the idea that, judging by his keeping on trying, Sidekick hadn't got hold of the book he was after; but, for that matter, neither had we. And—this was the most provoking thought of all—Sidekick could steam away from Sepatonk Island a free man. Free and clear and with all hands of us kissing him good-by, so to speak. I had meant to nab that fellow. Yes, I had; and show the folks who made me constable that I was on my job.

Whereas now— Godfreys, but it hurt my pride!

Well, and then, when it was about as dark as it could be and the tide was out as far as it could go, the change began; daylight commenced to show and the tide turned. I apologize to Captain Noah—right here and now I apologize to his memory.

I sat there, blue as a spoiled oyster, and, for the sake of doing something, I pulled out one of the upper drawers in my desk, reached in and opened the secret drawer behind it, and took out a folded paper. It was that letter Clarke and I had found in Kelly's pocketbook when we took the pocketbook from Half Pound down at his shanty. The letter beginning "Dear Pal Eddie" and signed "Legs."

I had kept that letter in the secret drawer, being mistrustful of the safe nowadays, and I had read it over and over—two dozen times, I guess likely. I had always had the notion that it might mean more than it looked as if it did. Kelly-Sanger had been so careful of it; he had planned to have Pound mail it for him providing he didn't show up to cross to the mainland on Pound's boat. Why, if it was nothing more than it made believe to be, would he have been so anxious to have it mailed? I had had the notion, from the start, that there was some kind of message in it—to a fellow who knew how to make it out.

I can imagine anybody reading what I am writing now grinning to himself and saying: "Yes, yes! Detective story stuff. Poor old Ownley's circulating library softening up his brains." Maybe so, but my brains were still soft, so far as that letter was concerned.

I had worked over it every way I could think of. One of my last season's boarders had left me a book of "Cryptograms," those kind of puzzles where one letter means another letter, like T meaning E and so on. I had got to be pretty good at doing those in the book and the ones they print in the Sunday newspaper. I had learned all about "letter frequency" and "terminations," meaning "ing" and "ion" and the like of that. But this Kelly stuff, if it was a cryptogram at all, wasn't that kind. All the frequencies and terminations in creation didn't make sense of it.

There was one book I got from the Brandt library that was called "The Black Room"—or some such name—and it was all about code messages in time of war, or between different countries, and such. The man that wrote it could make sense out of *any* kind of gibberish, him and those working for the Government with him. But I wasn't in their class, not by a hundred sea mile. If the Kelly letter was as complicated a code as the Black Room messages, I might as well chuck it into the stove—it was too many for me.

I didn't believe it was as complicated as all that. Considering who had written it and the kind of person it was written to, I didn't believe it could be *too* hard. It took experience and education and special training to write complicated code, and, judging by the letter itself, neither Kelly nor pal Eddie had education enough to give them brain fever. No, if there was a message hid in that letter, it ought to be findable. The trouble with that was that I hadn't been able to find it.

And now, sitting at that desk of mine, and down in the depths as I was, I gave it another try. From my other readings and puzzlings I had come to the conclusion that the letter was too long to have a code all through it. If a message was hid anywhere, it was liable to be short and in just one part—a sentence or two, maybe. And it had always seemed to me that the likeliest part was where that # sign came in.

"Give them *all* the double cross. The good old #."

That is how it went, and I couldn't see any reason for the # sign unless it meant something to the fellow who got the letter—the one who knew the code, I mean. There wasn't any other signs anywhere in the whole thing. Why was this one where it was? It wasn't needful. It meant "double cross," of course, but "double cross" had been spelt out already. No, I had believed—and I still believed —it was there for some purpose, it meant something.

That part of the letter started off like this: "Them old spiels of Mikes don't ever work. I'd can Windy too and with Hank and Eli's new gags plain tripe and N.G. the end's here, Ed, for I'm keen for man who is just as live at runing down buyers and free spenders as anybody."

Now another thing that made me think the message might be somewheres along there was because that part of the letter was kind of different from what had gone before. All the beginning was plain news, as you might say, telling about how he—Kelly—came to be on Sepatonk and about finding Sidekick was there too and playing sick—and so on. Full of crook slang and tough talk, but meaning something. Right after the # mark, though, it started off in a kind of jumble about Mike and Windy and Hank and Eli, folks that wasn't mentioned afore, nor afterward either. And one word "runing"—meaning "running" of course—was spelt wrong. It was the only piece of bad spelling in the letter.

My notion was that, maybe, those names were in there, not because they meant anything, but because they *had* to be to make the code run right. Or because they were easier to put in, in a hurry, than other everyday words. See what I mean?

So I had worked over that part of the letter again and again, getting nowhere. I tried to think of books and stories I had read with code messages in them. *The Gold Bug,* of course; but that was just a simple cryptogram and easy enough to solve if you had learned the trick. *The Giant Raft,* by Jules Verne—I loved that yarn

when I was a youngster—but the code there, and in a
lot of stories I had read since, was built around a name
or a number or a page in a dictionary or directory, all
too tough for me to get at, ever. And too tough for Kelly
and his pal to contrive and handle, or I missed my guess.

It was just then that I happened to remember another
book I had read years ago. *Colonel Quaritch, V.C.*, that
was its name, or something like it. A man named Haggard wrote it, the one who wrote *King Solomon's Mines,*
as fine a yarn of fighting and finding treasure as I ever
read or ever calculate to. Well, in this Quaritch book, as
I remembered it now, there was a letter which a man
had left for his son, or those who came after him, which,
to the average person reading it, was just a nice good-by
letter, but, all the time, hid in it, in a kind of code, was
a message telling where a million or so in gold cash was
buried. I liked that story and I have never forgot it.

I remembered it then, sitting at my desk that late
afternoon, and I remembered what kind of code was used.
Simple enough, too; just taking the first sentence and
counting off every three letters, or something like that. The
third letters, taken by themselves one after the other, spelt
out "Dead Man's Mount"—and that's where the gold was
hid.

So—as I said afore, just to be doing something—
I began counting letters in that part of the Kelly stuff
beginning with the # mark.

"Them old spiels of Mikes don't ever work," etc.

I tried first counting every other letter. That gave me:
H—M—L—S—

No sense to that and no need to go any further.

Then every third letter, same as in the Quaritch book.
E—L—P—I— Another flop.

I hadn't any hope, but I kept on. Every fourth letter now.

T—O—P—S—I—D—E

I said something, I don't know what, and counted again. Yes, it was right. Not much sense really, but "top side" was English, anyhow. I went on, counting every fourth letter.

A few minutes later I was standing on my feet, trying to believe I wasn't dreaming and finding it hard to believe. The *tide* had turned—it certain sure had!

I knew now that Kelly-Sanger *had* hid the Primer that night afore he died.

Not only that, but I knew where he had hid it.

IV

Luck! Amazing blind luck, that is what it was; I don't take any credit for it at all. The luck of remembering the Haggard book just at that time, and then—without any real hope, mind you—starting in to try the code that had worked in that old story. Just luck; but if anyone does read this yarn of Dick Clarke's and mine, I can't see how he or she can help feeling that, by all that is right and proper, some good luck was due us after all the other kind we had run afoul of.

Of course Hettie Bassett vows and declares it wasn't luck at all. She says it was that poor dead Kelly sinner's departed spirit influencing me and trying to make atonement. Maybe so. *If* so, and if my saying "Much obliged" will make Mr. Kelly any happier wherever he is, he can consider it said—and hearty, too.

My first thought was to gallop out and locate Dick

Clarke, and then he and I would head straight for the Primer. But Dick wasn't in his room, nor in the hotel anywhere, so I came back to my office again. I was sore tempted to go to the hiding place by myself, but I couldn't make that seem fair. It was Dick's book really, and he, not me, ought to be the one to first put hands on it. I paced up and down the little room, spelling out the message over and over and crowing vainglorious over every letter of it.

And then another thought began to get hold of me. We had got the Primer—or as good as got it; I was almost certain sure of that—but we hadn't got the rascal who was responsible for the heft of our trouble. The scamp who was behind the stealing in the first place, who had knocked out Perry Hale and scared poor Anne Francis half to death. The one who must be, right that minute, laughing in his sleeve at us and planning more deviltry, no doubt. We hadn't got him; we didn't have so much as a good hint at who he was. If we only could get *him*. Then our crowing would be worth while. But how? How?

If we could use that Primer as a bait, we might, maybe, get a bite from the fish we were after. How could we do it? If—

Well, I won't go over all the crazy notions that kept coming into my head and sliding out again. Most of them were no good, but there was one that, the more I thought of it, sounded halfway promising. It wasn't sure, but there did seem to be a chance in it. *If* Sidekick was a boarder in the Ownley Inn and the bait was dropped in front of him, he *might* rise to it. Anyhow, I couldn't see how we could lose anything by trying.

I sat down at my desk and wrote out eight copies—one for each of our boarders—of that part of the Kelly letter beginning with the # and ending with the word "anybody." The message was in that section; what came afore and what came afterward wasn't important and didn't have any code in it. I made eight copies, and I marked each one with a tiny initial, so small and in such a place that nobody who didn't know would ever notice it. Each copy was on the same kind of paper and of the same size as the other. I put them in my pocket and waited till supper time. It wasn't a long wait, but to me it was plenty long enough.

All hands—the boarders and Dick—were at the supper table, and, when we had finished eating, I stood up and said I had a favor to ask of all hands. It wasn't very important, I said, but it might help make me feel better satisfied with myself. A friend of mine out West, I said—you would have thought my middle name was Ananias the way I went on—a friend of mine out West, I said, who knew I was interested in puzzles and cryptograms and such, had sent me a cryptogram that he was willing to bet I couldn't read. It was simple, so he vowed, and anybody could read it if they knew the key. I considered myself so everlasting smart at such things that he calculated he would see if the smartness was real or just bluff.

"Well," I went on, "I have had that thing—only a few sentences it is—for weeks and I haven't dug my way into it yet. I hate to give up and have this friend guy me forever and ever, amen, so I didn't know but some of you folks would be willing to try and help out. This is about the last evening we'll have together this season—you'll all be packing and busy tomorrow night—and I wondered if any of you would spare a few minutes, after supper in the living room, going over the thing and seeing what you could make out of it. I know some of you are mighty smart at cryptogram puzzles. You, Mr. Holley—you have helped me afore. And the Commodore now—he is as good a crossword man as we've got. And Doctor Grover and Miss Hunter and Miss Fay—you are all, or have been, teachers of one kind and another. Suppose I give you each a copy of this thing, would you look it over for me? Provided you haven't got anything better to do this evening, of course."

They all laughed and most of them said they would. Old Mr. and Mrs. Foster backed out afore the start. Foster said he was no good at foolishness of that kind and that his wife was worse than he was. I didn't press them; I never had counted them in my school of fish anyhow. Drake said he was willing to spend half an hour at it but he wouldn't be much help, he knew. And, anyhow, he had an engagement for later in the evening. I could guess who the engagement was with.

Grover and House didn't seem very het up over the notion, but they didn't refuse right out. I handed around my copies of the part of the Kelly-Sanger letter.

"You'll notice," I said, "that some of the language in this letter is pretty tough, and the spelling isn't all it ought to be. It is supposed to be part of a letter a gangman in New York somewheres is writing to his crook partner in Chicago. Don't let the names and slang shock you, Miss Fay, nor you, Miss Hunter, will you?"

The Hunter schoolmarm giggled and vowed she was thrilled. The Fay one declared it sounded too romantic for anything. Old Souse growled and twiddled his mustache. Grover smiled that thin-lipped smile of his and Holley asked if I had a sharp pencil.

"Nobody is to compare notes," I said. "Work on your own and better luck to you than I have had."

Another lie, of course, but Ananias was going smooth by now. Dick came up to me; he had his slip in his hand.

"What in the devil is all this, Ham?" he whispered. "What are you up to?"

"Up to snuff, I hope," I whispered back. "Turn yourself into a railroad crossing sign and look and listen. May nothing come of it, anyhow."

For twenty minutes or so there was a great scratching of pencils and a rustling of papers. Then, one by one, the would-be cryptogramers began to quit work. The Commodore was the first to abandon ship. He came up to me and handed over his paper.

"Not quite myself tonight, Ownley," he said. "Brain is a bit fuzzy, I'm afraid. Usually this sort of thing would be child's play, but— Give it to me tomorrow, will you?"

He strutted out, leaving a faint smell of alcohol behind him. Drake next. He was sorry, but he must go, he said. He chucked his slip into the wastebasket.

The Hunter-Fay combination had, in spite of my orders, been working together. There was a lot of Oh-ing and Ah-ing but no results so far. They gave it up pretty soon, heaving their slips in to the basket, too.

"It is perfectly fascinating, Mr. Ownley," Grace Hunter said; "but my head is in no condition for such a problem tonight. I have had *such* a tiring day."

Nobody left in the living room now but Grover and Holley and Dick and me, and Grover was the next out. He got up from the table in the corner where he had been sitting by himself.

"Not my strong point, I'm afraid, Ownley," he said. "Mathematics or geometry—yes; but this sort of—er—nonsense—no."

He crumpled up his slip and threw it into the waste-basket with the rest.

"I shall retire early tonight," he told me. "Mean to have a long day in the open air tomorrow."

He went out into the lobby. Holley didn't last long, either.

"Oh, rats!" he said, getting up. "Give me a respectable crossword, and I am with you, Ham; but all this rot about 'spiels' and 'tripe' isn't up my street at all. Sorry, but I guess you better call in a butcher."

Dick was over by the window pretending to puzzle like the rest. When the living room was empty, except for us two, he came across to me.

"What *is* this?" he wanted to know. "Why did you show them this thing? If anyone of them should be Side-kick you might have—"

"I know, I know," I told him, in a hurry. "Tell you everything pretty soon. Just now, though, you stand by the door and cough or snort or something if anyone of them starts to come back."

He went to the door and stood looking out into the lobby. I went around to tables and chairs and waste-baskets collecting the slips of paper that had been left. With them in my hand I hurried to Dick.

"Stay where you are for a spell," I whispered. "If anybody goes outdoor I want to know it. Stay here until all hands go up to bed. I'll be in the back office."

When I got to that office, I shut the door and went over my slips one by one. I counted them. Six I had given out—the Fosters not having taken theirs—and only five I had now. Five—and a slip of blank paper. I knew where I had got that blank slip, and the initials on the others told me which one of the regular slips was missing.

Somebody had kept the slip I handed out and, when making believe to throw it away, had thrown away the blank instead.

Somebody had done that, and I knew who it was. Why had he done it? Why, because he might have recognized the names in the letter or—yes, he might have recognized the code. He might have seen it afore. He, or his partners, might be in the habit of using it.

By the Lord Harry! *Sidekick!*

It was just eleven that night when Dick and I came down to the lobby together. I hadn't told him about my working out the message in the Kelly letter. Mean of me, maybe, but I wanted him to see for himself what I hoped we were going to see afore that night was over.

"Don't ask me, boy," I said. "You will know everything pretty soon, I promise you. I want you to have the fun of being surprised. Take my word for it that it will be a surprise and fetch good news with it. Now follow the old man and stand by for action."

Dick, when he came to the office, had reported that all hands had gone up to bed, everybody but Charlie Drake, who was still out. The lobby was deserted, but, just as we got to it, the front door opened and Obed Silver, the night watchman, came in. There was a man with him, a square-shouldered, stocky-built fellow I had never seen afore.

"Oh, Mr. Ownley," says Obed, "this gentleman has just come over from the mainland in a motorboat. He was asking for the hotel and so I fetched him up here."

"Good evening," said I. The stocky man said "Good evening. You are Mr. Ownley?"

"That's my name—yes, sir."

"I see. Well, Mr. Ownley, my name is Brady."

I looked at the card he handed me. What was printed on it and what was written underneath made me whistle out loud. I didn't say much, though, on account of Dick. He would ask a million questions, I knew, and there wasn't time to answer them. "Well, well!" I gave Brady what I hoped was a warning look. "I think I know why you're here, Mr. Brady, but you can tell me about it later. Right now we're busy. Not that you aren't welcome. You're as welcome as the rich, long-lost son that shows up in the theater show just when the mortgage is going to be fore-closed!... Dick Clarke, shake hands with Mr. Brady.... And now, come on quick, both of you."

Dick was trying to ask the questions I had been afraid of when I shoved the pair of them out of the front door. I hung back just long enough to warn Obed Silver that if he told a soul I was out or who I was with I would kill him. Then *I* hustled out.

PART VIII

The Little Book

Told by
Dickson Clarke

I

HAM OWNLEY led the way with the stranger, Brady, and I tagging along behind. We had to walk in Indian file, as Ham was following the narrow path through the pines that led to Hale's. It was almost pitch dark, the sky overcast with low, scudding black clouds. There was a little bite in the air, almost the first warning of approaching autumn.

There was no talking. The pace was fast, and we needed all our attention to keep from falling over each other or over some inequality in the footing. I could not see, but I could sense—perhaps it was from the odor—the thick-growing, stunted little scrub pines pressing in on us from either side. I thought I spotted, but could not be sure, the place where Anne and I had met and talked only a couple of mornings before. It seemed to me as though ages had passed since then.

My heart was thumping when we came out into the open at last, but not from the exercise. Something in Ham's face before we started out, something in the swift sure purpose with which he was moving, made me believe that this was to be no ordinary adventure. Who was the man, Brady, that Ham had been so glad to see? I was no expert in such matters, but for some reason Brady brought the words "police officer" to my mind. Were we going to make an arrest? Was this, perhaps, after all the agony of groping and disappointments, to be the end of the trail?

A light or two gleaming in the dark showed that everybody was not yet asleep in Perry Hale's house. I had thought that surely must be our destination, but I was wrong. Without hesitation Ham veered away from it at an angle and crossed the broad lawn. Oyster shells crunched under my feet, and I knew we were following the drive. The low, dark mass just ahead of us was the Hale garage. Ham slowed his step and we approached cautiously.

The big double doors were closed, but an ordinary one alongside opened when Ham turned the knob, and we all stepped cautiously inside. A moment passed while we listened, but there was no sound. Then Ham used his flashlight briefly to examine our surroundings.

The place was boxlike, barren, and, except for Perry's old sedan, untenanted. The floor was cement, splotched with drippings of oil. In one corner was a heap of tin cans, empty crates, and the rest of the mixed junk that usually seems to be found in garages. A cluttered, home-made workbench ran along one wall. A closet projected from a corner in the rear. It proved to contain nothing but a lawnmower, hoes, rakes, and other garden implements, but Ham looked it over very carefully before closing the door again. He even directed the beam of his light under the car and into its interior before he was satisfied.

"Nothing here," he said in a low tone. "Not yet, anyhow. That's all fine and dandy. We may not have much time though. We've got to find a place to hide. That closet's a pretty cooped-up place for three of us to roost in. Hard to see out of, too."

"How about the car?" asked Brady. "Two of us can get in the back seat and one in the front. If we keep down low nobody can see us unless they deliberately look."

"I guess the car's the ticket," said Ham. "I'll take the front seat. You two get in back."

I couldn't contain my curiosity any longer. "What are we waiting for?" I demanded. "For somebody to come in here, I gather. But what's he coming here for, and what are we going to do after he comes?"

Ham climbed into his place behind the steering wheel and motioned us to ours in the rear. "Leave the doors on both sides open a crack," he ordered. "We may have to jump out of the car in an awful hurry."

"Nobody ever tells me anything," I mumbled complainingly, although I was greatly excited. "Don't we even get any instructions?"

"Yes." Ownley spoke rapidly and in a guarded tone. "If things go the way I figure, and the way I want 'em to, somebody will be coming in here before long—somebody you and I, Dick, and maybe even Mr. Brady, here, are mighty anxious to see. Now don't ask me his name, because I'm not downright positive of it. If he just *comes,* that'll be enough for me."

"And then what?" I asked. "Do we grab him the minute he shows up?"

"No." Ham was very positive about that. "Whatever else we do, we don't do that. We scooch down and try our best to keep out of his sight until we find out what he wants in here. *Then* we grab him, and grab him hard!

Wait till I give the signal though. When I yell, you boys jump!"

"What about this man?" asked Brady, opening his mouth for just about the second time. "Is he dangerous? Is he apt to be armed?"

"He's dangerous, all right," said Ham slowly. "If he had half a chance he'd do anything he could to get away. What I'm counting on is that he won't suspect anybody has got here afore him. I'm hoping he'll think he's the only hen on the roost and not be looking for trouble."

"If he's looking for trouble," said Brady grimly, "he'll get plenty. I'm heeled."

"Good!" said Ham, and I felt another little shiver travel up my backbone. "Let's hope there won't be any shooting, though. There's been enough rough stuff on Sepatonk Island lately to last us for a couple of hundred year."

My curiosity was anything but satisfied. It was, in fact, just reaching the boiling point. "What about the Primer, Ham? Will he—?"

"Shh, shh, Dick." Ham stopped me firmly. "I'd like to answer all you want to ask, and afore this night's done I hope I can. But right now is no time for talking. The man we're waiting for may not be along for a couple of hours—or at all. On the other hand, he may heave in sight any minute. If he does come, and hears us talking in here, he'll run away before anybody can say Jack Robinson. We've got to be still as a stopped clock from this minute on. No smoking, either."

It was the no smoking edict, strangely enough, that bothered me most during the time we had to wait. I smoke my share of cigarettes, I know, but I can go to the theater or to the movies and sit for a couple of hours without missing one. We didn't have to wait two hours in the

Hale garage, either, probably not much more than one; but before it was over I would have paid big money for the privilege of putting match to tobacco. Nervousness may have accounted for my craving, or perhaps it was the normal human desire to do what is forbidden.

I wasn't the only one that chafed under the delay. I couldn't see Ownley hunched in the front seat, but I could hear him move every now and then, and more than once I caught the gleam of his flashlight as he turned it on to look at his watch. Once I heard him mutter under his breath, impatiently. Brady, sitting beside me, did not move. He was so still that he might have been asleep or carved out of a block of granite, but I knew he was neither. I wondered if training in police work was responsible for the man's iron control, or whether he was just built that way. Anyhow, I began to respect him, and the thought that he was armed was comforting. Brady might be a handy man to have about if the fellow we were waiting for tried to get tough.

I'm not sure what time it was when something finally happened. Ownley says it was about one o'clock in the morning. For all of me it might have been four. The back seat of Perry's sedan was probably as comfortable as that of most automobiles, but I had stayed in one position for so long in an attempt to emulate the frozen Brady, that my right leg was asleep from the hip down. I had just cautiously moved it, to be rewarded by a stinging, prickling pain, when there was a heavy crunch on the oyster shells just outside the garage doors.

The noise probably wasn't very loud, but to our straining ears it sounded as though a bomb had been exploded. I heard Ham give a low, warning hiss, and I felt Brady, beside me, stiffen. I forgot all about my craving for a smoke, and even about the unpleasant seminumbness of my leg. I held my breath, with some vague feeling that by so doing I might shrink my big body into a smaller space.

There was a couple of more footsteps outside and then a tiny metallic rattle as though someone were fumbling with the knob of the door. A little creak and I knew the door had been opened. The click of a heel on cement and another, louder creak told their own story. Somebody had come into the garage and had closed the door behind him.

I did not move or breathe and I dared not try to look. Through the excitement in my brain flashed a picture of Kelly lying dead in the pines, and of Perry Hale sprawled unconscious at his desk with an ugly wound on the back of his head. If this man was the one we had been looking for, he was no one to pop up and yell boo at.

For a moment nothing happened, and then suddenly the garage was lighter. The man had turned on a flashlight. I could see the robe hanging on the rail against the back of the front seat, my own legs, Brady's square-toed black shoes. The beam of light moved. First it searched the entire place in a quick, exploratory circle. Then it centered on the car and hung there. I tensed my muscles for a leap should the intruder discover something wrong, but he did not. Apparently satisfied, he took his light away and proceeded on his business.

That business took him, with much less cautious footsteps, to the window in the wall furthest away from me. The garage was not plastered, or even sheathed, so that the window frames projected inward, boxlike, from the clapboards. Our man—he was only a dark shape—examined the frame briefly. Then he dragged over a near-by empty wooden box and stood up on it. He raised his arm over the top of the frame, and, from what I could see without exposing myself too much, seemed to be groping in the recess behind.

Whatever it was he was searching for, and about that I was beginning to have definite and very exciting suspicions, he did not find it; for after a little time he gave up and jumped down to the floor again. Without hesitation he picked up his box, moved around back of the car, and approached a similar window on the other side of the garage.

He was much closer to me, now, only a little more than an arm's length away, but I could not determine his identity. As I watched, he put down the box and repeated his previous actions. This time, however, he had success. He had no more than stretched his hand over the top of the window frame when I heard him give a little muffled exclamation. When his hand came down again, it was holding something. It was a small something, but indistinguishable.

I saw Ownley rise up ever so slightly from his position, and I knew that it was about time for action. I was on the side nearest our man and I must be the one to grapple with him first. I planted my feet firmly and reached out to take hold of the inner handle of the door.

The man was down on the floor again, standing sidewise to us, with the object in his hand and the beam of the flashlight falling directly on it. It was a small, flat, dark parcel he was holding, and I thought it gleamed dully. Could that be because it was oilcloth wrapped? I had no chance to answer the question, for just then Ownley gave the signal.

"Get him, boys!" he yelled at the top of his voice. "Hang on to him tight!"

It was confusion after that.

Leaping like a sprinter from the starting line and shoving the door open ahead of me, I popped out onto the garage floor, grabbing for my man as I did so. My intentions were good; but my leg and foot, as I have mentioned before, were more than half asleep, and they almost cooked my goose. I felt nothing as my right shoe hit the cement, and I staggered wildly. My hand caught hold of the man's sleeve, and I spun him half around; but I could not hold on.

Cursing, he pulled away, and I, tripping over the box he had been standing on, crashed to the floor ignominiously out of action. It was then that Brady's usefulness asserted itself. He must have been out of that car a split second after me, for even as I scrambled to my hands and feet my ears told me that he had succeeded where I had failed. There were sounds of a sharp scuffle, punctuated by grunts and heavy breathing. Then there was a metallic clatter as something fell to the cement floor, and a sharp exclamation from Brady. "Got you, you rat!" he growled fiercely. "Stand still if you don't want to get plugged!"

"Don't shoot!" begged a voice hoarsely. "I give up! I won't move!"

"Got him, Mr. Brady?" asked Ham excitedly, his flashlight directed at the closely entwined pair. "Hold him tight! Dick will help."

"Don't need any help," said Brady savagely. "If he moves, I'll drop him in his tracks and be glad of the chance. The punk had a gun and tried to use it! Turn on the lights and let's have a look at him."

"Lights? I wonder where the switch is." Ham moved the light of his torch along the walls. "Ought to be one alongside the doors. Yes! Half a jiffy, Mr. Brady."

He walked swiftly across the floor and put out his hand. There was a little click, and the whole place was suddenly brightly lighted. "Now!" he said, turning around. "Now let's see what kind of fish we caught on our hook!"

We all looked at the man who stood scowling and motionless under Brady's heavy hand. I gasped aloud when I saw his face, and my gasp was a mixture of sheer astonishment and bitter disappointment. "Why!" I said weakly. "This isn't anybody. There is some mistake. This is just— just Doc Grover!"

II

"Doctor Oscar Grover!" Ham repeated the words after me slowly and grimly. "Why, so it is, just as sure as I'm alive! It's Doc Grover, one of my star boarders at the Inn! Somehow I'm not so terrible surprised as I might be. And you think catching him is a mistake, do you, Dick?"

"Of course it's a mistake!" The captive didn't move a muscle but he was fast getting his bearings. "It's not only a mistake," he blurted indignantly, "it's a sheer outrage! What is the meaning of it, I'd like to know? What possible right have you to leap out like this at an innocent, peaceable person?"

"Peaceable, eh?" Brady shook his victim slightly as he growled the words. "One of you pick up that gun for me, will you? It's there on the floor under the runboard of the car. Loaded, is it? I thought so!" He shook Grover again harder. "Peaceable, are you? If I'd given you half a chance, you'd have shot me down like a dog!"

"Why not? Why shouldn't I?" Grover was rapidly gaining self-assurance. "Any citizen has a right to defend himself—especially against unwarranted attack like this. Why—"

"Heave to, Oscar." Ham's expression was not what I should have called sympathetic. "Don't be in too much of a hurry to get all het up under the collar and sorry for yourself. Maybe you'd like to tell us what you're doing here, in Perry Hale's garage, in the middle of the night, with a pistol in your pocket that, so far as we can judge from your actions, you were ready to use."

Right then my brain began to function again. I remembered the little package that Grover had been holding in his hand before the fireworks began, and I wondered where that package was now. It did not take me long to discover, for it was lying on the floor practically at my feet. I pounced on it with an exclamation, and, as the others watched, I tore at the wrappings.

Inside the oilskin was heavy brown wrapping paper. Inside that was a cardboard box. Inside that was some tissue paper, and finally—a dingy little book! Almost incredulously I looked at it as it lay in my hand. Almost reverently I opened it for a final glance to make sure.

"It's the Primer, Ham," I said as quietly as possible, although I'm sure my voice must have trembled. "It's Doctor Payson's Primer!"

"So!" Ham seemed to take this wonderful bit of news for granted, almost. "So it's that pesky little book at last, eh?" He kept his eyes on Grover. "Well, Oscar, you've asked us what it means, our jumping out at you like this. Now I cal'late I'll ask you what *this* means. The book that Dick, there, has got is stolen property. It was robbed from the Knowlton Library at Bainbridge University. How does it happen *you* have it?"

Grover shrugged and I could see that his familiar lofty and superior attitude was coming back to him by the minute. "I have it because I had brains enough to find out where it was hidden. If it is stolen property, this is complete news to me. I warn you, Ownley, to be careful what you say and do. You gave us a puzzle to do this evening. I took my copy to my room, and, using the brains God has given me, I found the answer. Apparently something, I had no idea what, was in this garage. I was curious, naturally, and decided to see if anything *was* hidden here, and what it might be. It seems to be a book, which is a complete surprise to me."

"Why," demanded Brady, who seemed to have a one-track mind, "did you bring a loaded thirty-eight automatic with you?"

"It was late at night." Grover shrugged again. "I thought it best to be on the safe side, and events seem to have justified the thought."

"Let's let that wait for a minute," said Ham. "We'll ask you later, Oscar, for a look at your license to carry a gun. First off, I want to know something else. What were you going to do with whatever you found in this garage?"

"I hadn't got so far as to consider that." I could see that Grover felt more and more sure of his ground. "I should, of course, have handed it to you tomorrow morning, telling you where and how I found it. Now will you kindly take your hands off me, whoever you are? Ownley, I shall hold you and Clarke responsible for this outrage—this assault on my person!"

At this point Brady suddenly put back his head and

laughed loudly. "Well, well!" he said with deep satisfaction. "It certainly is worth a trip on from Cleveland to hear that line of talk again. Sounds just as dignified and smooth and injured innocent as ever." He shook Grover back and forth almost playfully, as though dealing with an old friend. "Well, well, Herb! My old college chum, Herb!" Brady was all geniality. "And how is the literature and art racket going these days?"

"Know him, do you, officer?" Ham asked sharply.

"I'll say I know you, don't I, Herb? Just as slick a bluffer as you ever were, aren't you? And still working the old book racket! Glad to see you, my boy! The people in the Cleveland museum will be glad to see you, too. They've been looking for you for a long, long time."

Grover twisted around then and looked Brady squarely in the face. Then he grunted, his shoulders sagged, and all the bluster seemed to go out of him. When he spoke again, he didn't seem like the same man who had been living at the Ownley Inn. Even his voice had changed. "Hell!" he grunted. "It's George Brady. Can't I ever shake you? You coppers give me a pain in the neck."

"Tough luck, old timer." Brady spoke in a fatherly but admonitory tone. "If you boys would stop being naughty, us coppers would have a lot easier time."

"Skip it," said Grover and turned to Ham. "Are we going to hang around this place all night? That Inn dump of yours is bad enough, Ownley, but even that is better than this. Let's go there. I want a drink. In fact, I think I *need* one."

III

We were undoubtedly a triumphal procession, returning to the Inn in the dead of night, but were about as quiet and decorous a one as could be imagined. The whole place was shut up tight as a drum and our sole welcoming committee consisted of Obed Silver, the night watchman. He met us in the lobby looking more than half asleep at first and then not a little frightened.

"What are we going to do with the Doc, here?" Ham asked Brady. "Or Herb, or whatever his right name is? It seems to me you and I ought to compare notes a little bit before we have him up on the carpet for a heart-to-heart talk."

"Why don't you let me go to bed?" Grover asked sulkily. "I'll promise not to run away, and even if I broke my promise there wouldn't be any place for me to run."

"Nothing doing, buddie," said Brady shortly. "I know you from way back, and I wouldn't trust you as far as I could throw you. You're a valuable and slippery piece of goods; and now that I've got you, I'm going to see that you don't get mislaid again."

Finally, and over Grover's most violently expressed objections, he was plunked down in a chair out in the Inn kitchen and securely fastened to a steam pipe by means of a pair of handcuffs that Brady produced from his pocket. Obed Silver, more frightened than ever, but with a story to tell that would last him the rest of his life, was left to watch, and the rest of us trooped into Ham's little office.

First, of course, we examined and gloated over the little Primer that had been the reason for so much heartache and violence. To me, after all I had been through, it seemed a thing of supreme beauty, and I felt like kissing it and hugging it to my bosom. To the others, however, and especially to Brady, it was just a funny little old book. "It beats me," said Brady, shaking his head. "It certainly beats me. I can understand how these thugs can go around sticking people up to get their hands on a bunch of diamonds. Those things are worth important dough, and they look like something. But this—"

He grunted contemptuously, but I didn't care. It was Doctor Payson's pride and joy, and having it in his hands again would make him happier than anything else in the world. So far as I was concerned I couldn't have found a finer pot of gold at rainbow's end. I wanted to telephone Payson immediately, but finally agreed to Ham's suggestion that I wait until the next morning.

"You'll have plenty to keep you busy until then," said Ham with a little sigh, "and I doubt if any of us get much sleep this night. We've got an awful pile of things to talk over and decide, and they won't wait. First off, Dick, perhaps I'd better make you a little better acquainted with Mr. Brady here. You may not know it, but—"

"But he's a police officer." I finished the sentence for him. "I guessed that much. Ordinary citizens don't usually go around armed and with handcuffs in their pockets."

"That's right." Ham nodded. "He's from the Cleveland police, and he's here on account of a letter I wrote a little while ago to a friend of mine on the Boston force. That right, ain't it, Mr. Brady?"

Brady admitted the charge, and Ham explained to me about the letter. After the death of Kelly, or Sanger, or whatever we chose to call him, Ham had written to his Boston police friend. In the letter he had given as close a description of Kelly as he could from memory. He had also enclosed some snapshots of all the guests at the Inn. There were likenesses of Holley, House, Drake, Hale, Folger, and of course Grover.

"What the Boston folks did with my letter," said Ham, "I don't know. They must have done something, though, because here's Mr. Brady—just about as welcome a visitor as anybody could ask for."

The Boston police, from Brady's story, had done plenty. They had gone through their records and their Rogues' Gallery, and it wasn't long before they turned up something. Our quiet, scholarly Dr. Grover was not, it seemed, altogether an unknown character in the world of crime. His real name was Herbert Hayward, but in the past he had operated under the names of Herbert Lane, Henry Lane, Grover Newland, and some others. To the crook fraternity he was sometimes known as "Paper Herb" or "Frisco Bookie." The records showed that he was an educated man of good family. To the police of the nation he was known as a thief of valuable objects of art and of rare books in particular. He had been in prison twice. At the present time he was wanted, and had been wanted for a year and a half, in Cleveland for the theft of a Cellini chalice, taken from a private museum there. The chalice was still missing, and the supposition was that Grover had sold it to a private collector, no one but he knowing whom.

"He's clever at getting rid of the stuff he steals," said Brady, "and he knows either by reputation or first hand every fence and every ask-no-questions collector in the country. He slipped up on the Cleveland job, though, and we've been looking for him ever since. It'll be a long time before Herb gets out of the pen, even not counting whatever he's done on Sepatonk Island. So much for Hayward, or Grover, as you know him. Now about his pal—the man that died here."

"I suppose," I said, "that Kelly was another of the same breed of cats."

"It looks that way. From the little Mr. Ownley wrote in his letter and from the fact that he was apparently mixed up in this job with Hayward, our guess is that his real name was Frank Perelli. He sometimes traveled as Frank Princa, and was known to his buddies as 'Chicago Frank,' or just plain 'Legs.' "

"Legs!" I exclaimed. "That's the name that was signed to the letter, Ham! The letter that had the message in it!"

"That's right." Ham nodded. "It looks as though he was the one. Doesn't seem to be much doubt about it."

"One other thing," said Brady. "About that boatman—the one that was drowned off the *Nellie B.* during the hurricane that washed Perelli ashore here. The Boston people checked up in Bainbridge and they think they know him, too. If their calculations are right, he was an ex-convict who had just served a year and a half for armed robbery. He was suspected, with Perelli, of looting a couple of yachts in Chicago waters. It all seems to tie up. Now what's the case against Grover, or Hayward, here on Sepatonk? How much can you prove about that?"

"That's just it." Ham sighed. "We're practically sure that he has done enough on this island in the past few days to send him to state's prison for the rest of his natural life—if we could prove it. Trouble is that I'm not at all dead certain that we could—not so's it would hold water in a court of law."

"You never can tell," Brady observed. "Sometimes circumstantial evidence will take you a lot further than you might think. Let's hear the story."

Ham Ownley told it, and when he had finished Brady whistled. "Whew! You've had action on this little sand pile in the last week or so, haven't you! Mysterious death, safe breaking, assault, not to mention another assault mixed up with abduction. It's a shame that gold penknife got away from you. If you had that and could prove it was Grover's, we'd have that gent right where we want him."

"We would," said Ham with a shrug. "*If.* We haven't got the penknife and we haven't got any other evidence that I can see. We caught him tonight with stolen goods in his hands; but if he sticks to the story he told us at the start, I don't see what we can do to him. He looks to me as though he might get off scot free."

"No." Brady shook his head. "He's not sitting so pretty as all that—not by a long shot. We've got enough on him in Cleveland to send him up for a stretch. And, as for Sepatonk: remember that gun he was carrying when we nabbed him a little while ago? That wasn't there for decoration, I can promise you that. It was for business, and if I'd been a little slower or less lucky it would have been used. He tried to use it hard enough, and I'll swear to that. That's something else he will have to do time for."

"It's not enough," I said savagely. "It isn't enough by a long shot! You don't seem to realize the sum total of what this man has done. It was his brain that was directly responsible for the nearly killing of Dr. Payson and for the theft of the Primer. He slugged Perry Hale. Worse than both of those he brutally attacked a girl I'm very fond of, shoved her down a flight of cellar stairs, and left her there to rot, for all he cared. The very thought of it makes me fighting mad. Do you mean to tell me that out of all that, the only things he'll have to answer for are stealing a chalice in Cleveland and threatening you with a gun just now? That isn't justice, and it isn't right. The man is a dangerous menace. Why, for all we know he may be an out-and-out murderer!"

"Murderer?" asked Brady sharply. "What do you mean by that?"

"Wait just a minute," said Ham cautiously. "Murder is a hard word. It's a hard word to say, and in this case it would be nigh impossible to prove—even if we were sure murder had been done."

Brady wanted to hear the details and Ham gave them to him. He told about our finding Kelly dead in the pines; about the fact that his pockets had apparently been picked; about the lump on the back of his head. "Doctor Farmer," he said in conclusion, "and his coroner here, called the death an accident. Maybe it was, but Dick and I aren't so sure. Maybe Kelly didn't fall down. Maybe he was *hit*, just the way Perry Hale was hit. In that case it would be out-and-out murder, but we can't ever prove it."

"Prove it or not," I insisted stubbornly, "it's my belief that Grover is a murderer! A murderer as well as a lot of other things—and all he's going to get is a short sentence for carrying concealed weapons—that is, so far as his Sepatonk career goes."

"Hm!" said Brady, greatly interested. "This is something else again. Let's think about it for a minute. Just for the sake of argument let's say that in the process of robbing Kelly, Grover did hit him on the head, and that as a result of the blow Kelly died. That's murder, and Grover knows it well enough. In that case, what is Grover worrying about right this minute out there in the kitchen? I'll tell you, gentlemen. He's worrying about the electric chair and nothing else! These rats are all alike. They're tough and brave and all that until they run up against a murder rap. Then the thought of the hot seat gets them. They fold!"

"What good does that do us?" I asked unhappily, realizing the truth of what Ham had said a short time before. "We haven't any evidence of murder. We can't prove anything."

"Maybe not." Brady, I could tell, was doing a lot of fast thinking. "On the other hand we may be able to bluff a murder charge and to darn good advantage. Especially if Grover has a guilty conscience. He doesn't know, remember, what evidence we have or that we may have turned up. I think I'll have a little talk with Mr. Hayward-Grover right this minute. I'll never be able to make him confess killing Kelly, of course, whether he did it or not. He's a crook, but he'll be too smart and too scared for that. Perhaps, however, I'll be able to put enough of the fear of the Lord into him to make him confess all the rest of the stuff in order to escape facing a murder rap. It's worth trying, anyhow. Let's have the gent in, and turn on the heat!"

I have to hand it to Brady, without reservation, for the job he did on the so-called Oscar Grover. Grover was no easy mark, and during his sojourn in the kitchen he had undoubtedly studied his position and arrived at the conclusion it was pretty good. Anyhow, he was confident and truculent when he first appeared in Ham's office, and seemed to be daring us to do our worst.

That attitude didn't last very long, I can tell you, because Brady went into his act without wasting a minute. He ignored the Primer and the various sluggings and opened proceedings by slapping a flat accusation of murder into Grover's teeth. I thought that Grover was going to faint. He went white as a sheet, and he almost shouted his vehement denial. He swore by all his gods that he had never so much as laid a finger on Kelly, and defied us to prove that he had. The man's excitement and fear were so extreme that he convinced me then and there that he had slugged Kelly, even though he might never suffer for the crime.

Brady handled him cleverly. He said that Grover's protested innocence meant nothing since he also protested innocence of all the other recent crimes, crimes which we could definitely prove he had committed. He hinted, also, that we had evidence in the matter of Kelly's death that we weren't revealing. He talked about Grover's record, and about his known dealings with the deceased Kelly, or Perelli. He took the gold penknife from the end of Grover's watch chain and put it carefully away. He said that Anne could swear it was the knife she had found in the library the night Hale was attacked, and that it was the same knife that had been taken from her after the clambake, when she herself had been attacked. He pointed out the similarity between Kelly's injuries and Hale's. He painted so black and convincing a picture before he was done that he had *me* believing that Grover could be convicted of murder.

"You've got one chance, Herb," he said flatly at last, "and that is to tell the truth, and all of it. You say you didn't kill your pal. All right, prove it. Tell everything that you have done down here, without leaving out a single thing, and perhaps you can get out of the murder rap. I'm not promising anything, mind you, but it's your only chance. Sing, or I'm telling you that just as sure as my name is George Brady, you are going to burn!"

Well, Grover did not give in at once. He denied everything over and over and swore that he was being framed. In the end, however, sheer fright got the better of him. "All right," he said bitterly. His face was deathly pale and sweat was running down his cheeks. His hands were trembling. "I never touched Frank Perelli. I'm not a murderer, and nobody is going to frame me into being one. I'll talk."

He talked.

IV

Oscar Grover's confession took a long time and needed a good deal of prompting; but it was time well spent, for when it was finished we knew practically all of the things that had been hidden from us up until then. Most of those things, as it turned out, we could have guessed correctly, even without Grover's help, but with it we had certain knowledge of them.

Grover said that he had read in the newspapers about the Knowlton Library's discovery of the Primer, and about its great monetary value. That was all the incentive he needed, and he immediately set to work perfecting his plans. Granting that he could steal the Primer, his next step would be to sell it, and for such a purpose he already had at hand a comprehensive list of possible buyers, made up of the names of most of the private collectors in the country. From this list he selected several prospects to whom he sent letters. Signing a false name, he said that there was a possibility of his getting hold of a *very* early New England Primer—he gave the approximate date—and asked if his correspondents were interested. Several replies came in, including one from Perry Hale. Grover had never previously done business with Hale, but he knew him by reputation as a wealthy and not too curious buyer of really rare items. A little investigation showed that Perry Hale spent his summers on Sepatonk Island.

Having laid his foundation and having located a possible purchaser, Grover immediately got in touch with Perelli, who had done some jobs for him before and who was more than ready to serve again. The pair got together and laid their plans for the theft of the Primer from the Knowlton Library. Perelli was to do the actual stealing and to be given a flat price for the job, acting merely as a hired thug and not as a real partner in the crime. Grover had somehow learned, he would not tell how, but we suspected a friend at Columbia University, that Professor Semphill was planning to come to Bainbridge to examine the Primer; and Grover's plan was to have Perelli get there first, disguised with white wig and glasses and posing as Semphill's secretary.

Grover swore that he and Perelli had planned no strong-arm business at all. Perelli was merely to knock off Dr. Payson's glasses, and to take advantage of the latter's extreme near-sightedness by substituting a fake for the real Primer. After the substitution he was to come directly to New York and to meet Grover there.

What Perelli actually did, Grover knew no better than we. We knew that Doc Payson's spare pair of glasses forced Perelli to use violence and then flee. Perelli did not, however, go to New York to meet Grover, and apparently had not planned to do so. Instead he met the boatman, Blake, and with him set out on the *Nellie* B. for an unknown destination. Grover's theory, and it sounded reasonable, was that Perelli was either dissatisfied with the price he had been offered for the job, or that he had learned of the Primer's value and had decided to sell it for his own profit. Anyhow, he never got wherever he was going. The hurricane saw to that, washing him up more dead than alive on Sepatonk Island, Blake being drowned.

Grover, meanwhile, was waiting at the appointed rendezvous in New York, but Perelli failed to show up. Not knowing what had happened, Grover decided to go back to Sepatonk Island, where he had taken up residence so as to be near Perry Hale. He had not revealed himself to Hale as the seller of the Primer, intending to do so only after he had the book in his hands. He hoped now, that Perelli, knowing his address, might get in touch with him on Sepatonk.

When he got to the Island, he heard of the wreck of the *Nellie B.* and of the castaway with the large sum of money and the mysterious flat package. It meant nothing to him, naturally enough, until one morning when he was playing dominoes in the Inn lobby with Holley and Drake. At that time Dr. Farmer, a bystander, happened to mention that the sick man at his house had a twisted arm. The combination of the twisted arm and the flat package was enough for Grover. He suspected the castaway to be Perelli, and he intended to find out if he was right.

Seeing Dr. Farmer's patient, however, was a difficult and fairly risky job. He made one or two attempts but had no luck until the night of Perelli's death. That night he pretended to go to bed and sneaked out of the Inn via a supposedly locked store room on the second floor and a trellis outside its window. Hurrying along the path to Dr. Farmer's house, he found the light on in the castaway's room, and, looking through the window, recognized and was recognized by Perelli.

The account of what happened immediately after that is merely Grover's story, and while I don't believe the important part of it, others may. Anyhow, Grover said that he and Perelli talked briefly in whispers through the window and that Perelli then came outside. The pair walked a short distance into the woods where they stopped to talk. Grover admitted that the talk wasn't friendly and that he accused Perelli of double-crossing him. He swore once more, however, that there was no fight. He said that Perelli was very weak and "half nuts" and that in taking a step backward he stumbled and fell, hitting his head. Grover, being a nice kind of lad even on his own admission, didn't wait to see how badly Perelli was hurt. He merely searched Perelli's pockets hastily, found nothing, and hurried away.

Grover was, of course, the man I had heard in the bushes that night.

When the smoke all blew away, Grover still did not have the Primer, and was more than ever determined to get it. He heard, as did practically everybody else on the Island, that Dr. Farmer had intrusted the dead man's belongings to Ham Ownley, and that Ham had put them in the Inn safe. He assumed, naturally, that the Primer was among them, and lost no time in cracking the safe. He found no Primer, but he mussed up Ham's belongings, much to the latter's puzzlement.

At that point Grover was in as bad a fix as Ham and I had been at the same time. He had no inkling of what to do next, and was marking time, when chance brought him to the lavatory next to the library in Hale's house on the afternoon when Perry and I were having our remarkable conversation at cross purposes. He heard a few words by accident, and stayed to hear more by intent.

From what he learned he drew the same mistaken conclusion that Perry had. He inferred that I was the one who had the Primer, and that I was about to sell it for the twenty-five thousand dollars in cash that Hale evidently had on the premises.

He thought, then and there, that he saw a literally golden opportunity. The Primer, if he could get it, would be a valuable asset, but a slightly troublesome one, in that it would still have to be sold. Twenty-five thousand dollars in cash, however, was something else again, and something that Grover was determined to have.

He had heard me say that I would give Hale my answer after twenty-four hours had passed, so he knew he must act quickly. Late that same afternoon he telephoned Perry and, disguising his voice, said that he was Dick Clarke. Stating that he had decided to meet the proffered terms, he made an appointment for midnight that night in Perry's library. At that time he agreed to deliver the book in exchange for the money.

Things looked very simple to Grover, and as the action unfolded, they looked increasingly simple. When he sneaked up, armed and masked, to the Hale house at midnight, he found the French door to the library wide open and Perry seated with his back toward him, at the desk. This presented an unhoped-for opening, but one that he had no intention of passing up. He would not now, as he had planned, hold up Perry at the point of a gun and take the money. Instead he would sneak in quietly, hit his unsuspecting victim over the head with the butt of his automatic, steal the money, and vanish without anybody so much as having seen him.

It was a good plan, and up to a certain point it worked. He knocked Hale out without any difficulty, but a locked desk drawer prevented him from snatching the money without delay. He was searching Perry's person for the necessary key when he heard me in the living room outside. That changed things. He straightened, catching and breaking his watch chain on a projecting knob of one of the desk drawers as he did so, and ran from the room.

In the darkness outside he was brought up short with the realization that he had met with a serious, if not fatal, misfortune. His watch chain was broken, and the little gold penknife that he carried at the end of it was gone. It must be lying, he realized, on the library floor—a very damning piece of evidence indeed.

There was nothing that he could do. Helplessly he watched me enter the library, switch on the lights, and examine Hale. He saw Anne come in, and heard us talk. He saw me leave. I must have passed, in fact, within a few feet of where he was standing. He saw Ted Folger's arrival, and the removal of Perry Hale to his bedroom. Worst of all, he saw Anne stoop down, just before she finally left the room, pick up the precious little knife, and absently thrust it in a pocket of her dressing gown.

The next day could not have been a very pleasant one for Grover. Having heard a large part of my conversation with Anne the night before, he knew that his crime had been laid at my door. That was some help, but the knife remained a very real menace. Questions would some time be asked about that knife, and once they were asked the hue and cry was certain to start.

Grover had a certain kind of nerve, I'll have to admit that. He did not hire a motorboat and sneak away from the Island the next day. Instead, he calmly held his ground, acted as though nothing had happened, and waited developments.

The developments came at the clambake that night, after I had given up and had gone home to bed. Grover said that he had been about to go home, too, when he heard Anne ask for me. When told that I didn't seem to be anywhere about, she had shrugged her shoulders indifferently and said that it didn't really matter. Then she added a few careless words of explanation that were to bring upon her a rather terrible experience. She said that she wanted to see me merely because she had something of mine in her pocketbook—something that I had dropped without knowing it, and something that I would probably want to have back.

Grover realized instantly that Anne was talking about his gold penknife, and that she was under the impression it was mine. He also realized that if that knife ever reached me I would deny owning it, with possibly very unpleasant results to himself. The situation, as he saw it, was fairly desperate, and required the desperate step he instantly determined to take.

What happened after that has been told. Luck once more played into Grover's hands, for Anne, instead of going home with Barbara Taylor, as she had planned, changed her mind at the last moment and started to walk back alone through the pines to Hale's. Grover overtook her, struggled with her, tore the pocketbook out of her hand, and thrust her down the cellar stairs of the abandoned house. Then he went home with the damning gold penknife safely in his pocket, and, I have no doubt, a serene conscience.

The state of his mind can be seen from his actions the next morning. He had missed his chance to get Perry Hale's twenty-five thousand dollars, but the Primer was still presumably in my possession, and fair game. While Ham and I were desperately searching for Anne, Grover improved the shining hour by ransacking my bedroom at the Inn. He did not find the Primer, of course, but he did find a letter I had written to Doc Payson in which I stated that the little book was still among the missing.

In Grover's mind, that practically closed the case. Perry Hale's money was forever out of his grasp. The Primer was missing; and, so far as he could see, it was permanently missing. There was nothing for him to do but be philosophical about his hard luck, and to wait until the Inn closed the next day. Then he could take himself off to the mainland, leaving behind a spotless reputation.

It was in that frame of mind that he had come down to dinner in the evening, and it was only with the most desultory sort of interest that he tackled the puzzle which Ownley presented for solving to his guests. In about ten seconds, however, his attitude changed. The text of the enigma, plus a certain familiar little symbol, caused his blood pressure to jump up plenty of notches.

Pleading boredom, he went to his room almost at once, and in a short time had solved the riddle. Then, when he thought the coast was clear, he used the storeroom and the trellis once more, and took the path to Hale's. Straight to the garage he came, and straight to the New England Primer, and straight to the welcoming arms of Mr. George Brady.

"That's the whole story," said Grover, earnestly, when he had finished, looking from first one to the other of us as though begging us to believe. "I've told you everything I've done, and everything I know. I've told the truth—all of it. I never laid a hand on Frank Perelli. I'm not a murderer—so help me God!"

V

Well, Oscar Grover may not have been a murderer, but he certainly had admitted being about everything else there was on the crook honor roll. He had told enough about himself, I was mortally certain, to keep him in the jug where he belonged, for the rest of his days. Brady must have felt the same way, for, when the confession was finished, he couldn't get Grover out of the way fast enough.

He and Ham had a brief consultation as to the best method of keeping the prisoner safe. The Sepatonk lockup was suggested but that didn't satisfy Brady. It might be a sturdy enough place, he admitted, but, knowing his captive, he intended to take no chances. It was finally decided to put Grover to bed in his room at the Inn, with one arm handcuffed to the iron bedpost. "He can rest fairly comfortably there," said the policeman, "and he won't be lonesome. Mrs. Brady's little boy is going to be sitting right at the side of the bed with a gun in his hand. If I ever let this downy bird slip through my fingers now, I'd hang myself to the nearest crabapple tree!"

He and Grover went away, with Obed Silver acting as guide. Ham, seated at his desk, sighed. "Well, Mr. Dickson Clarke, it looks as if we were running for home at last with a following wind. The little Primer book is in your hands, and pretty soon it'll be back in the Knowlton Library where it belongs. The crook that hit your boss, Dr. Payson, is dead. The crook that cooked up the whole scheme —the one that slugged Perry Hale and played his dirty tricks on Anne Francis—is arrested. All our questions are answered and all our puzzles solved. All in all it has been what you might call a busy day." He yawned, glanced at his watch, and uttered an exclamation. "Godfrey mighty! It's nigh four o'clock in the morning. If Hettie Bassett catches me up at this time of night, she'll think I've gone to perdition for good and all, at last. Let's turn in, Dick. What say?"

"Applesauce!" I snorted. "You're just as excited as I am, Ham Ownley, and you wouldn't be able to sleep any better. I promise you I'm not even going to make the gesture of trying—not until I know the whole story."

"Whole story?" Ham looked at me with childlike innocence. "Why, what story is there left to tell? Oscar Grover has been talking himself black in the face for the last couple of hours; and so far as I'm concerned, he's answered all the questions that have been bothering me."

"Maybe so," I said grimly, "but what isn't bothering you doesn't help me any. I'm still completely in the dark. How did you get on Grover's trail? How did you manage to catch him? How did you know he would go to Perry Hale's garage tonight? Did you know the Primer would be there? Those are a few of the things I want to know. You've been traveling a lone trail all day long and I've been playing marbles in a corner. I want to know how you did it all."

"Well, Dick," said Ham, giving in with a smile, "I suppose your questions are natural enough, and I'll try to answer them; but so far as how I did it all goes, I'm not quite sure, myself. Luck was part of it, scare was part of it, and pride was another part."

"Scare?"

"Yes." He nodded. "I was scared to death that the Inn would close up tomorrow, and that everybody would go away with the little Primer book still missing, and with the dirty dog that pounded Perry Hale over the head and shut Anne up in the cellar of an empty house, still free. If that had happened, I'd never have heard the end of it, and rightly so, too. Perry Hale has already done a lot of talking and complaining about my not getting the regular police from the mainland to help. I hadn't sent for 'em for what I thought were good reasons, but that wasn't much help. The thing was right in my lap. It was up to me. That's where the pride part came in. I made up my mind that even if there weren't a half-dozen Philo Vances snooping around on Sepatonk, we still can wash our own dirty clothes. There were times today, I'm willing to admit, when I thought the clothes were going to stay dirty, but it all turned out all right finally."

He told me then about all the questions he had written down on paper that morning and about how he had set about trying to answer them. His most likely suspects, as he saw it, had been Drake and Folger. Drake loomed particularly large because, off and on for some time, he had been out late at night, and had been very secretive about his actions. Drake he learned from Obed Silver, had been out the night Perry Hale was hit on the head. That looked good, but Obed's further revelations about Charlie Drake's girl had promptly and permanently exploded that bubble. "Charlie Drake with a girl!" said Ownley disgustedly. "He ought to be old enough to know better, but it seems he ain't. He'll never know how close that precious girl of his came to getting him arrested for being a thief and a head knocker!"

Holley entered the picture briefly, for he, too, had been out on the night of Hale's trouble, but an innocent visit to the local poolroom explained that. Folger alone remained, and he not for long. Ham felt quite strongly that

Ted did not fit into the picture, and an examination of his movements on the night of the clambake showed, almost to a certainty, that he had not been the person who had attacked Anne.

"All my suspects were gone," said Ham ruefully. "Things were bad, and they got worse when I found out about that trunkroom key, and about the trellis outside the trunkroom window. One look at the trellis showed me somebody had been using it for a ladder, and one minute of thought told me that all the alibis I had fixed up for the folks at the Inn weren't worth a puff of smoke. Any one of them could have gotten in and out any time of night without anybody knowing a thing about it. I was in a fine old fix when I found that out." He laughed. "I thought I was in the chowder for fair."

"I don't blame you," I said. "I'd have given the whole thing up there and then."

Ham, however, had not given up. In the back of his mind all along, it seems, had been the thought of that letter that Kelly, or Perelli, had written to his Chicago pal. He felt sure that somewhere in that letter were concealed directions for finding the Primer; and when all his other clews had failed, he set out in desperation to see if he could solve the puzzle.

He has already written the steps that he took along those lines, so I won't repeat them. His great interest in detective stories and in newspaper cryptograms helped him. The symbol in the letter, the ♯, looked like a probable starting place, especially since the following text was rather involved and obscure. He tried one thing after the other, with infinite patience, until finally he found the answer.

"It wasn't so much of a puzzle, after all," he said deprecatingly. "Not when you had worked it out. Here, take a look. Every fourth letter spells out a message."

He tossed me a piece of paper that had a copy of the vital part of Kelly's letter. From the ♯ on it read: "Them old spiels of Mike's don't ever work. I'd can Windy, too, and with Hank and Eli's new gags plain tripe and N. G. the end's here, Ed, for I'm keen for man who is just as live at runing down buyers and free spenders as anybody." With every fourth letter underlined it looked like this: "Them old spiels of Mike's don't ever work. I'd can Windy, too, and with Hank and Eli's new gags plain tripe and N. G. the ends here, Ed, for I'm keen for man who is just as live at runing down buyers and free spenders as anybody."

When the underlined letters were put together, the message read:

"TOP SIDE WINDOW HALE GARAGE HERE ON ISLAND."

"You see?" said Ham. "Easy as pie."

"Easy as pie," I said with genuine admiration. "Once you know how! 'Top side window Hale garage here on island.' So that was the message. And when you had it, you knew where the Primer was hidden! You knew, and yet—"

"I know." Ham nodded. "I know just what you mean. You're wondering why I didn't holler the news out loud, and run up there to get the little book. Well, that's just what I was cal'lating to do, until I stopped to think. Then it come over me that, while I was pretty sure of being able to lay my hands on one of the two things we wanted, the other one was just as far away as ever. We still didn't know who our crook was, or how we were ever going to lay hands on him. I wanted that crook, Dick; so I let the Primer stay where it was for a while—it was safe enough there—and did some more tall thinking."

The result of that thinking was that Ham Ownley laid a trap. On account of the trellis outside the storeroom window, together with some other things, he felt reasonably certain that the person he was after was one of the Inn guests. If that were true, then the crook might possibly be familiar with the code used in Kelly's letter and be able to solve it. *If* he solved it, Ham felt that there was a very good chance of his giving himself away.

Ham, therefore, prepared a number of copies of the vital parts of Kelly's letter. Each copy was to go to a specific guest and each was marked with the customer's initial in small letters on the back. After dinner he handed out his puzzle and stood by to watch the results.

They weren't, to all appearances, very satisfactory. No one seemed to be a great hand at doing puzzles, and the interest in this particular one waned quickly. Grover gave up just about as soon as the rest. He rose from the table, where he had been sitting with his back to the room, and announced himself baffled. Then he twisted his sheet of paper and ostentatiously tossed it into a wastebasket. The others did, or had done, approximately the same thing.

Ham was apparently defeated, but he did not give up. At the first opportunity he gathered together the discarded copies of the message and examined them. Almost immediately he struck oil. One of the copies was missing, and, using the initials in a process of elimination, he discovered that the missing one was Grover's. The paper that Grover had so obviously discarded was not the one that had been handed him. It was just a blank sheet of stationery. He must have taken Kelly's message with him when he went up to his room.

"Wow!" I exclaimed excitedly. "That fixed it, of course! You knew that Grover was your man. And yet—"

"And yet I didn't go upstairs and arrest him. That's right, I didn't, and the reason was that I didn't have a scrap of real evidence. To arrest Mr. Grover I had to catch him red-handed at something, and that's why I waited. I went outside and watched that trellis, but nothing happened. Finally I decided it wasn't safe to watch any longer. I went back into the Inn, and you know the rest. You and Brady came along, and the three of us went to Hale's garage, where we held a kind of surprise party, as you might say, for Mr. Grover. That's the whole story, Dick. It was luck, most of it. Just plain bull luck."

"Luck nothing!" As the thing sank in, I was more and more admiring. "It was wonderful, Ham! You did a swell job if anybody ever did one. I can't believe it yet! You certainly deserve a medal."

"No." He shook his head with a smile. "I don't deserve any medals, and I don't want none. All I want right now is a night's sleep." He looked at me. "I suppose all *you* want is to get the little Primer book back to the Library. Well, there's nothing to keep you from doing that, now. Your business on Sepatonk is finished. It's finished, that is—"

"That's right." I grinned. "There *is* one other small detail remaining. I'll attend to that the first thing to-morrow."

VI

It was late afternoon, and Ham Ownley was seated at his desk in the little office. The Inn was officially closed, and the guests were gone. Gone, too, were the policeman, Brady, and his prisoner. Ham was in his shirt sleeves, and there were dark circles of weariness under his eyes; but he looked up with a cheerful smile as Anne and I walked in.

"Come to say good-by, I suppose," he observed regretfully. "Well, I'll hate to say it, because I've taken a kind of liking to you two young folks. Still and all, the world has to move, and I suppose you have to get back, Dick, to your job at the Library."

"No," said Anne. "Dick is all through with his job there. He's going back home and start in at his real job of gentleman farming."

"Quite to the contrary," I said firmly, winking at Ham. "In two weeks I'm going to take a job that Anne's father has gotten for me in the canning business."

Anne tapped her foot. "You're going to be a farmer."

I corrected her. "What you mean is that I'm going to be a canner."

Ham looked so confused that I was forced to laugh. "Don't mind us, Mr. Ownley," I told him. "We're just arguing, which is our natural state. But we didn't come here to bother you with our arguments. We came to ask you to marry us—right now!"

"Marry you? *Me?*" Ham's jaw fell open. "Now?"

"Of course," said Anne calmly. "It'll be dark in a little while, and we've got to get Dick's cottage fixed up for a honeymoon before then."

"I see," said Ham weakly. "I see."

"You can do it, can't you?" I asked. "You're a justice of the peace, as I understand it."

"I can do it, of course. But—but don't you want a regular parson?"

"No," Anne shook her head. "We want you, or the whole deal is off. Get on with it, will you, please?"

Ham sat there for a little time, thinking. Then a broad smile spread slowly across his face. He got up from his chair and came around the desk, holding out a hand to each of us. "Marry you?" he inquired. "You bet I'll marry you, and I'll marry you so it'll take for keeps! To tell the truth, marrying you is the one job I'd really like to do, right now."

He shook hands, delightedly, with me, and tried to with Anne, but she kissed him instead. "Now let me see," he said, clearing his throat importantly as though not embarrassed at all. "Where in the everlasting nation do I keep my license blanks, and the prayer book?"